The Contradictions of Media Power

The Contradictions
of Media Power

DES FREEDMAN

B L O O M S B U R Y
LONDON · NEW DELHI · NEW YORK · SYDNEY

Bloomsbury Academic

An imprint of Bloomsbury Publishing Plc

50 Bedford Square	1385 Broadway
London	New York
WC1B 3DP	NY 10018
UK	US

www.bloomsbury.com

Bloomsbury is a registered trade mark of Bloomsbury Publishing Plc

First published 2014

Library of Congress Cataloging-in-Publication Data
Freedman, Des, 1962-
The contradictions of media power / Des Freedman.
pages cm
Includes bibliographical references and index.
ISBN 978-1-8496-6073-0 (hardback) – ISBN 978-1-8496-6069-3 (paperback) –
ISBN 978-1-4725-8983-5 (ePub) – ISBN 978-1-8496-6610-7 (ePDF) 1. Mass media–
Political aspects. 2. Mass media–Social aspects. 3. Mass media–Influence. I. Title.
P95.8.F729 2015
302.23 – dc23
2014010313

ISBN: HB: 978-1-8496-6073-0
PB: 978-1-8496-6069-3
ePub: 978-1-4725-8983-5
ePDF: 978-1-8496-6610-7

Typeset by Integra Software Services Pvt. Ltd.
Printed and bound in Great Britain

To Wickford's finest export – always

Contents

Acknowledgements

Part of Chapter 1 appeared in *International Journal of Communication* (2014); part of Chapter 2 appeared in *International Journal of Cultural Policy* (2012); part of Chapter 3 appeared in *International Journal of Press/Politics* (2010); and part of Chapter 5 appeared in *Westminster Papers in Culture and Communication* (2009).

I couldn't have written this without the support of my wonderful colleagues in the Department of Media and Communications at Goldsmiths. Everyone, in very different ways, is working on the relationship between media and power, and I have always been inspired by the range of perspectives that inhabit our department. Another source of inspiration has been my involvement with the Media Reform Coalition, and I would like to thank all the campaigners who have been with us since 2011.

I would also like to thank the following for their fantastic feedback and support: Michael Bailey, Nick Couldry, James Curran, Aeron Davis, Emily Drewe, John Downing, Katie Gallof, Paolo Gerbaudo, Rodrigo Gomez, Deborah Grayson, Jennifer Holt, Deepa Kumar, Guillermo Mastrini, Bob McChesney, Toby Miller, Hallvard Moe, Angela Phillips, Victor Pickard, Manuel Puppis, Justin Schlosberg, Mila Steele, Damian Tambini, Gavan Titley, Peter Thompson, Daya Thussu, Mike Wayne, Dwayne Winseck, Andreas Ytterstad and Yuezhi Zhao. I'm so grateful to my Dad for his enthusiasm for every project I'm involved with, while Chris Nineham has illuminated me about media power for longer than I can remember and I look forward to his book on the subject. For academic solidarity and friendship, I'm completely at the mercy of the 'Northerners' (Natalie Fenton, Dave Hesmondhalgh, Gholam Khiabany and Milly Williamson), and for everyday confusion I'm indebted to the 'Southerners' (Kirstie, Stanley and Dexy), who can now have me back if they still want me.

1

Approaches to Media Power

If you have a readership of 3 to 4 million, even if the newspapers are behaving in the most totally proper way, that's power, and I think – I don't know any other way of describing it.

TONY BLAIR, EVIDENCE TO LEVESON INQUIRY, 28 MAY 2012

It was a normal, run-of-the-mill encounter in a central London restaurant. In 2007, Rebekah Brooks, the then editor of Britain's best-selling daily newspaper, the *Sun*, and subsequently the chief executive officer of News International, News Corporation's UK news division, was having lunch with Sir Ian Blair, head of the Metropolitan Police, when she enquired into the possibility of borrowing one of the Met's 100 horses. Later the same day, Brooks contacted Scotland Yard's head of public affairs to make the necessary arrangements. The following year, a 22-year-old retired horse called Raisa was loaned out to Brooks. Then, just before he was elected prime minister in 2010, David Cameron, a fellow member of the 'Chipping Norton set' (referring to a particularly picturesque area of the British countryside where both the Camerons and the Brooks have houses), went riding on Raisa with Brooks' husband Charlie, an old friend of his from the elite private school Eton. The anecdote provides a powerful symbol of the network of compliant relationships between the press, politicians and the police that were to be so thoroughly exposed in the debates that followed the phone hacking scandal that broke in July 2011 (Mair and Keeble 2012). It is a wonderfully lucid story of class, privilege and influence in contemporary Britain that speaks to the entanglements of private and state power that we see in many countries across the globe.

Since journalists at the *Guardian* newspaper first revealed that staff working for another popular News International title, the *News of the World*, had hacked into the mobile phone of a murdered teenager, the British public has witnessed a series of unprecedented events: the closure by Rupert Murdoch of the offending newspaper; the resignation of two of the most senior police officers in the land along with the departure of top News Corp executives; the abandonment of News Corp's bid to assume full control of Britain's biggest broadcaster, BSkyB; the setting up of a major public inquiry into press standards – the Leveson Inquiry – which heard evidence of the complete failure of regulatory frameworks to hold to account those newspapers who breached agreed codes of conduct; the existence at the *Sun* of a 'culture of illegal payments' involving a 'network of corrupted officials' (Akers 2012); the increasing use of other illegal practices (such as bribery and 'blagging', the unauthorized obtaining of personal information) that went well beyond the *News of the World*; and the systematic failure by the Metropolitan Police to investigate phone hacking allegations.

What is the narrative thread between these revelations? Do they reflect an ethical breakdown at the heart of the British press or are they the product of a rise in cynicism that, at least in the UK, has been blamed for the degeneration of both political and media culture (Blair 2007, Lloyd 2004)? Do they reflect, on a broader scale, an individualization of public culture leading to the dissolution of civic bonds that might have otherwise held sway (Beck 1992)? Or are they, as some editors and journalists have argued (for example Kampfner 2011), not at all representative of systemic patterns but merely the actions of a single company, News International, that was allowed to accrue too much influence and therefore to cast a shadow across the rest of the press? Do these revelations speak to a problem that goes far beyond Britain: the emergence of highly influential but barely accountable media organizations or moguls who play a central role in public life? For Nick Davies, the *Guardian* reporter who broke the original story, the whole sequence of events 'never was simply about journalists behaving badly: it was and is about power' (Davies 2012: 1). Indeed, it is about one specific type of power that has now entered mainstream vocabulary: media power.

Yet, despite its increased use in political, academic and professional circles, it is far from clear precisely what we mean by media power. It is hardly controversial to suggest that the media are powerful social actors but what is the nature of this power? Does it refer to people, institutions, processes or capacities? Does media power relate to the economic prowess of the largest media corporations like Google, News Corp, Disney and Time Warner or to the political influence of particular 'media moguls' like Rupert Murdoch, Silvio Berlusconi and Sumner Redstone? Does it refer to the media's capacity to shape attitudes and modify individual behaviour or to make possible new forms of social action (or even to prevent these possibilities from taking place)? Does it suggest an ability to promote the sharing of common meanings or to entrench divisions? Does it point towards the media's tendency to interpret the world according to their own material interests and therefore to reinforce largely privileged ideological positions or does it hint at the new possibilities of mediated interaction that have been facilitated by the growth of social media?

We need a definition of media power that is both sufficiently clear to capture the dangers it can pose for democracy and sufficiently complex in order fully to evaluate its channels, networks, participants and implications. This book aims to unravel this puzzle and to identify a model that may be of particular relevance to those countries with 'pluralist' political arrangements and intensively marketized economic systems where the configuration of media power is such that it is formally separate from, but intertwined with, the state. It proposes a definition of media power that refers not simply to the authority of specific actors or institutional structures but to their interactions; just as power itself is not a tangible property visible only in its exercise, media power is best conceived as a relationship between different interests engaged in struggles for a range of objectives that include legitimation, influence, control, status and, increasingly, profit.

Elements of the puzzle

Power is a slippery term and, as John Downing notes (2001: 12), 'potentially one of the more vacuous concepts in social and cultural analysis'. That power refers to a transformative capacity shared by humans is hardly headline news, but issues concerning its generation, circulation and impact are rather more controversial. In part this is because of a division between two key ways of understanding power – a consensual 'power to' and a more coercive 'power over' – that reveal a tension between understanding power as a means of individual regulation or as a source of domination (Parsons 1963, Scott 2001). The former account is widely identified with pluralist perspectives that view power as an essential mechanism of social organization and cohesion. There may be conflicts and hierarchies but, where they exist, power nevertheless operates 'in the interest of the effectiveness of the collective operation as a whole' (Parsons 1963: 243). Power is understood here as a medium used to reconcile different actors in situations in which they encounter each other – it is 'the *means* of acquiring control of the factors in effectiveness; it is not itself one of these factors' (1963: 234).

Radical theorists, on the other hand, take the opposite approach and view power as a key factor in the ability of one actor to exercise her interests at the expense of another actor. Power is not a formal technique for conflict resolution so much as a property that is unequally distributed between actors in such a way as further to distort, not to balance, their relationship. Yet, while there is not necessarily a contradiction between 'power to' and 'power over' (given that the latter takes for granted the existence of the former), pluralists, according to Steven Lukes (2005: 34):

> focus on the locution 'power to', ignoring 'power over'. Thus power indicates a 'capacity', a 'facility', an 'ability', not a relationship. Accordingly, the conflictual aspect of power – the fact that it is exercised *over* people – disappears altogether from view. And along with it there disappears the central interest of studying power relations in the first place – an interest in the (attempted or successful) securing of people's compliance by overcoming or averting their opposition.

This book adopts a radical view of power, not least because I believe that any full account of media power has to confront the very unequal allocation of resources that are attached to mediated interactions. This is of course not to suggest that every such interaction is constituted or characterized by the desire of one actor to dominate another but simply to acknowledge the acutely uneven capacity of the right to speak (as well as the ability to listen) in contemporary market-driven societies. This disparity in communicative resources is acknowledged by different theorists of media power – including Joseph Turow, who argues that power involves 'the use of resources by one organization to gain compliance by another organization' (Turow 1992: 24), and Manuel Castells, who emphasizes the 'relational capacity that enables a social actor to influence asymmetrically the decisions of other social actor(s) in ways that favor the empowered actor's will, interests and values' (Castells 2009: 10) – and is at the heart of the analysis of media power that is proposed in this book.

In these circumstances, Steven Lukes' (2005: 16–29) celebrated account of the three 'faces' of power is useful not only in focusing attention on the different dynamics of power but also in proposing some of the ways in which media themselves might be implicated in social reproduction and coordination. The first 'face' refers to a pluralist conception of power as the successful mobilization of resources in visible decision-making situations; the second, to a more critical notion of the ability to influence what is discussed (or what is not discussed) in the first place and therefore directs us to examine the control of the decision-making agenda; and the third (and hidden) 'face' consists of the realm of ideology – the idea that power is associated with the capacity (though not necessarily the exercise of that capacity) to shape the preconditions for decision-making in order to 'secure compliance to domination' (2005: 111). Given its explicit relevance to 'formal' instances of decision-making, I examine Lukes' typology in more detail in Chapter 3 when discussing the relationship between media policy and power.

Lukes later comes to recognize that this model, first developed in 1974, is perhaps too limited as it focuses exclusively on power as domination and ignores, in particular, following Foucault (1977, 1980), 'the way in which power over others can be productive, transformative, authoritative and compatible with dignity' (Lukes 2005: 109) and how the media might provide a site both for the exercise of and resistance to power. Yet Lukes continues, even after this modification, to focus on power's relationship to securing compliance and to treat the media as important architects of social consensus. He mentions the media as major institutions through which 'thought control' (2005: 27) takes place and he speaks of the 'power to mislead' which consists of everything from 'straightforward censorship and disinformation to the various institutionalized and personal ways there are of infantilizing judgment' (2005: 149). Here, the 'power *to* mislead' is combined with an assumed 'power *over* audiences' to generate what we might call the 'power *of*' the media to secure, in Lukes' terms, compliance to existing social relations.

Now this idea of the 'power of' the media is far from new and has long been asserted in terms of the impact of specific technologies on historical events: the impact of books on the Reformation, of pamphlets on the French Revolution, of the press on the emergence of the US democracy where De Tocqueville, for example, granted it not just constitutional but constitutive power: 'its influence in America is immense. It *causes* political life to circulate through all the parts of that vast territory. Its eye is constantly open to detect the secret springs of political designs and to *summon* the leaders of all parties in turn to the bar of public opinion' (de Tocqueville 2003: 167, emphasis added). The nineteenth-century French sociologist Gabriel Tarde attributes a similar power to the press in the rolling out of European modernity. Newspapers, he argued, change the fabric of politics, starting new conversations, stirring up 'united movements of minds and will' and nationalizing and internationalizing private opinions and the 'public mind' (2010: 304, 307). According to the historian Paul Starr, media technologies had, by the 1920s, formed a 'new constellation of power' and were, by now, 'increasingly a source of wealth' and 'formidable institutions in their own right' (2004: 385). Since that point, the power of radio, film, television and, latterly, the internet to amuse and distract, to mobilize and publicize, to integrate and inform, and to educate and enrage has grown exponentially. This 'power of' specific media remains a central area of interest.

In the last seventy years, however, the notion of a holistic *media power* has emerged, characterized less by specific properties of individual technologies than by a new collective media influence that expresses the salience of information, symbols and knowledge in the contemporary world. Since the early twentieth century, those technologies that are now understood together to form 'the media' have grown in scale and influence, requiring a rethinking of their impact on modern societies beyond their individual histories (for example, Castells 2000, McLuhan 1964, Thompson 1995, Williams 1968). Today, despite the fact that power remains unequally distributed across different media platforms, few people would dispute the premise that the media, as a distinct entity, can, as John Corner puts it, 'exert a significant degree of power over both public and corporate perceptions and therefore bring about changes to the "action frames" within which they operate' (2011: 15).

Yet, two problems follow from this. First, there is little agreement about the extent of media influence and about the power of the media as an independent variable. There are those who argue that the power of media power is itself overstated. Michael Schudson, for example, acknowledges that news has the ability to amplify particular perspectives and to confer 'public legitimacy' (1982: 19) on individuals and institutions but nevertheless insists that this influence is too often exaggerated. 'It is not media power that disengages people but their belief in it, and the conviction of their own impotence in the face of it' (1982: 17). Media power, according to this perspective, is far more indirect and elusive, closer perhaps to the 'limited effects' theory of communication that replaced the 'hypodermic model' in classic accounts of media sociology (McCullagh 2002: 152–153).

This line of argument has emerged recently in relation to the UK phone hacking scandal, where a growing number of journalists have reacted to the current crisis by insisting that we have little to fear from concentrated media power. According to the *Financial Times* columnist Philip Stephens, 'there has always been something faintly hysterical about the charge that British politics has been held helpless hostage to the Murdoch empire. He has never been as powerful as his enemies imagined' (Stephens 2011: 13). Simon Jenkins continues this line of argument in the *Guardian*, claiming that the damage that could ever be caused by the media is relatively minimal: 'Has anyone been murdered? Has anyone been ruined? Is the nation gripped by financial crash or pandemic, earthquake or famine?' (Jenkins 2011: 35). For these commentators, media power is a conspiratorial phenomenon that exists only in the mind of its accusers. Media, after all, are only as powerful as readers and viewers allow them to be and, indeed, it is increasingly argued that *concentrated* media influence has met its nemesis given the decentralization and fragmentation of power in the digital communications environment (Jarvis 2009), a debate to which I return in Chapter 4.

But there are also those who warn against underestimating media power and therefore ignoring the extent to which social relations have been increasingly 'mediatized'. This flows from a series of very different conceptual starting points: from Foucauldian analyses that see power as an all-pervasive feature of contemporary life that operates through bodies and subjects just as much as it does through institutions and governments (Bordo 2003, Miller and Rose 1997); from postmodern accounts that posit media technologies as the main textures of everyday life in an age of hyperreality and simulation

(Baudrillard 1994); from post-Marxist accounts, such as those of Stuart Hall (1986), that see 'ideology' as the 'cement' of any late capitalist social formation and that endow the media with tremendous definitional power; and from technologists who see digital media as innately disruptive and ultimately empowering (Downes 2009, Negroponte 1996). This latter expansive (and optimistic) view of dispersed media power reached its apotheosis in claims made about the 'revolutionary' role of social media in the Arab Spring of 2011, the emergence of 'Twitter Revolutions' and the rise of networked protest that culminated in the Occupy movement (Mason 2012). Manuel Castells (2009, 2011) has famously described this as 'media counterpower'.

The media are, of course, neither omniscient nor redundant, neither all-conquering nor vanquished. We need instead a view of power that recognizes the media's own capacities for both transformation *and* misrecognition but locates them in relation to other actors who participate in struggles over the allocation of resources. As John Corner argues (2011: 19),

> There are very good reasons, historical, political and sociological, for seeing media institutions and processes as exercising their powers *systemically*, that is to say within the terms of a broader pattern of determining relationships with other sources of power, the vested and often elite sources of which they routinely serve to maintain, whatever the localized tensions and questioning that might also occur.

This is most helpful when considering some of the revelations uncovered in the course of the phone hacking scandal in the UK: for example, that ten out of forty-five staff in the press office of the Metropolitan Police used to work for the *News of the World*; that News International executives 'enjoyed close social ties to Scotland Yard's top officials' and that the police commissioner dined eighteen times with company executives during the time when Scotland Yard refused to launch a full investigation into phone hacking (Van Natta 2011); that Rupert Murdoch has had 113 private meetings with prime ministers and opposition leaders since 1988 (Rogers and Burn-Murdoch 2012); that Prime Minister David Cameron found time to host seventy-five private meetings in Downing Street with figures from the media in the fourteen months from May 2010 to July 2011, twenty-six of which were with representatives of News Corp alone; that News Corp met with the chancellor George Osborne sixteen times and the education secretary Michael Gove seven times during the same period; that the culture secretary Jeremy Hunt met with News Corp seven times, including two meetings at the time of the proposed takeover of BSkyB by News Corp (BBC 2011). Indeed, the *systemic* nature of the problem was acknowledged by none other than the prime minister, who, in his initial response to the phone hacking allegations in July 2011, declared that 'it is no good pointing the finger at this individual journalist, or that individual newspaper. It's no good, actually, just criticising the police. The truth is, we have all been in this together – the press, politicians and leaders of all parties – and yes, that includes me' (Cameron 2011).

The question that follows from this concerns not the allocation but the *location* of media power: whether it is a capacity reserved for media institutions themselves or whether it is a resource hegemonized by those whose interests lie primarily outside the media, in other words with organizations whose main output is not necessarily symbolic. Does media power refer to the 'concentrated symbolic power of media institutions' (Couldry 2000: 192) or to the ability of *other* state, corporate or civic actors to use communicative activities as a valuable resource with which to assert their own interests? What is the relationship between the 'power of' the media and the possibility of cementing 'power through' the media (Couldry and Curran 2003: 3–4, Hackett and Carroll 2006: 21–31)?

This is an issue that has been taken up by Manuel Castells, who provocatively suggests (2007: 242) that 'the media are not the holders of power, but they constitute by and large the space where power is decided'. Media institutions, according to this perspective, are not the main protagonists but the hosts of power struggles, making available their platforms and channels for the genuine power-holders of international finance, business, politics and war. Castells develops this line of thought in his comprehensive account of communication power (Castells 2009) where he argues that, because of the centrality of information and communication processes in influencing minds and securing legitimation, 'communication networks are the fundamental networks of power making in society' (2009: 426). Power, a ubiquitous feature of informatized capitalism, comes to be closely associated with the ability of capital, politics, subjectivity, terror and resistance to be programmed into these networks. Castells is clear: the media are *not* power-holders themselves (they are more important than that) but, instead, 'constitute the space where power relationships are decided between competing political and social actors' (2009: 194).

This notion of the media providing the terrain for other actors to contest power is widely accepted. Indeed, many excellent historical accounts suggest that media have, for example, assisted in the consolidation of existing, or the emergence of new, 'power centres', such as the rise of Catholicism in the Middle Ages (Curran 2002: 56), stimulated new politically motivated reading publics (Leonard 1986) or acted as 'mighty levers' in the development of liberal democracy (Starr 2004: 402). Despite their contribution, it appears as if media, intimately tied to the play of power, spend more time *servicing* power than actually accruing it for their own purposes. Media power, according to this view, is like a junior partner in a coalition dominated by more established social forces like religion, armies, politicians or corporations. Consider the claim by Stuart Hood, in his wonderful history of British television, that the media 'can make crucial interventions at critical moments in the history of a society … but they are never likely to be, on their own, the instruments of a social change which depends on a shift in the power structure of society' (1980: 116). The following questions flow from this: What constitutes the 'real' power structure of any society? Do the coercive abilities of the state, the economic resources of big business and the political authority of government somehow trump the symbolic power of institutions including the church, schooling and the media? Are there primary and, therefore, secondary instruments of power in which the media fit only into the latter category? What are the specific dynamics of the relationship between media and other agents of change and can we trace a causal or rather a more incidental or associative connection?

Refuting this kind of hierarchization of power, John Thompson (1995: 13–18) suggests that there are four forms of power (political, economic, coercive and symbolic) and argues that the ability to wield power in one area depends, at least partly, on the capacity to exert influence over another. Confidence in the political system, the ability to go to war and to trust current economic arrangements all require legitimacy and consent (or at least, following Lukes, compliance) that can be partially secured through ideological institutions like the media. 'Symbolic activity', writes Thompson (1995: 16), 'is a fundamental feature of social life, on a par with productive activity, the coordination of individuals, and coercion.' So, instead of endowing symbolic and material forms of power with different levels of impact, Thompson attempts to assess the ways in which they are mutually supportive and overlapping in 'the murky reality of social life' (1995: 18).

How does this relate to a materialist conception of power – that in Marx's terms, it is not 'the consciousness of men that determines their being, but, on the contrary, their social being determines their consciousness' (Marx 1963: 67) and, further, that this social existence is fundamentally shaped by economic forces? Firstly, despite Thompson's claim that symbolic power is used to naturalize other forms of power, it does not follow that this is always the case. Governments do not always secure consent from their populations to go to war, and financial systems are not always seen as legitimate; more significantly, the existence of covert operations, private lobbying and closed networks of privileged individuals (think back to Raisa, the horse we met at the beginning of this chapter) suggests that symbolic power is not a precondition for the operation of other forms of power.

But it is also important to stress that social relations, in their entirety, include ideas as well as economics, mental as well as physical production, the 'economic base' as well as the 'ideological superstructure'. This does not mean that the media are confined to a superstructure that passively reflects its economic foundations but instead that the two domains are intimately tied together. As the Marxist philosopher Franz Jakubowski puts it, the 'material' and the 'ideal' dimensions of social reproduction are equally 'real' and each reacts on the other to form 'inseparable moments of a unity' (Jakubowski 1976: 57). The key is not to separate ideas or culture from the circumstances and tensions in which they are generated: 'Economic relations are the foundations of social life and prevail in the last instance. But in any analysis of an individual situation it is social being as a whole that has to be taken into account – the economic and political relations certainly, but also the existing social ideologies and the intellectual tradition' (1976: 59). While ideology is neither all-pervasive nor insurmountable, that does not stop it from being productive and 'constitutive of the social relations of production' (Miller 2002: 252). Media power, according to this perspective, is structurally tied (but not subordinated) to wider patterns of privilege and control: 'Accounts of the world and evaluations of it emerge from material experience as well as from the media and other symbolic systems' (Miller 2002: 253).

Consider Aeron Davis' meticulous analysis of the consumption and use of media at 'elite' sites of power: in financial markets, parliaments and corporations (Davis 2007). Davis examines not the large-scale impact of mainstream media on mass audiences, the basis of many media studies texts, but the precise ways in which information and communications are integrated into the decision-making processes and lived cultures of some of the most powerful groups on the planet. Crucially, while the book is initially framed around a separation between media personnel and 'those in power' (2007: 14), Davis finds that the saturation of elite sites by media people and processes has started to break down this division. Journalists, he argues (2007: 175):

> are not simply reporting on political and economic processes and sites of power. They are immersed in them. They are a physical component of the information networks that form in elite sites of power. In constantly going between sources, who are also key media subjects and audiences, they are part of the elite circuits of information exchange and dialogue.

This 'immersion' ought not to suggest that elite power has somehow been made visible and its dynamics fully exposed but simply that mediation is a process that is at the heart of even some of the most 'closed' networks. This points to the existence of a more intricate relationship between media and power that recognizes the economic foundations of social relations but also acknowledges 'media power' as a vital (although far from the sole) factor in sustaining and reproducing current patterns of power. What is the point, therefore, of arguing that there is power first and then the mediation of power? Instead, at a time when media power (a) is increasingly the subject of public debate and (b) seems to have such a profound influence on social reproduction more broadly, it is vital to understand its dynamics, its capacities, its limits and its contradictions by neither insulating it from nor reducing it to other forms of power.

Political, economic and cultural dimensions of media power

I have raised so far only a few elements of the puzzle of media power: whether it operates autonomously or rather in conjunction with other spheres of influence; whether it is always mobilized through its component parts or whether it refers to a more collective understanding of media as a set of institutions and processes; whether its own power is over or understated; and whether it refers to a physical property to be possessed or a relationship to be dominated. A further source of confusion relates to the fact that media power is played out in very different fields of the social world and will therefore assume different forms. In order to address this confusion, I want briefly to discuss three ways of framing media power in the liberal democracies of the West: through a democratic lens, through a concern with its economic potential and through a focus on the symbolic practices and textual operations that characterize media flows.

Given the significance of ongoing controversies concerning the impact on the communications landscape of giant companies like News Corp, Google, Mediaset, Facebook and Apple, let us start by considering how they may be affecting democratic life. Media power has frequently been seen in terms of the ability of one group or a single individual to command such a sizeable presence in and control of the media environment, and thus the public sphere, that it undermines both the pluralism of voice and diversity of opinion necessary for a democracy. This form of power is based on the notion that audiences are all too often susceptible to media influence and that too much 'power' in the hands of a single organization or individual (or a small group of individuals) is undesirable and undemocratic. This is the view taken, for example, by the leader of the British Labour Party, Ed Miliband, in his response to the News Corp hacking scandal, where he argued that Rupert Murdoch's grip on the British media needed to be dismantled.

I think it's unhealthy because that amount of power in one person's hands has clearly led to abuses of power within his organisation. If you want to minimise the abuses of power then that kind of concentration of power is frankly quite dangerous. (Quoted in Helm, Doward and Boffey 2011)

The danger Miliband refers to is not simply the corruption of an internal culture – as could happen in any business – but, through the media's political influence, the ability to wield power over public life and the 'national conversation' in quite unaccountable ways. The emblematic figures of this particular understanding of media power range from William Randolph Hearst in the early twentieth century to more recent figures including Murdoch himself; Roberto Marinho, the founder of the Brazilian Globo network; the German publisher Axel Springer; and, perhaps most notoriously, the Italian media mogul turned prime minister, Silvio Berlusconi, who, until his departure from office in 2011, best epitomized the definitional confusion between 'media' and 'politics'. Given the association of all the above 'moguls' with explicitly conservative political views, media power according to this perspective poses not just small ethical or administrative problems but constitutes a major source of ideological support for existing frameworks of power and privilege.

Concentrated media power, therefore, is antidemocratic both because it hands definitional, analytical and interpretive power to unelected organizations and because it undermines the ability of citizens to acquire and exchange the range of information and ideas necessary to take informed decisions about public life. However, it is also dangerous because it distorts the logic of the media industries themselves, transforming them from vehicles of symbolic interaction to increasingly significant engines of capital accumulation. Consider Rupert Murdoch's response in 2009 to calls for a bail-out of news organizations as they struggled to cope with the combined impact of a huge drop in advertising revenue and the structural challenge posed by the internet. Welcoming the collapse of companies that failed to adapt to the new digital age, Murdoch argued that 'they should fail, just as a restaurant that offers meals no one wants to eat or a car-maker who makes cars no one wants to buy should fail' (Murdoch 2009). This is the same vision of media – as commodities that measure their success simply using market criteria – as that famously espoused by Federal Communications Commission (FCC) chairman Mark Fowler in the early 1980s when he described television as 'just another appliance. It's a toaster with pictures' (quoted in Horwitz 1989: 245).

Media power is conceptualized here primarily in relation to economic activity: both in general terms concerning the growing share of gross domestic product earned by the 'creative' and 'cultural' industries and, more precisely, in relation to forms of concentration that distort market systems rather than, as previously mentioned, undermine democracy. Organizations that are too large or that operate as monopolies are said to stifle competition and restrict innovation, thus interrupting the free flow of market forces. There is, therefore, a need for regulatory bodies, whether nationally based, like the Federal Communications Commission (FCC) in the US or Ofcom in the UK, or supra-national, like the European Commission, to monitor the emergence of anti-competitive 'blockages' in media markets and to respond with the appropriate regulatory tools: competition law, media ownership rules or media-specific public interest obligations. The rise of neo-liberalism as a political-economic regime (Couldry 2010, Harvey 2005, Mirowski 2013) together with the enormous growth in the information and communication technology sector has, of course, radically changed what governments and regulators are likely to define as uncompetitive (or indeed unacceptable) but, nevertheless, an economic understanding of media power is increasingly deployed by policymakers, investors and regulators.

This economic perspective on media power has been challenged on several fronts. First, there are those who argue that the digital world has shifted power away from concentrated to dispersed forms of ownership, a central premise of the argument that I tackle in Chapter 4. As we shall see, Alvin Toffler's notion of an epochal 'power shift' (Toffler 1990) was predicated on the emergence of 'power mosaics' where 'one thing is certain: The notion that a tiny handful of giant companies will dominate tomorrow's economy is a comic-book caricature of society' (1990: 232). We see an even more recent illustration of changing patterns of media with Chris Anderson's analysis of the increasing irrelevance, under digital conditions, of the traditional 'blockbuster economy' (Anderson 2009). Of course, these arguments do not by themselves question the association of media power with productivity, growth and innovation but merely suggest that we should concern ourselves with how best to stimulate dynamism and creativity and not to worry about issues of size and scale when thinking through the economic implications of contemporary media. These approaches challenge the often negative connotations of media power – that it is, by definition, a *problem* as we saw above – and replaces it with a notion of fragmented media power as something positive and, indeed, emancipatory that is evidence of both ideal trading conditions and maximal audience interaction. Indeed, according to John Corner, while concentrated media power is usually seen as 'bad ', and as a problem to be corrected, 'good' media power has to be described in totally different terms – as 'communicative capacity' (2011: 37) – and is thus often not characterized as power in the first place. This is an interesting contrast to the pluralist model where 'the threat of coercive measures, or of compulsion, without legitimation or justification, should not properly be called the use of power at all' (Parsons 1967: 331).

Second, and perhaps more fundamentally, there are those who argue that, just as power in general is far too extensive and productive a concept to be 'reduced' to primarily economic features, the power of the media – institutions, channels and texts that rely above all on symbolic interactions – is even less reducible to economic imperatives. Nick Couldry, one of the most prolific recent theorists of media power, is determined to establish the 'analytic separation' of media power from other domains and notes that, all too often, the concept of media power in contemporary media studies 'is either absent or collapsed into its supposed determinants in economic or state power' (2003a: 41). Following Bourdieu (1991), Couldry (2000: 4) argues that media power refers to the 'concentration in media institutions of the symbolic power of "constructing reality" (both factual representations and credible fictions)'. For Couldry, media power is not a tangible object, possessed by institutions and circulated to beguiled audiences but a social process organized on the basis of a constantly renewed distinction between a manufactured (and rather dazzling) 'media world' and the 'ordinary world' of non-media people. One of the key roles of the media is precisely to make this distinction seem entirely natural thus legitimating their symbolic power as key institutions through which we come to make sense of the world. Couldry, in virtually all of his work, assesses the 'local practices' (2000: 155) in which this naturalization of media power takes place, whether through the ritual of major media events (2003b) or the ubiquitous format of reality television (2009).

Couldry's work on media power is a sophisticated exploration of the interaction of institutional structures, modes of representation, access to media technologies and broader issues of political authority and civic engagement, framed by an interest, in relation to an earlier point, with the location rather than the allocation, of media power. He sees power in a particularly dynamic way: as a contingent force, open to political contestation precisely because it is never settled, always in the process of being reproduced and always trying to act 'natural'. But what are the implications, given his argument that media power 'is both a cultural and an economic phenomenon' (2000: 194), of an emphasis on rituals, memory and myths over questions of economics, policy and regulation, particularly in the context of Thompson's warning that there are no clear-cut distinctions between different forms of power (1995: 18)? Precisely in order to do justice to the complex relationship between the cultural and the economic – and in recognition of the material impact of ownership and corporate influence on the impact of media institutions, the capacities of media audiences and the possibilities of media content – can a robust account of media power afford not to privilege these kinds of issues?

John Corner deliberately focuses on the interaction between the political, economic and the cultural in the play of media power arguing that it is a kind of 'soft power' with 'matters of power essentially turning on issues of form and subjectivity' (2011: 3). While this requires great attention to textual and aesthetic detail, Corner is keen not to marginalize political or economic dimensions, arguing that there are both structural and discursive components to media power and is quite right to locate media power in tension with, and in relation to, other forms of power. His account avoids media-centrism and, as I have already noted, contributes to a systemic, rather than an atomized, view of media power. Furthermore, he is quite clear about the relevance of economic factors and market forces on transformations taking place in both political and media culture.

Yet, Corner is preoccupied, above all, with evaluating the discursive mechanisms through which media power is reproduced. Rather than examining the interaction of institutional and text-level factors, he calls for a focus on the 'localised dynamics of form and interpretative practice [that] still figure importantly within power flows and should continue to be one focus for making further conceptual and methodological progress' (2011: 45). Of course, this is a matter of choice and perspective (and Corner's writing on television, screen documentaries and photography is very stimulating), but this approach tends in practice to forego macro-level analysis for an emphasis on 'conditions of subjectivity, of awareness, knowledge and affective orientation' (2011: 15).

These more culturally focused accounts of media power require detailed exploration of textual processes and discursive mechanisms. For Couldry, this involves the investigation of practices such as framing, ordering, naming, spacing and imagining (2000: 42), while for sociologist Ciaran McCullagh, media power operates through the practices of agenda-setting, imitating, sourcing and representing – all of which help to 'shape the nature of social consciousness and the nature of public opinion' (2002: 151). However, given that media power is also about owning, regulating, censoring, controlling, decision-making and profiting, how do we incorporate these processes into a full picture of the significance of communicative activity for the contemporary world? Indeed, given the huge questions currently being posed about the ethical basis, financial sustainability, political influence and democratic implications of contemporary media activity, is there an argument actually to *emphasize* macro-level analysis in order to get to grips with the underlying dynamics of media power?

In the light of the exposure in cases like the Leveson Inquiry of the anti-democratic relationships between police, press and politicians, the continuing scandal over campaign finance in the US and the popular mobilizations in Mexico against the grip of the two main TV channels on public life, we need to make a strong case for moving beyond the 'local' and the 'textual' and to turn our attention to the major social institutions and processes that circulate and embody media power in the world today. This involves a focus on, for example, ownership patterns, resource allocations, governance arrangements and policy and regulatory regimes in conjunction with an analysis of the means by which these embodiments of media power work to naturalize their own status and legitimize their own interpretations. Effectively, this is a plea to combine Lukes' emphasis on the ideological dimension of power with a detective-like obsession with the dynamics of the material environment in which media are produced, distributed and consumed.

Four paradigms of media power

I now want to identify four paradigms – of consensus, chaos, control and contradiction – within which these dimensions of media power co-exist but where each theorizes the play of media power in quite different ways. These are perspectives, in other words, that map not simply how media power 'works' but how we might conceive of it as a social process in its own right. As with any conceptual model, it is open to challenge – there may be additional paradigms, theorists may belong in more than one category, they may have been put into the wrong category or perhaps there are simply too many connections between each of the categories to make them analytically meaningful – but I believe nevertheless that it will help to clarify what is at stake in theorizing media power and therefore to develop a sufficiently robust analytical model both to understand and to help to democratize the relationships to which it refers.

Paradigms are useful ways of organizing together discrete elements into theoretical frameworks in order to analyse social phenomena; they are not naturally occurring categories but purposeful ways of ordering the world so as to make better sense of it (Sparks 2007a: 15–17). As such, they map quite closely onto pre-existing categories of media scholarship where the consensus paradigm may be considered to relate to liberal pluralist communication studies; the chaos paradigm to fan studies and cultural studies; the control paradigm to media political economy; and the contradiction paradigm to Marxist-influenced critical media industry studies and participatory perspectives. However, specific 'disciplinary' approaches to media analysis should not be seen as homogeneous nor reduced to a particular orientation, not least in their attitude towards power. The four paradigms discussed in this section, while also not free of internal distinctions and ambiguities, nevertheless provide a more focused approach to questions of *power* and allow us better to examine the relationships between the economic, political, technological and cultural forces that shape the dynamics of media power as they operate, albeit in quite specific ways, across different genres and platforms.

Consensus

The consensus paradigm relates to a long-standing and highly influential notion of power that, in advanced liberal democracies, power is widely distributed, pluralistically organized and contributes to a relatively stable social arrangement. Responding to criticism, posed particularly by theorists like C. Wright Mills (1959), that American society in the mid-twentieth century was dominated by a military, political and financial elite, pluralists argued that the

US politics was instead a competitive arena in which different interests vied for power and influence but in which there was no single dominant voice, no undue concentration of power. In Robert Dahl's study of the political system of New Haven, Connecticut, *Who Governs?* (Dahl 2005), politics is dominated by coalitions – by rival groups of actors and interests, none of whom could be said to exercise complete control. According to Dahl, 'there was no clear center of dominant influence in the [political] order. No single group of unified leaders possessed enough influence to impose a solution' (2005: 198), certainly not the economic or social 'notables' who had only a limited and shifting impact on New Haven politics. Pluralist politics, argues Dahl, is characterized by its 'dispersion of political resources', the 'disappearance of elite rule' (2005: 85, 86) and the emergence of polyarchy, a benign mode of democratic politics.

Yet, despite the multiplicity of beliefs and the variety of channels through which to mobilize these beliefs, a degree of mutual understanding and harmony was still evident to Dahl inside American society. This was not imposed by the 'notables' nor was it spontaneously present in the minds of citizens; instead, members of the political class and the bulk of citizens are engaged in an ongoing dialogue that 'generates enough agreement on rules and norms so as to permit the system to operate' (2005: 316). The consensus reached is not permanent and nor is it particularly stable but the process of consensus-building is nevertheless vital to the functioning of American democracy. Consensus, concludes Dahl (2005: 316), 'is not at all a static and unchanging attribute of citizens. It is a variable element in a complex and more or less continuous process.'

This conception of consensus has long underpinned pluralist arguments concerning the integrative function of the free press as well as the exercise of sovereign power. Dahl acknowledges in *Who Governs?* the rather modest role of newspapers in fostering pluralism but perhaps the most famous expression of consensus in relation to media power are the rationale for media performance that are proposed in *Four Theories of the Press* (Siebert, Peterson and Schramm 1963) to describe the American and British media systems. This remains the classic exposition of liberal advocacy of the 'freedom of the press' composed primarily of a 'libertarian' approach where newspapers are seen as 'a partner in the search for truth' but where '[t]ruth is no longer conceived as the property of power' (1963: 3). The libertarian model was modified in the twentieth century to deal with the growing permeation of society by electronic media and a new 'social responsibility' model emerged reflecting the view 'that the power and near monopoly position of the media impose on them an obligation to be socially responsible' (1963: 5). Both rationale, however, were predicated on an unyielding faith in market forces to nurture media systems that informed and entertained audiences, that were based on professional values of independence and impartiality and that provided a necessary check on government power. A market-driven media is, from this perspective, one of the guarantors of a pluralist consensus.

This approach resonates in more recent accounts of the democratic role of the media. For example, in Dayan and Katz's notion of integrative 'media events' (Dayan and Katz 1994) – ceremonial coverage of 'unique' public occasions like state funerals, major sporting events, scandals and political earthquakes – audiences are enthralled and transformed by the live coverage of these unprecedented events. 'These broadcasts *integrate* societies in a collective heartbeat and evoke a *renewal of loyalty* to the society and its legitimate authority' (1994: 9). We can also identify the consensual dimension of media power in some non-market structures, for example in accounts of public service broadcasting as an institution that serves to produce cohesive viewing and listening publics with distinctive identities but common interests. For Paddy Scannell, organizations like the BBC 'brought into being a culture in common to whole populations and a shared life of a quite new kind' (1989: 138), and they remain a central part of British democratic life. Indeed, he attributes unprecedented generative power to the media: 'What was *public* life before broadcasting?' he wonders (1989: 135).

A consensual media system requires adequate competition between its different outlets and thus the free interchange of all players in an open market. Media economist Ben Compaine describes the patterns of ownership in the largely commercial US media system as 'extremely democratic' and notes that the media tend 'to be run not to promote an ideology but to seek profit' (2001: 4). Private ownership is therefore viewed as a steward of plurality with regulation, mostly confined to the broadcast sector, needed only as a last resort in order to deal with specific blockages (for example, monopolies or oligopolies) and to redistribute media power across a wider number of players. Indeed, despite moves to liberalize media systems and to roll back curbs on ownership concentration (Freedman 2008), there remain restrictions on media ownership and forms of public media in almost all countries. This 'mixed economy' approach reflects the enduring appeal of calls for 'choice' of outlets and 'variety' of media content in contemporary democracies, facilitated by a free market but underwritten by the use of limited state power.

In sum, this consensus paradigm relates to a liberal functionalist perspective on media, described by James Curran as one where the media's role is 'to assist the collective self-realization, co-ordination, democratic management, social integration and adaptation of society' (Curran 2002: 136). In the light of recent exposures of the illegal and unethical behaviour of the press, of desperate attempts to boost ratings at all costs, and of the hypercommercialization and globalization of large parts of the media, this approach may appear better suited to an earlier period of media history. However, even with the emergence of digital technologies and 'empowered' consumers, it is stubbornly resistant to change and remains the default language of policymakers wishing to nurture 'open' and 'competitive' media markets. Indeed, it is precisely this approach – in which economic liberalism is seen to promote individual liberty and democratic pluralism – that underpins the arguments of the UK news proprietors seeking to maintain self-regulation in the light of the phone hacking crisis. For example, in one of its many attacks on calls for a new, tougher regulatory regime to promote ethical journalism, Britain's top-selling newspaper, the *Sun*, opined that: 'Ours may be a rough old trade, sometimes scurrilous and always noisy. But without its freedom to dig dirt, embarrass the great and good, and tell unpalatable truths – and, yes, occasionally get it wrong – British democracy risks grievous damage' (31 October 2012). Despite warnings from theorists like Onora O'Neill (2004: 8) that '[a]ccording unrestricted freedom of expression not only to individuals but also to powerful institutions, the media among them, is not necessary for but damaging to democracy', this form of media power continues to be invoked as a vital requirement for free speech and social cohesion.

Chaos

Recent structural and geopolitical shifts have forced an updating of the some of the foundational elements of pluralist accounts of power. While globalization and digitization have contributed to the erosion of fixed spatial boundaries and the rise of a disembedded and decentralized form of capitalism built on abundance and not scarcity, a range of events – for example, the collapse of Communism, the spread of democratization, the growth of public relations and the weakening of deference towards elites – have precipitated a new and highly volatile paradigm: cultural chaos (McNair 2006).

The chaos paradigm is based not on the role of singular factors like class, hierarchy and wealth in sustaining unequal social relations but on ideological diffusion and structural uncertainty. This reflects the dispersed and 'fluid' properties of power in a digital age. According to McNair (2006: 200), power

> ebbs and flows between locations and centres, spreading amongst societies along the channels and pathways provided by communication media. Power *pools*. It evaporates, dilutes and drains away as environmental conditions change. Communication in the medium through which power resources are disseminated, and leaky channels of communication therefore mean less secure power centres.

Traditional systems of gatekeeping and ideological control have, therefore, largely dissolved allowing for more interrogative forms of journalism and a flourishing of perspectives, including even the promotion of radical voices – such as Michael Moore and Naomi Klein – that would previously have been kept to the margins.

The paradigm finds its perfect expression in the collapse of an 'old media' logic in the face of the digital media revolution, a situation in which business models, modes of production and consumption patterns which were relatively stable for many years have now started to break down. We are shifting from being a population of established newspaper readers and viewers of scheduled television programmes to an amorphous group of promiscuous consumers that takes its news from diverse outlets, watches television at times (and on platforms) that suit its convenience and not those of the networks and generally cannot be relied upon to demonstrate brand loyalty for very long. Bob Garfield describes this as 'The Chaos Scenario' (Garfield 2009) and argues that we are witnessing a seismic shift in media power relationships.

> The first element of The Chaos Scenario ... creates an inexorable death spiral, in which the fragmentation of audience and DVR ad skipping lead to an exodus of advertisers, leading in turn to an exodus of capital, leading to a decline in the quality of content, leading to further audience defection, leading to further advertiser defection and so on to oblivion. (2009: 38)

Although, judging by the revival of the advertising industry, an overall increase in television viewing and, perhaps most surprisingly, a recent increase in network news audiences in the US (Friedman 2012), the death of 'old media' is somewhat premature, the enormous growth of social media has clearly contributed to a tremendously uncertain, but no less refreshing, atmosphere of confusion in which power, it is argued, operates in far less hierarchical ways – proof, for its advocates, of the ability of forms of technological power to mediate, unsettle or reconstitute social relationships.

It is, of course, far from novel to associate the internet with an ability to disrupt the wider communications environment. Indeed, for many years it was viewed as a rather uncontrollable and energetic toddler who fails to adhere to the more ordered practices of the adult world. Consider the words in 1996 of District Judge Dalzell when throwing out the Communications Decency Act, a highly controversial attempt to regulate obscenity online:

> The absence of governmental regulation of Internet content has unquestionably produced a kind of chaos, but as one of the plaintiffs' experts put it with such resonance at the hearing: 'What achieved success was the very chaos that the Internet is. The strength of the Internet is that chaos.' (ACLU vs Reno 1996)

The internet has since grown from an anarchic toddler to a snarling teenager with the ability still to unsettle everything around it. Larry Downes claims that disruptive technologies like the internet, based on very low transaction costs and virtually infinite capacity, undermine established business practices and that '[c]onfronted with the weird economics of information, the core principles of public law, private law, and information law are being turned upside down' (Downes 2009: 269).

Not everything is to be welcomed in this brave new world but, generally speaking, theories of chaos are seen to express more adequately the fractured and decentralized forms of media power facilitated by digital technologies. Jeff Jarvis describes this as a 'power shift' (2009: 11) in which 'the shift from mass [to niche] is really a shift of power from top to bottom, center to edge, them to us' (2009: 67). *Wired* editor Chris Anderson makes a similar point about what he sees as an 'inversion of power' (2009: 99) from traditional manufacturers and advertisers who are rapidly losing control to newly empowered audiences: 'The collective now controls the message' (2009: 99). According to Anderson, we are seeing the transformation of power from label to band, publisher to author, price to free, 'watercooler' moments to dispersed sharing, mass to niche and rigid to elastic, while, for Tapscott and Williams in their description of 'Wikinomics', digital 'weapons of mass collaboration' are 'ushering us toward a world where knowledge, power, and productive capability will be more dispersed than at any time in our history' (2008: 12).

This corresponds to McNair's conception of a far more fluid social and ideological environment in which traditional mechanisms for ensuring compliance have broken down under the impact both of communicative abundance as well as an increasing unwillingness to 'toe the line'. This has significant political consequences as, for Henry Jenkins, the process of convergence makes it much harder for elites to impose their authority. He contrasts 'old media's' 'power to marginalize' with today's bottom-up 'power to negate' (2006: 278) that is facilitated by new peer-to-peer networks, characterized by 'prosumption' and underpinned by a collapse of deference. 'Democracy has always been a messy business' he argues, but today's 'politics of parody', in which citizens use digital tools in creative and autonomous ways to express their cynicism towards 'official politics', is a perfectly logical response to the changing dynamics of authority (2006: 293). The most dramatic illustration of this view of dispersed media power – and of the interconnections between political, economic and technological contexts – is, as I have pointed out earlier in this chapter, to be found in claims made about the 'revolutionary' role of social media in the Arab Spring of 2011 and the possibilities for networked protest (Castells 2011, Mason 2012).

In his view of power as a highly volatile and diffuse phenomenon, McNair appears to oscillate between a Foucauldian approach, where power is seen as productive and all-pervasive, and a 'new economy' version of earlier pluralist accounts where, for example, Cater writes about the 'mobile and transitory' nature of power in highly segmented decision-making situations (1965: 4), just as Freeman (1965: 25) highlights the 'complex and pluralistic committee matrix within which so many decisions are reached in a decentralized fashion'. Moreover, McNair admits that the chaos paradigm is not immune from the influence of powerful gatekeepers in the sense that key actors remain determined to stamp their authority on the digital world. The problem is that, given digital abundance and ideological fragmentation, they will find it virtually impossible to secure this objective: 'The chaos paradigm does not abolish the desire for control; it focuses on the shrinking media space available for securing it ideologically' (McNair 2006: 4).

This is an interesting point, although just how difficult it is to secure some semblance of order online is up for debate, as I explore in Chapter 4. As the web grows into adulthood, the desire to control it is increasingly evident and the search for order increasingly important. In a situation in which the internet is expected to contribute some $4.2 *trillion* to the GDP of the world's twenty biggest economies (Boston Consulting 2012), it is not surprising that we see attempts to regulate the chaos and to classify the confusion: Google categorizes the web, Wikipedia orders knowledge and Facebook organizes friendships. This is partly a matter of the cyclical nature of technological evolution (Spar 2001, Wu 2010) where technologies pass through different stages of development from anarchy and uncertainty through consolidation to the re-establishment of rules and the reallocation of property rights. It is also, however, evidence of the profoundly contradictory nature of technological innovation under capitalism – that it benefits the public so long as it rewards those who own or control it – and is thus likely not to stay permanently in a state of chaos.

Control

The underlying pluralism of the consensus and chaos paradigms has triggered responses from theorists who believe that, far from achieving social integration, providing a 'neutral' window on the world or fostering the flourishing of diverse voices, there *is* such a thing as a 'dominant media' bloc that uses its control over symbolic resources to naturalize hegemonic ideas and to confine public discussion to a narrow and artificially maintained consensus. Brian McNair describes this as the 'control paradigm' and argues (2006: 3) that it is

premised on economic determinacy, whereby ruling elites are presumed to be able to extend their control of economic resources to control of the cultural apparatuses of media, including the means of propaganda and

public relations, leading to planned and predictable outcomes such as pro-
elite media bias, dominant ideology, even 'brainwashing'.

While this simplifies and caricatures many of the arguments of 'control
theorists', it does at least point to some of the mechanisms and impacts
that are relevant to this conception of media power: the capturing of
media agendas, the commodification of innovation, the deployment of
propagandistic techniques and the circulation of partisan media content aimed
at securing compliance with existing social relations. Furthermore, McNair's
emphasis on the paradigm is certainly justified considering the influence that
it has long exerted over critical academics and audiences and its status as a
comprehensive account of the media's failure to perform the task attributed
to them by pluralists: to hold power to account.

However, it vastly exaggerates the homogeneity of those who are said
to operate within the paradigm and glosses over important distinctions in a
field characterized by a wide range of different perspectives. There are instead
many different varieties of what McNair suggests is a fairly uniform approach
to media influence on the part of these critical theorists. The 'hardest' edge
of the paradigm is best expressed by the propaganda model as developed
by Edward Herman and Noam Chomsky in *Manufacturing Consent* (1988).
For them, the mainstream news media are a crucial tool for legitimizing the
ideas of the most powerful social actors and for securing consent for their
actions: they are the ideological lynchpins of the dominant class and thus
a crucial constituent of state power. Through a combination of capitalist
property relations and an orientation on profit; the existence of advertising
as a key source of capital; the domination of elite sources; sustained attacks
on any material that challenges these sources and elite agendas; and the
construction of an 'enemy' (whether Communism or Islamism) around
which populations (and media agendas) can unite, the mainstream media
environment is structured in such a way as to control dissent and steer public
action towards the interests of ruling elites. Herman and Chomsky provide a
detailed empirical analysis of, for example, news media coverage of the US
interventions in Central America and South-East Asia to make a convincing
case that the 'societal purpose of the media is to inculcate and defend the
economic, social, and political agenda of privileged groups that dominate the
domestic society and the state' (1988: 298).

David Edwards and David Cromwell of Media Lens, an online group
dedicated to correcting the distortions of corporate news, adopt the
propaganda model in their rebuttal, primarily, of 'liberal' news outlets (such
as the *Guardian* and the BBC) that, they argue, provide effective cover for
what is, overwhelmingly, a partisan and conservative set of interests.
Interestingly, the problem lies not simply with a corporate media system,

described by Edwards and Cromwell as constituting 'a propaganda system for elite interests' (2006: 2), but with the individualism and complicity of citizens who refuse to withdraw their support for instruments of class rule that are instead disguised as professional journalistic values. 'Control is maintained', they insist (2006: 187), 'not by violence, but by deception, self-deception, and by a mass willingness to subordinate our own thoughts and feelings to notions of "professionalism" and "objectivity".' The media, according to this perspective, are seamlessly integrated into existing structures of power with the result that 'media performance overwhelmingly promotes the views and interests of established power' (2006: 178).

The propaganda model occupies only part of a broader theoretical movement at the heart of the control paradigm – media political economy – that assesses the structuring relationships between economic organization, political contexts, institutional forms, textual possibilities and consumption patterns *across* media genres (Murdock and Golding 2005). For Vincent Mosco, political economy actually 'asks us to concentrate on a specific set of social relations organized around *power* or the ability to control other people, processes and things, even in the face of resistance' (Mosco 2009: 24). This is a highly productive line of inquiry that attempts to knit together what are often seen as disparate elements of the social world through, above all, privileging the material relations of power that shape the possibilities and contours of media at any one time (Curran 2002, Garnham 1990, Golding and Murdock 2000, McChesney 2004, H. Schiller 1989, D. Schiller 2007, Smythe 1981). It is based on the notion, paraphrasing Marx somewhat, that forms of social consciousness correspond to the sum total of capitalist relations of production and it has led to illuminating critiques of vast areas of media output (see Wasko, Murdock and Sousa 2011 for a comprehensive selection).

Of course, just as there are multiple shades of political economy analysis, there are many other approaches within the control paradigm that refute any notion of a uniform, top-down, smooth exercise of power although that does not mean that they escape from its overall logic. For James Carey, power refers to the ability to hegemonize definitions and allocations not of economic phenomena but of *reality* which he describes as a 'scarce resource': 'Once the blank canvas of the world is portrayed and featured, it is also pre-empted and restricted' (1992: 87). Pierre Bourdieu conceives of symbolic power in terms of its ability to construct reality and endows it with almost magical qualities: the 'power of constituting the given through utterances, of making people see and believe, of confirming or transforming the vision of the world and, thereby, action on the world and thus the world itself' (1991: 170). Even more significantly, Bourdieu sees symbolic power as a highly efficient means of naturalizing certain preferred interpretations of the world and of legitimizing classifications based on those with most access to that power.

Symbols are the instruments *par excellence* of 'social integration': as instruments of knowledge and communication ... they make it possible for there to be a *consensus* on the meaning of the social world, a consensus which contributes fundamentally to the reproduction of the social order. (1991: 166)

This is not the comfortable, democratic consensus discussed by Dahl and his fellow pluralists nor the rather more frazzled and energetic expressions celebrated by chaos theorists but a distilled version of class interests. Whether this process works in relation to the media by including or marginalizing specific perspectives, by shaping and framing social narratives, by influencing what narratives are told in the first place or by privileging certain individuals with greater symbolic resources (and therefore life chances) than others, it seems to me that this is still part of a quite pervasive and critical 'control' paradigm.

Contradiction

The final paradigm, and the one that most effectively addresses both the relational and material aspects of media power, is a modification of the control paradigm. While it accepts that media power is an *interested* force, a set of relationships intimately tied to the reproduction of existing relations of power more generally, it seeks to avoid the functionalism with which control theorists are often (and sometimes rightly) associated. Far from media institutions working seamlessly as 'totalitarian structures of power' as recent advocates of the propaganda model have argued (Cromwell and Edwards 2006: 187), they are rather a series of groups and institutions that, while overwhelmingly tied to powerful interests (and of course the hacking scandal provides an exemplary illustration of this), are not immune from the movements and ideas that circulate in society at any one time and that seek to challenge these power structures (Kumar 2008). Crucially, as the Italian Marxist Antonio Gramsci, reminds us, '[a] given socio-historical moment is never homogeneous; on the contrary, it is rich in contradictions' (1985: 93). What significance does all this have for the study of media power?

To provide a meaningful answer, we need to go back to Marx's conception of contradiction as a key feature of capitalist society. Throughout his writing, Marx combines a tribute to the revolutionary achievements of capitalism with an analysis of why it is systematically unable to make available the full potential of these achievements to its subjects. While the capitalist class has played a 'most revolutionary part' in human history, it has done this, not because of the 'genius' of individual scientists and technologists or the bravery of pioneering entrepreneurs but because it is a system based on a structural need to innovate, expand and accumulate.

> The bourgeoisie cannot exist without constantly revolutionising the instruments of production, and thereby the relations of production, and with them the whole relations of society. Conservation of the old modes of production in unaltered form, was, on the contrary, the first condition of existence for all earlier industrial classes. Constant revolutionising of production, uninterrupted disturbance of all social conditions, everlasting uncertainty and agitation distinguish the bourgeois epoch from all earlier ones. (Marx and Engels 1975: 36)

Yet, just as Marx was enthralled by capitalism's dynamism, he was appalled by the means by which it is obliged to sustain itself: through destructive competition between different companies, intensive exploitation in order to extract maximum profits; increased alienation as workers are systematically separated from the fruits of their labour; and a disastrous lack of coordination which leads to bouts of overproduction and regular periods of crisis. These processes are for Marx the terrible price to be paid by the majority of people for the wonderful technological advances experienced – albeit unequally – under capitalism.

Marx highlights these contradictory tendencies within capitalism – for example, between the interests of workers and capitalists, between the social relations and productive capacity of the system, between socially useful production and production for exchange and, crucially, between the social aspect of labour and its private appropriation – not as incidental but key both to capitalism's expansion *and* its demise. As Marx writes in the *Grundrisse* (1973: 77), reflecting on processes that are familiar to many media economists:

> The [capitalist] division of labour results in concentration, co-ordination, co-operation, antagonism of private interests and class interests, competition, the centralization of capital, monopolies and joint stock companies – so many contradictory forms of unity which in turn engenders all these contradictions.

Contradiction, as Ellen Meiskins Wood puts it (2002: 278), is therefore 'capitalism's basic operating principle, in a way that is true of no other social form. It is the source, at one and the same time, of both the capitalist system's unique dynamism and its constant self-subversion'. While other theorists identify contradiction as a feature of all social systems, especially in terms of the relationship between humans and nature (for example Giddens 1979), Wood insists that capitalism alone is predicated on such an inflammable and generative set of tensions (see also Harvey 2014).

These contradictions are played out both at the level of institutions and ideas, material as well as symbolic practices. For Marx, popular consciousness 'must be explained from the contradictions of material life, from the conflict existing between the social productive forces and the relations of production' (Marx 1969: 504). Gramsci, in trying to understand the failure of revolutionary movements in the inter-war period, discussed how there was a battle going on in the minds of ordinary people between what he called 'common sense', ideas generally distilled from the capitalist class, and 'good sense', the formation of a more progressive set of ideas developed in the course of struggling against that class. In particular, he spoke of a *dual consciousness* that reflects this ongoing battle. The worker

> has a practical activity, but has no clear theoretical consciousness of his practical activity, which nonetheless still involves understanding the world in so far as he transforms it. His theoretical consciousness can indeed be historically in opposition to his activity. One might almost say that he has two theoretical consciousnesses (or one contradictory consciousness): one which is implicit in his activity and which really unites him with his fellow-workers in the practical transformation of the real world; and one, superficially explicit or verbal, which he has inherited from the past and uncritically absorbed. (Gramsci 1971: 333)

This is particularly helpful in thinking about the media as a set of institutions and practices that are implicated in the regular advocacy of 'common sense' and the transmission of ideas 'inherited from the past'. But the model also suggests that, when pushed to do so by popular mobilizations and mass struggles, the media may be able (albeit in fragile and temporary ways) to articulate strands of 'good sense' and enhance prospects for change (Ytterstad 2012).

This is especially the case in moments when capitalist hegemony, understood by Gramsci to refer to the various forms of class leadership at any one time, is threatened and unstable. Of course, hegemony understood properly is never absolute and fixed but corresponds to the uneven consciousness of ordinary people under capitalism. 'We have to emphasize', argues Raymond Williams (2005: 38), 'that hegemony is not singular; indeed that its own internal structures are highly complex, and have continually to be renewed, recreated and defended; and by the same token that they can be continually challenged and in certain respects modified.' Indeed, that is surely one of the prime objectives of media power: all the time to seek fresh ways of naturalizing the media's own authority.

But while hegemony is never stable, it is vital to highlight the importance of these interruptions to 'normal' practice: 'The production and reproduction of society is never guaranteed, automatic or mechanical, and the problematics of the phenomenon are often best revealed in moments of conflict and contradiction and in the rare but powerful episodes of coercive violence, social disorder and chaos' (Carey 1992: 110). There have been several examples of how, in recent years, small portions of the mainstream media, despite their frequent involvement in the amplification of powerful voices and reproduction of existing relations, have also provided space to more critical or 'marginal' perspectives (such as in relation to class, gender or ethnicity). For example, in one case that I will return to in Chapter 5, the popular tabloid newspaper, the *Daily Mirror*, adopted a radical stance against the rush to go to war with Iraq in 2003 at a time when the UK audiences were clearly not satisfied with official explanations and media frames justifying a war, and marched in their millions urging the government not to invade Iraq (discussed in Nineham 2013). Other examples include sympathetic coverage of the 1997 strike by United Parcel Service (UPS) workers by mainstream media in the US (Kumar 2008), favourable reporting in the Danish media of environmental campaigning (Ytterstad and Eide 2011) or even the appearance of an opinion piece by anti-capitalist Occupy representatives in the pages of the business daily *Financial Times* (25 January 2012). None of these examples occurred because of any inherent pluralism in the mainstream media. The degree to which there are different positions expressed in the media relates to the need, in a competitive market, to address (in however skewed a way) both the interests of different audiences and the existence of conflicts among capitalist elites as well as pressure placed on mainstream media by countervailing forces.

There are, as a result, multiple contradictions within the commercial media: a simultaneous desire for a narrow consensus and yet a structural imperative for difference; a situation in which audiences are treated as commodities but in which they do not always play this role; a tendency for those who work within the media not to rock the boat (for self-protection and advancement) but, in exceptional periods, to do precisely this. We need, therefore, a methodological approach that tackles the mainstream's embedding in elite networks of power but also compensates for the control paradigm's 'inability, or perhaps reluctance, to acknowledge how these contradictions account for instances of creativity, resistance and change' (Havens, Lotz and Tinic 2009: 238; see also Hesmondhalgh 2013: 45). We need to integrate analysis of the 'quotidian practices and competing goals' of the media industries (Havens et al. 2009: 236) with the larger political and economic contexts in which these practices take place, and we should neither reduce one to the other nor pretend that micro-level interactions are immune from the impact of the tensions that mark the dynamics of broader social forces.

An approach to the media that focuses on their internal contradictions can highlight not simply the ways in which everything from Hollywood movies to network news and from social media to soap operas are involved in generating 'common sense' but also how popular mobilizations – not in the discursive sense discussed by some media scholars (for example Fiske 1989) – might help to produce forms of 'good sense' inside the media. Recognizing and acting upon these contradictions is necessary, as Mike Wayne puts it (2003: 261), 'if we are to avoid sliding into some species of functionalism or pessimism'. This requires an approach to media power that emphasizes structure *and* agency, contradiction *and* action, consensus *and* conflict; an analytical framework that recognizes the existence of unequal power frameworks but acknowledges that they are not forever frozen; and a perspective that takes seriously the activities of producers and audiences while recognizing the existence of uneven consciousness. In short, the contradiction paradigm is needed to compensate for the misplaced optimism of pluralism, the occasional functionalism of the control paradigm and the unwarranted celebrations of the chaos scenario. Media power, according to this perspective, may be comprehensive but it is nevertheless always unstable and contestable.

Conclusion

These four paradigms provide the organizational foundation for the rest of the book. Chapter 2 considers the role of media elites and the implications of concentrated media ownership given contemporary neo-liberal circumstances and addresses many of the concerns that are closest to political economy in reflecting on the media's status as mechanisms of social control. Chapter 3 provides an assessment of the terms and conditions on which media policymaking is based and necessarily confronts pluralist assumptions concerning decision-making power that I discussed in relation to theories of consensus. Instead, I argue for an emphasis on the silences that permeate policymaking – particularly in relation to pluralism and net neutrality – and that distort the process in favour of those best able to shape both what questions are posed as well as which ones are not to be tabled at all. Chapter 4 examines the claims made by advocates of the chaos paradigm that digital media have helped to fracture accumulated concentrations of media power and to usher in a new volatile yet decentralized media environment. I examine the argument that there has been a fundamental redistribution of power given the rise of digital media and focus on the continuing relevance for the communications environment of power blocs (as opposed to 'power mosaics') and gatekeepers (despite the process of disintermediation). Chapter 5 then focuses on contradictions in contemporary capitalist societies to explore how resistance to media power is most effectively posed and looks at challenges both to mainstream media content, notably in the light of anti-war coverage in the popular press, and to existing media structures in the context of struggles for media reform.

The book argues that media power is a pervasive and difficult concept. It is too often used as shorthand for the political influence of a particular media mogul *or* the cultural impact of a specific technology *or* the affective dimension of a particular text; media power is viewed either as an irrepressible force *or* as a diversion from more substantial threats to democracy and citizenship. What I will attempt to show is that media power, particularly as found in neo-liberal societies of the West, is not reducible to a single characteristic nor traceable to a single source (despite the undoubted impact of a Murdoch or a Berlusconi); it does not 'belong' to Hollywood, Silicon Valley, Madison Avenue or what used to be known as Fleet Street (although it is most certainly mobilized in all those contexts); neither does it emerge spontaneously out of the communicative interactions of ordinary people (even though many people may claim to be 'empowered' by their use of media technologies). It refers instead to a set of relationships that help to organize the deployment of the symbolic resources that play a vital role in social reproduction and that, in conjunction with other institutions and processes, help to structure our knowledge about, our ability to participate in and our capacity to change the world.

The crucial point, however, is that these relationships are situated in an environment in which access to the media – as with access to all kinds of resources at institutional and societal levels, including health, education and employment – is fundamentally unequal and reflects structural disparities of power in wider society. Not all audiences are equally desirable to advertisers; not all individuals have the same capacity to start up a publishing venture despite being formally 'free' to do so; not all readers have the same access to editors and owners should they wish to complain about something; and indeed not all citizens are able to afford the £250,000 necessary to secure a private dinner with the British prime minister David Cameron in order to discuss urgent matters of public policy (Leigh 2012: 1). Media power is both a consequence and an increasingly significant component of continuing, and stratified, processes of social reproduction. It is not simply about *either* gently persuading *or* forcibly coercing individuals to do things they would otherwise choose not to do but about the material coordination of flows of information, communication and culture such that persuasion and coercion – as well as expression and interpretation – are most effectively able to take place.

2

Elites, Ownership and Media Power

Forgot to tell #Leveson that it's unreasonable to expect individuals to spend £millions on newspapers and not have access to politicians.

EVGENY LEBEDEV, OWNER OF THE *INDEPENDENT* NEWSPAPER, TWEET, 23 APRIL 2012

This book argues that media power is best understood as a relational property – the ability, in competition with others, to hegemonize the resources concentrated inside the media – but the popular shorthand for media power, as previously noted, often refers to those individuals who sit at the top of the largest communications corporations across the globe. People like News Corporation chair Rupert Murdoch, CNN's founder Ted Turner, Globo's Roberto Marinho, Kalanithi Maran, chairman of the Sun Group in India, Koos Bekker, CEO of South African media conglomerate Naspers, the Mexican telecommunications billionaire Carlos Slim and the German publisher Axel Springer are the latter-day expressions of power and influence that was, in earlier times, characterized by William Randolph Hearst, Frank Gannett and Lords Beaverbrook and Rothermere.

The 'media mogul' phenomenon is most acutely articulated when control of media interests is directly combined with the exercise of political power as with the former New York City mayor Michael Bloomberg (founder of Bloomberg News), former Thai premier Thaksin Shinawatra and, perhaps most notoriously, the former Italian prime minister and media giant Silvio Berlusconi. According to Paul Ginsborg, Berlusconi 'attempted to do what no other media magnate had ever done before him: to unite very significant media ownership to national political power' (2005: 62). Partly through his control of Mediaset, a conglomerate with interests including commercial television, publishing, advertising and football, Berlusconi managed to dominate the Italian political scene for some twenty years, fusing media and political power in an unprecedented fashion. Even where the roles are not quite so obviously meshed together, media moguls have long relied on relationships with leading politicians to secure and maintain their power – from Thaksin's friendship with former Interior Minister Chalerm Yubamrung that helped him launch Thailand's first pay-TV service (Lewis 2007: 27) to Roberto Marinho's close contacts with the generals who ruled Brazil until 1985 (Margolis 1998: 146) and from Rupert Murdoch's personal relationships with Margaret Thatcher and Tony Blair to the association of Canal Plus founder Andre Rousselet with former French president Francois Mitterrand, who, according to Tunstall and Palmer (1991: 158), used to discuss media policy during their regular Monday morning rounds of golf.

Media moguls are, therefore, intimately connected to other powerful actors in networks that were famously described by the US sociologist C. Wright Mills as a 'power elite' (Mills 1959). This refers to a small group of people who occupy commanding positions across the economy, politics, culture and authority and who impose their world views and everyday regimes on those who lack 'elite' power. In a direct challenge to pluralist accounts of a society in which 'equilibrium is achieved by the pulling and hauling of many interests' (1959: 242), Mills sought to highlight the interconnections that allowed elites to come together in order to reign over the rest of the population. Some ten years later in the UK, the Marxist political scientist Ralph Miliband embarked on a related project, aiming to study the unequal distribution of power in the contemporary state in order to confront the assumption that 'power, in Western societies, is competitive, fragmented and diffused' (1969: 2). In *The State in Capitalist Society*, a book actually dedicated to Mills, Miliband discusses the 'social composition of the state elite' (1969: 68) and examines the processes by which state power is legitimized.

What is so important for us is that both writers prioritize emerging mass communication systems as vital components of elite rule and provide a key intellectual underpinning for later approaches to media scholarship, embodied by the control paradigm, that view the mainstream media in a similar light. Whether it is Herman and Chomsky's propaganda model (Herman and Chomsky 1988), Robert McChesney's critique of media concentration (McChesney 2000) or sections of the media political economy tradition developed in the UK (see Murdock and Golding 1977), there remains an influential view of the existence of a cohesive group of people whose privileged access to, and membership of, the 'upper' layers of society ensures that the media 'function' to secure and reproduce the interests of this elite. The provenance of this idea can be traced back not only to classical Marxism's development of a critical political economy but also to the approaches of Mills and Miliband, both of whom sought to expose the connections and cultures that lay at the heart of elite power.

This chapter explores 'power elite' theories in relation to the role that media institutions and personnel play in 'manufacturing consent' to capitalist relations. It considers the role and relevance of elites in contemporary circumstances and attempts to identify distinctive features of a neo-liberal media power elite (as well as to reflect on the continuing salience of the concept of neo-liberalism). Finally, it focuses on whether ownership is a sufficiently meaningful proxy for media power, particularly in its concentrated form, and addresses the political influence that is mobilized through elite control of the media. It concludes that elite theory is a fantastically valuable, though in the end perhaps limited, tool for understanding the implications and exercise of media power.

Power elite theory and the media

Mills' argument that power was centralized inside elite circles was a jolt against the complacency of liberal pluralist accounts of the US society that stressed the latter's vigorous competition for power and influence and its self-regulating ability to overcome inequalities and democratic blockages. Instead, Mills claimed that in an increasingly bureaucratized society, control of key institutions was dominated by a narrow group of people drawn from three sectors of American public life. 'By the power elite, we refer to those political, economic and military circles which as an intricate set of overlapping cliques share decisions having at least national consequences' (1959: 18). The book goes on to catalogue and evaluate the social composition and organizational structure of the groups that inhabit this elite including the 'very rich', the 'corporate chief executives', the 'warlords', the 'political directorate' and even the 'celebrities' who are lauded inside the media as the most exquisite symbols of prestige and status at any one time. The emphasis for Mills was, therefore, on the dynamics of membership of the elite rather than on its impact.

One of the leading proponents of pluralism, Robert Dahl criticized *The Power Elite* for its failure empirically to evaluate 'a series of concrete decisions' (1958: 466), the core of the visible first 'face' of power identified by Lukes (2005). This gets to the heart of the differences between pluralists and more radical voices as Mills makes the point explicitly that power is not to be measured only in its visible form. Mills, presaging Lukes' other 'faces' of power, was more interested in the elite's *capacity* to act more than the actions themselves: 'their failure to act, their failure to make decisions, it itself an act that is often of greater consequence than the decisions they do make' (Mills 1959: 4). This is a claim that I shall return to in my assessment of 'media policy silences' in the next chapter.

Dahl also challenged Mills' tendency to exaggerate elite consensus, a point that was picked up by Daniel Bell, who cast doubt on the levels of coordination that were implied by Mills' thesis: 'Except in a vague ideological sense, there are relatively few issues on which the managerial elite are united' (Bell 1958: 248). The idea of a cohesive power elite was, for pluralists, a crude and conspiratorial explanation of the complexities of American democracy. Mills, however, had no illusions that the elites agreed on everything but insisted that their shared interests ultimately served to override any differences between them. He recognized the frequent tension inside elite groups and spoke of the 'often uneasy coincidence of economic, military and political power' (1959: 278). For Mills it was a question of priorities: any 'conflicts of policy' were simply not as crucial to the reproduction of power relations as the 'internal discipline and communities of interest that bind the power elite together' (1959: 283). This can, of course, be seen as a highly instrumentalist narrative of power structures but the idea that conflicts within the elite are tempered by the recognition of their common interests is hugely significant for our understanding both of the durability and the contingency of elite power.

Mills' friend, Ralph Miliband, did not set out specifically to study elites, bureaucracies or corporations as such but to investigate the structure of the state in relation to an emerging managerialist form of capitalism (Miliband 1969). The book was intended to be a more explicitly radical critique of power designed to warn against mild-mannered, parliamentary efforts to reform the state. For Miliband, 'the state in these class societies is primarily and inevitably the guardian and protector of the economic interests which are dominant in them' (1969: 265–266). Yet, like Mills, he ended up painting a picture of economic and state elites (though not necessarily vested in government) who occupied central positions of power. Also like Mills, he acknowledged both the tensions marked by the existence of a 'plurality of economic elites' (1959: 47) as well as their eventual convergence around a set of shared determinations.

> This 'elite pluralism' does not, however, prevent the separate elites in capitalist society from constituting a dominant economic class, possessed of a high degree of cohesion and solidarity, with common interests and common purposes which far transcend their specific differences and disagreements. (1969: 47–48)

Any sectoral or partisan divisions are, therefore, liable to be marginalized in favour of the overall strategic interests of the dominant class.

Not surprisingly, given the different political and economic contexts of the US and the UK, Mills and Miliband use rather different terminologies – for example the latter speaks far more about class and capitalism than does Mills, who is more likely to write of 'higher circles' and a countervailing 'society of publics'. Miliband draws extensively on Marx while Mills remains closer to traditional sociological categories. Yet, while Miliband avoids talking about a 'ruling class' and focuses instead on the role of dominant and subordinate classes, an approach that was criticized by some on the revolutionary left as a form of elite stratification theory (Balbus 1971), Mills asserts that a 'Marxian doctrine of class struggle' is 'closer to reality than any assumed harmony of interests' (1959: 300). Whatever relationship each may have had with Marxism, however, they share a view that media and communications play a central role in the nurturing and reproduction of elite power and here I want to draw out three areas that are relevant to this claim.

First, both highlight the fluidity of roles within the elite and note the interpenetration of state and market actors (a position that becomes very important in later discussions of neo-liberalism). Indeed, both use the same term to describe the movements between different sections of the elite. Mills describes the 'interchangeability of position between the various hierarchies of money and power and celebrity' (1959: 12) while Miliband identifies the 'interchangeability between government service of one kind or another and business [which] is particularly characteristic of the new brand of "technocrats" who have been spawned by the economic interventionism of the "neo-capitalist" state' (1969: 125). Indeed, so valuable is the role of the technocrat, the 'innovator' in today's language, that they are able to 'glide' between sections of the elite in such a way that 'the boundaries between these worlds are increasing blurred and indistinct' (1969: 126). The existence, for example, of a 'revolving door' between private and public sector elites and between senior politicians, lobbyists and regulators demonstrates how futile it is to counterpose the actions and interests of the capitalist state with those of industry. They are, as Miliband puts it, 'partners in the service of a "national interest"' (1969: 125) in which media moguls are as implicated as oil barons.

Second, the convergence of interests between state and market elites and the notion that the power elite itself is an 'interlocking directorate' (Mills 1959: 8) is all the more significant in an age when information and communication are set to play an increasingly important role in cementing power relations. For Mills in particular, the *dynamics* of power are inseparable from the *means* of power and therefore the technological innovations and mass communications of the 1950s served only to centralize and 'enlarge' elite power. 'As the institutional means of power and the means of communications that tie them together have become steadily more efficient, those now in command of them have come into command of instruments of rule quite unsurpassed in the history of mankind' (1959: 23). Just as nuclear weapons demonstrated the ability of a tiny number of people to wreak havoc on the lives of millions, mass communications – in the hands of an elite – is not simply an adjunct to but constitutive of elite power; the ability to hegemonize flows of information and knowledge becomes less a technical detail than a crucial component of control. In fact, it becomes an objective in itself: 'The ends of men are often merely hopes, but means are facts within some men's control. That is why all means of power tend to become ends to an elite that is in command of them' (1959: 23). It is hardly surprising, therefore, that 'some of the higher agents of these media are themselves either among the elites or very important among the servants' (1959: 315).

The fact that media proprietors and commentators may populate this 'interlocking' yet cohesive elite and that media technologies are central to the reproduction of elite power does not take away from the fact that what preoccupied both writers, and what they devoted considerable space to evaluating in their analyses of power, was the media's *ideological* role in naturalizing elite rule – the central premise of the 'control paradigm' discussed in the previous chapter. Miliband argues that the media help to 'legitimize' the power of dominant classes while for Mills, the media are instrumental in turning what he sees as an almost Habermasian rational and robust public into a far more passive and atomized 'mass'. The highly commercialized US media, a system that included among its industries, public relations, advertising, Hollywood and network television, 'have helped less to enlarge and animate the discussions of primary publics than to transform them into a set of media markets in mass-like society' (1959: 311). To use the language of the Frankfurt School (Adorno 2001), commercial media provide a tool 'used' by the elite to fragment, distract and disempower its citizens. Miliband, in a moving tribute to Mills written shortly after his death, argued that it was the social relations of capitalism – and not a generalized hostility to technology or industrialization – that motivated his friend's analysis. 'What he loathed about America was not its industrial strength, but the mess which a profit-oriented society had made, and cannot but make of its human and material powers; not America's cars but their built-in shoddiness; not television but its commercialised misuse' (Miliband 1962).

Miliband himself also engages quite extensively with institutions of promotion and persuasion and discusses their role in encouraging popular identification with capitalist society. He is, however, particularly absorbed by what he sees as the key agency of 'political socialisation' (1969: 218): the field of communications. Some twenty years before Herman and Chomsky's discussion of the 'filters' that make up the propaganda model (Herman and Chomsky 1988), Miliband provides three filters of his own to help explain how the mass media in liberal democracies 'work in the same conservative and conformist direction' (1969: 227). First, there is the problem of concentrated ownership of the media industries and the likelihood that the owners will have 'ideological dispositions [that] run from soundly conservative to profoundly reactionary' (1969: 228). The second source of pressure is the impact of advertising which inculcates a generally favourable attitude towards business and distorts the media market against the interests of those who are deemed to be 'anti-business'. Finally, Miliband notes the pressure applied by government and state through news management techniques, the threat of sanctions and the media's incorporation into an official environment that militates against radical content. Where there is criticism of mainstream agendas, it tends to draw on controversies amenable to the elite and 'to remain within a safe, fairly narrow spectrum' (1969: 233). Influenced by Raymond Williams' devastating indictment of the growing commercialization of the British media that was written some seven years before his own work (Williams 1968), Miliband concludes that the media 'are both the expression of a system of domination, and a means of reinforcing it' (1969: 221).

As I have already hinted, these accounts of media power prefigure later analyses of the conservative ideological impulses and impacts of mainstream media, especially those that fall within the umbrella of the 'control paradigm'. As such they reflect some of the weaknesses – the exaggerations, the pessimism and the instrumentalism – that has also been thrown at political economy approaches (see McNair 2006). Mills in particular attributes far too much power to the media and far too little agency to viewers and readers whose very ability to act as enlightened individuals has been compromised by what he calls the 'basic psychological formula of the mass media today': the ability to 'give him [the audience]' identity, aspirations, hope as well as the (obviously false) possibility of escape (1959: 314). Both accounts lack a comprehensive engagement with media texts and media audiences and both are light on the empirical substance necessary to make such grand claims stick.

Yet, a careful reading of the two texts yields plenty of evidence that their 'functionalism' is not quite as intransigent as it might first appear to be. Neither claims that mainstream media have been completely monopolized nor do they claim that there is no possibility of resistance to media messages; neither dismiss the importance of the limited degree of freedom of expression that exists in advanced capitalist societies and both are sympathetic to arguments that higher levels of meaningful competition in the media might stimulate more critical output. Indeed Mills uses the term 'power elite' and not 'ruling class' precisely because he believed the former was better able to account for the 'noticeable degree of autonomy' (1959: 277n) present in the elite's ability to act decisively as a coalition of interests. As Aeron Davis puts it in a recent appreciation of the relevance of power elite theory, Mills believed that 'there was not simply a top class with a shared class consciousness that naturally cohered around the same interests. Elite power structures were more fragmented and complex' (Davis 2012).

Miliband stays closer to the traditional Marxist lexicon of class power but nevertheless argues that it is neither possible nor even necessary for the elite to achieve complete ideological domination. In fact, media coverage can have unintended consequences in conditions of wider conflict. Nearly twenty years before Daniel Hallin's seminal study of the reporting of the Vietnam War (Hallin 1986), Miliband noted that American TV coverage of the war played 'a considerable part in opening the eyes of many people to the crimes that were being committed in their name, and strengthened the resistance movement to the war' (1969: 237–238). Miliband takes the argument even further when discussing the role of journalists and media workers more generally. By and large these are not radicals straining at the leash to challenge elite views but Miliband insists that the 'leash they wear is sufficiently long to allow them as much freedom of movement as they wish to have' (1969: 236) so that, in their everyday activities, they do not even feel the leash – a position later adopted by Pilger (1999: 4) and Parenti (1993) among others. The system, he insists, can tolerate dissent but its prime function is to secure consent. In a statement that epitomizes both the nuances *and* the functionalism associated with both power elite and 'control paradigm' approaches, Miliband concludes that the media

> can, and sometimes do, play a 'dysfunctional' role; and the fact that they are allowed to do so is not lightly to be dismissed. But that, quite emphatically, is not and indeed cannot, in the given context, be their main role. They are intended to fulfil a conservative function; and do so. (Miliband 1969: 236)

Media power elites and neo-liberalism

Power elite theory was developed, refined and extended in the years following Mills' initial work. Theorists like Domhoff (1967), Dye (1976), Lindblom (1977), Sklair (2001), Williams (2006), Davis (2007), Rothkopf (2009) and Carroll (2010) sought to evaluate the composition, unity, influence and transnationalization of elites, amplifying both the benefits and drawbacks of an elite stratification perspective. For example, Davis' (2007) investigation of media consumption within elite circles and Carroll's (2010) exploration of the growth of corporate power are significant contributions to our understanding of the dynamics of elite networks. Williams' investigation of *Britain's Power Elites*, a twenty-first-century version of Mills shifted across the Atlantic, is more problematic, treating elites as a permanent fixture of *all* societies and *all* fields of activity. Williams speaks in Weberian terms of the 'iron law of oligarchy' (Williams 2006: 12) that operates more subjectively through local customs, perceptions and learned patterns of behaviour rather than any structural forms of social organization. Nevertheless, Williams is right to recognize the early twenty-first century as a 'period of elite consolidation' (2006: 217) and to highlight the emergence of a far more concentrated type of power that many others have come to describe as the central governing paradigm of our era: 'corporate libertarianism' (Pickard 2014) or, as it is more generally expressed, neo-liberalism.

Neo-liberalism has been most forcefully characterized by David Harvey (2005) as a project that, in its original iteration, was designed to provide wealth and confidence to a capitalist elite that had lots its way in the economic downturn of the 1970s. It referred to a system, benefiting from the rise of global patterns of trade and rapid developments in communications technology, that sought to cement free-market values and remove regulatory impediments for enterprise in order to 're-establish the conditions for capital accumulation and to restore the power of economic elites' (2005: 19). In the narrowest measure of the distribution of wealth and income, neo-liberalism appears to have performed extremely well for elites. In the UK, the top 1 per cent of the population has increased its share of income from 6 per cent in 1979 to 15 per cent in 2012 (Dorling, cited in Robinson 2012) while we can see a similar trend in the US with the top 1 per cent group upping its share of wealth from 19.9 per cent in 1976 to 35.4 per cent in 2010 (Domhoff 2013). This is actually slightly below global wealth distribution patterns where the richest 1 per cent owns 39 per cent of the entire world's wealth (Boston Consulting 2013). As David Rothkopf concludes in his study of the super-rich, power and wealth may have shifted away a little from the West since Mills' time but, in its place, we now have 'an elite occupying a global playing field that is for the most part unregulated by governments or law' (2009: 12).

Harvey (2005: 19) distinguishes between the ideal-type form (and fantasy) of *neo-liberalism* and the more concrete and purposeful practices of *neo-liberalization* which involve processes such as the deregulation of labour markets, liberalization of industries, outsourcing of services, championing of individual freedom, lowering of taxes, cutbacks in public expenditure and an assault on the legitimacy of the state itself. Of course, rhetorical attacks on 'big government' have not prevented neo-liberal actors from relying on state power to create and sustain the conditions necessary for capital accumulation. The state, according to Harvey, is needed to 'set up those military, defence, police and legal structures and functions required to secure private property rights and to guarantee, by force if need be, the proper functioning of markets' (2005: 2). State and market actors are, therefore, accomplices in the neo-liberal project – an intensification of the relationship that Mills described back in *The Power Elite* that '[i]f there is government intervention in the corporate economy, so is there corporate intervention in the governmental process' (1959: 8).

However, in order for neo-liberalization to succeed, market logic had to be internalized and naturalized as the most desirable and productive philosophy underpinning *all* human activity, extending beyond market exchange and governmental processes and into far more intimate domains. Neo-liberalism has become a frame for the analysis not simply of the economy but of a wide range of political, intellectual and cultural fields, not least the media which have been increasingly subject to neo-liberal pressures – witness the fostering of policies based on privatization and marketization (Freedman 2008), the intensive commercialization of media content (McChesney 2004), the restructuring of telecommunications (Schiller 2000) and the reorganization of media ownership (Fitzgerald 2012). Furthermore, the media have also been complicit in *producing* neo-liberal subjects through, for example, their constant scheduling of 'reality' programmes which 'teach' neo-liberal discipline (Couldry 2010) or 'agony aunt' talk shows which preach individual self-reliance (Peck 2008).

Of course there is always a danger that neo-liberalism becomes the singular, grand narrative which provides an explanatory framework for the world's problems. In its repeated usage and its extension to *all* areas of social life, it may be seen to lose some of the analytical clarity. As I have previously argued, there is a risk that 'by talking about neo-liberalism as a steamroller laying waste to public culture and paving the way for market forces, more complex and precise accounts of the agents, arguments and mechanisms involved in neo-liberal practices may be sacrificed in order to emphasize, in this context, the undesirability of the project itself' (Freedman 2008: 37). The answer to this problem is that we confront neo-liberalism concretely and in relation to specific practices of neo-liberalization. This is not enough, however, for an increasing number of critics for whom neo-liberalism is a totalizing meta-narrative that fails to do justice to the very different configurations and contexts of elite power and capitalist enterprise in the world today. Their criticisms take three main forms: that neo-liberalism as a concept is overly generalized, potentially misleading or simply outdated.

Terry Flew suggests that neo-liberalism is now an 'omnibus term' and rails against the way in which it has 'come to be used in a highly mechanistic and reductionist way' (2008: 129), in particular through attributing neo-liberal properties to very different media systems such as those in the US and the UK (as in Freedman 2008). How can one analytical frame do justice to a system marked by rampant commercialization as well as one with a solid public service core? I would argue that Flew mistakes the specious unity of 'neo-liberalism' for the material practices of neo-liberalization which, in very different cultures and contexts, nevertheless share the same aim of implanting a market logic into social life. This can involve the intensification of already existing market pressures in a commercial environment as well as the introduction of market disciplines into public organizations (as we are seeing in the UK with the health service, education as well as public service media).

So while neo-liberalization has taken the form of attempts to liberalize media ownership rules in the US, there is little doubt that through such practices as the internal market, Market Impact Assessments and the Public Value Test (see Freedman 2008: 149–163), a public service broadcaster like the BBC has also been subject to neo-liberal restructuring. The starting points and outcomes may of course be different but the motivation remains the same: to subject virtually all areas of social life (the military appears to be somewhat exempt from these pressures) to market forces such that their worth comes increasingly to be measured in terms of profit, efficiency and 'value for money'. Neo-liberalization, as has already been pointed out, is not a monolithic process but a form of regulatory re-structuring that operates across distinct fields with very different outcomes, not least because such redistributive acts often face substantial opposition. 'Neoliberalism has not and does not pulsate out from a single control center or heartland; it has always been relationally constituted across multiple sites and spaces of "co-formation" ' (Peck and Brenner 2009: 1250).

Other critics warn that an emphasis on neo-liberalism is a distraction from the central problem of *capitalism* which, according to Garland and Harper (2012), has now been replaced in the radical vocabulary by what is effectively a slightly 'softer' option. Neo-liberalism, they argue, may have useful things to offer in assessing the impact of commodification, consumption and de-socialization, but it misses out on more traditional instruments of class rule such as propaganda and nation-building, especially in relation to the daily activities of 'liberal' news outlets or public service broadcasting. Neo-liberalism, as such, 'is a term that must be used with caution' (2012: 417) as it can, if loosely defined, provide a false description of the world – for example, one where the state is seen to be languishing in the shadows of corporate activity or where the key struggle is seen to be between neo-liberalism and 'a tepidly agonised hankering after a long-gone "fairer", "more democratic" capitalism' (2012: 414).

Once again, a robust understanding of neo-liberalism answers these points. Whatever the *rhetoric* may be about the disappearance of the state, neo-liberalism refers to a particular configuration of capitalism in which the state actively assists market actors to consolidate their grip on social and economic life (and which, therefore, is likely to require the use of propaganda and nation-building). In Mills' terms, this refers to the 'interlocking directorate' that runs the show and hardly presages the imminent decline of state power. This explains why, according to Mirowski (2013: 41), many proponents of neo-liberalism actually distance themselves from what they see as the 'outmoded classic doctrine of laissez-faire'. The counterpoint of neo-liberalism furthermore is not necessarily a romantic vision of capitalism but a different kind of social system that, by rejecting market principles as the overarching measure of success and happiness, privileges human cooperation and economic equality. Garland and Harper may well be right that there are some opponents of neo-liberalism who seek an accommodation with a 'fairer' form of capitalism, but it is hardly the case that by adopting neo-liberalism as a critical frame, you are destined to argue that 'a largely benign and neutral state needs to be reclaimed for democracy' (2012: 421). A neo-liberal critique, if understood in relation to capitalism's underlying structures, is a powerful tool in the armoury of those who oppose not simply market *fundamentalism* but the more general consequences of private property and exchange.

A third rejection of neo-liberalism as a relevant analytical frame is that the great economic crash of 2008 has effectively put an end to it. As the former chief economist of the World Bank and leading US economist Joseph Stiglitz has argued, '[n]eoliberalism like the Washington Consensus is dead in most western countries' (cited in Mirowski 2013: 32). Buffeted by the collapse of key financial institutions and the implosion of key financial markets, neo-liberalism has lost its glamour as well as its credibility and its death knell has been predicted by a series of leading economists (see Mirowski 2013: 31 for a series of obituaries). 'Neo-liberal market fundamentalism' for Stiglitz, was 'always a political doctrine serving particular interests. It was never supported by economic theory. Nor, it should now be clear, is it supported by historical experience' (Stiglitz 2008). The problem is that the beast refuses to die – notions of 'zombie neoliberalism' are rampant (Fisher 2013, Quiggin 2010) – and that both neo-liberal institutions and discourses continue to exert a huge influence across the globe. Precisely because neo-liberalism is neither a static nor a homogeneous phenomenon, it will attempt to reconstitute itself and to recover its poise by modifying its discourses and mechanisms while maintaining the same commitment to capital accumulation and market instrumentalism. For example, faced by a rising tide of opposition, William Davies argues that through practices like corporate social responsibility and social entrepreneurship, neo-liberalism is now 'being reinvented in ways that incorporate social logic, as a means of resisting critique and delaying crisis' (Davies 2013). The social is effectively being incorporated and neo-liberalized.

Neo-liberalism may have taken a battering but neo-liberal elites have neither disappeared nor have they declined in number – indeed the number of billionaires in the world appears to be increasing (Kroll 2013). Critiques of and movements opposed to neo-liberalism may have gathered pace around the world, but Mirowski is right to claim that '[n]eoliberal initiatives and policies still carry the day and, more to the point, most people still understand their own straitened circumstances through the lens of what can only be regarded as neo-liberal presumptions' (Mirowski 2013: 28). To the extent that this is the case (which does not necessarily imply that populations agree with these 'presumptions') and that today's austerity policies are not the refutation but the application of neo-liberal ideas, then it seems obvious that many major media outlets will have a role in both sustaining market ideologies through 'everyday neoliberalism' (2013: 89) and in acting as vehicles for the reproduction of neo-liberal social relations more generally. We need, therefore, to think about whether, and in what ways, neo-liberal media power elites are implicated in these processes.

The rise of the communications sector

First, it is clear that industries associated with the production, distribution and consumption of media are central to the broader circulation of capital across the globe. Communications conglomerates are not the poor cousins of 'core' parts of the global economy but institutions that preside over many billions of dollars of economic activity and, as such, there is little reason to doubt that the 'higher levels' of the media would be well represented in elite circles. Indeed, media interests are intimately related to even larger parts of productive activity through the provision of, for example, advertising, public relations and access to specialist information. The rise of digital technologies has only intensified the influence of communications such that innovations in biotechnology, financial services and weapons systems are, at least in part, increasingly wrapped up with media transformations (Der Derian 2009, Schuster 2006).

Media interests have long featured in the lists of the world's largest companies but as long as they remained 'pure' media companies, confined to publishing, broadcasting and movies, their presence was fairly limited. Given the huge growth of networked communication and multi-platform convergence, companies that straddle interrelated areas – such as technology hardware, computer software and telecommunications – now have a significant presence in both the Forbes 2000 and FT 500 lists of global giants and are increasingly popular with private equity investors (Castells 2009: 94). The FT list, which ranks companies by market value alone, counts fifteen media companies in its tally for 2013 (up from eleven in 2009) but the broader measure, as described above, yields some seventy-seven companies from twenty-five different countries, approximately 15 per cent of the total, including Apple at number one (Financial Times 2013). The Forbes list, which has a slightly more complicated metric involving sales, profits, assets and market value, contains just over 200 companies whose primary commodities relate to information and media, 10 per cent of the total (Forbes 2013a).

Media-related industries are, therefore, significant in number although still only a minority of a list that continues to be dominated by financial, energy, materials and insurance companies. This points less to the notion of a post-industrial society than to the integration of the media and information sectors into wider patterns of global trade. Indeed, the consolidation of these sectors coincided with the emergence of the neo-liberal project in such a way that they provided an essential element of the rejuvenation of the market system following the 1970s, both through the growth of communications markets but more significantly through their links to financialization processes (Martin 2002) that were seen to be driving the world economy. The restructuring of communications that took place throughout the 1980s – the privatization, liberalization and overall reconstitution of communications along a market logic (Horwitz 1989) – was the result of determined efforts by ruling elites to incorporate information and communication technologies into the heartland of the capital accumulation process. According to Dan Schiller, this signalled a step change in the dynamics, if not the priorities, of capitalism: 'At stake in this unprecedented transition to neoliberal or market-driven telecommunications are nothing less than the production base and the control structure of an emerging digital capitalism' (Schiller 2000: 37).

'Digital capitalism' is marked by continuities with rather than differences from 'analogue capitalism' and has proved to be just as vulnerable to booms and slumps as its predecessor. However, the latest recession, emanating from the financial crisis of 2008, appears to have negatively affected media consumers far more than the companies themselves. Spending on entertainment declined by 4.5 per cent in the US from 2009 to 2011 (Bureau of Labour Statistics 2012) while the average monthly spend on communication services (including mobile telephony) in the UK fell by over 7 per cent between 2007 and 2012 (Ofcom 2013: 4). Yet, the *Financial Times* reported that media (along with pharmaceuticals) was the strongest performing stock market sector in 2012 (Dullforce 2013) while *Forbes* noted that media had the best market growth of any sector in 2012 of some 20 per cent (DeCarlo 2013). In the US, the average share price of movie exhibition chains increased by nearly 47 per cent, cable and satellite distribution companies by 42 per cent, cable networks by 34 per cent, TV stations by 24 per cent while social media companies languishing with a mere 21 per cent rise (Lieberman 2013). Perhaps this simply represents the overvaluation of communications-related companies or the hope that a digital future will replenish the spirit of free enterprise or that 'fresh cycles of accumulation are feasible within this still expansionary zone' (Schiller 2011: 932); or perhaps it expresses the continuing ability of large communications companies to extract healthy profits from consumers even in difficult circumstances. Whichever is the case, the media sector looks set to continue dining at the top table of international business with its chief executives firmly implanted at the core of the global business elite.

The return of the media baron

The same lists that place media and information companies at the core of world trade also reveal that some of the wealthiest men (and a very few women) on the planet have made their fortunes from media-related activities. The Forbes list of the world's richest people consists of 1426 billionaires (worth $5.4 trillion) of whom sixty-eight (including only nine women) are identified as presiding over 'pure' media companies with a further eighteen in telecommunications and ninety-two in 'technology' – some 12.5 per cent of the total (Forbes 2013b). The world's richest man is Carlos Slim, the Mexican telecommunications magnate whose company, America Movil, controls nearly 75 per cent of Mexican fixed-line and mobile telephony. There is a similar trend in the UK where according to the *Sunday Times* (2012), media, film and sports interests comprise eighty-four of the richest 1000 individuals, the fourth largest number after property, finance and industry. Taken together with computers, telecoms and the internet, nearly 15 per cent of the 'rich list' is occupied by people who have amassed their wealth from information and media-related activities. Media barons, according to David Rothkopf (2009), join with heads of state, top military commanders, leading industrialists, private equity investors and oil potentates, among others, in a 'superclass' that wields enormous power over the rest of us.

These individuals constitute a 'media elite' comprised of family members, proprietors and chief executives that is surely more powerful and durable (although riven with tensions and conflicts) than the rather more fragmented and transient assortment of leading journalists, commentators, producers and commissioning editors who have a more supple relationship with media power – they may be indispensable in circulating ideas that chime with the values of neo-liberalism but often lack the allocative power that is the privilege of elites. This is despite the fact that many media 'insiders' are regularly accused by conservative voices of acting as a highly partisan 'liberal media elite' (see Lichter, Rothman and Lichter 1986). Of course, the distortion of the term 'elite' is itself part of a conservative news agenda where, according to Geoffrey Nunberg, references to the 'media elite' on Fox News are forty times more frequent than references to corporate elites. 'When Americans hear *elite* these days, they're less likely to think of the managers and politicians who inhabit the centers of power than of the celebrities, academics and journalists who lodge in its outer boroughs' (Nunberg 2009: 185). Michael Wolff, in his biography of Rupert Murdoch (Wolff 2008), describes how Murdoch attempted to present himself as an 'outsider' and to paint most editors and journalists as the real establishment figures. 'The elites, so-called [by Murdoch himself], have a good thing going, a monopoly of their own, and they don't want to let him in' (2008: 220). The fact is that Murdoch was 'never removed from the establishment – or, that is, never removed from power' (2008: 264).

Media elites at the level of Rupert Murdoch are extremely well rewarded, indeed better rewarded than in many other industries. In 2012, seven of the top twenty highest paid executives in the US were from media companies, a substantial over-representation of the economic performance of the sector. The average pay of the ten best-paid media executives was about $30 million a year in contrast to technology and finance CEOs who, according to the *New York Times*, averaged between $6 million and $14 million less (Carr 2013). Band and Gerafi (2013) estimate that compensation of CEOs in the copyright industries as a percentage of overall company revenue is more than twice as high as those in non-copyright industries and that the gulf between CEO pay in copyright and non-copyright industries is increasing – in 2012, this was a threefold gap with average compensation in the former sector at just under $30 million per year (2013: 3). No wonder that, despite the challenges and risks faced by media elites, it is clear that 'being a king in the media realm comes with a very lucrative crown' (Carr 2013).

Despite this handsome compensation to top executives, most of whom are in publicly quoted companies, there has been a significant shift in corporate structure as power is increasingly being vested in individual proprietors as opposed to CEOs or board members as in most public companies. This is particularly noticeable in the newspaper industry where there has been, in the last few years, a spate of takeovers by wealthy individuals. The billionaire investor Warren Buffet, number four in the Forbes rich list, bought a controlling stake in the Media General newspaper group in May 2012; the property developer Douglas Manchester bought the *San Diego Union Tribune* in November 2011, while a consortium of Philadelphia businessmen acquired the Philadelphia Media Network in April 2012. In Spring 2013, well-known conservatives, the Koch Brothers, attempted to take over the newspaper titles of the Tribune Group leading to protests in over a dozen US cities, while in August 2013, billionaire businessman John Henry, 974 on the Forbes list, bought the *Boston Globe* from the New York Times Group to add to his sporting portfolio which includes the Boston Red Sox and Liverpool Football Club. In the same month, Jeff Bezos, the founder of Amazon, surprised the whole industry with his purchase of the *Washington Post* for $250 million.

A similar process is underway in the UK where, according to the *Guardian*, '[p]roprietors and other private owners have been on the march since the beginning of the century, buying up and consolidating publicly quoted media companies' (Sabbagh 2011). The newspaper contrasts the sluggishness and conservatism of many bureaucratic, publicly traded media companies with the ability of private companies to manoeuvre more rapidly and flexibly. Groups like Northern and Shell, owned by the former pornographer Richard Desmond, and the Telegraph Media Group owned by the reclusive Barclay Brothers (423 on the Forbes list) are far more buoyant than, for example, Trinity Mirror, owner of two declining national newspapers and a slew of regional titles. Similarly, the Russian oligarch, Alexander Lebedev, having bought a controlling stake in the London *Evening Standard* and subsequently turning it into a highly successful freesheet, then paid in 2010 a nominal £1 to 'rescue' the

Independent stable of newspapers from rack and ruin. His tabloid title, *i*, is now the fastest-growing title in the sector.

Of course, there is a further distinction between public and 'controlled' public companies where, in the latter, a sizeable amount of shares are controlled by a single individual or where there is a dual class structure that allows the company effectively to be dominated by a single individual. This is particularly common with social media companies like Facebook, Groupon and Zynga, where the founders are able to benefit from an injection of capital while maintaining their overall control of the company. In the cases of social media, proprietorship may be seen as a means of maintaining a focus on innovation and retaining the 'vision' of the founder in order to extract maximum profits in a growing industry. In the case of newspapers, however, this is clearly not the case and the intervention of wealthy individuals signals a desire to see a return on their investment measured less in profits than in influence. Todd Gitlin, reflecting on the takeover of the *Washington Post* by Bezos, argues that 'we may be reverting to a world in which commerce is not the prime motivation for publishing' (Gitlin 2013). The era of a commercial and outward-looking press, supported by advertising and circulation and based on an ideology of professionalism and independence, 'now looks like more of an interlude than a permanent American fixture'. If journalism is to survive, at least in the US, then according to influential journalism scholars Leonard Downie Jr and Michael Schudson (2009), it will have to rely on a combination of subsidies, tax incentives and most crucially philanthropy. The rich, it appears, are likely to play a critical role in the future of media and to remain, by far, the most significant component of media power elites.

The role of the 'club'

The third dimension of the ability of media elites to naturalize and reproduce neo-liberal social relations lies in the networks and locations in which media power is cemented and extended. Mills described the shared educational backgrounds and higher circles in which elites mingled both professionally and personally and contemporary media folk have their own venues and routines in which either to seek common purpose or to negotiate differences. There is, of course, nothing surprising about this. Elites have a series of codes, institutions and protocols in which to insulate themselves from those outside and therefore to enjoy and profit from each other's company: clubs, board meetings, villas, yachts, festivals and parties. These are not necessarily conspiratorial or secret events but simply occasions on which elites are able to assemble and do business. Indeed, for those people who argue that the very concept of an elite is far too simplistic to do justice to the contingency and fluidity of power transactions in the contemporary world (for example

Castells 2009: 47), such events are useful in identifying the ways in which a range of interests can cohere around a shared set of values. Of course, the operation of power, as well as the decision-making processes of media elites, is not always visible or open to scrutiny and transparency, but that makes those spaces in which the powerful can be observed all the more valuable. So, just as the development of communication media has 'rendered power visible in new ways' (Thompson 1995: 5) through, for example, twenty-four-hour news and blogs, it is also true that media elites attempt to *use* their power precisely in order to shield themselves from unwanted publicity. The whole phenomenon of unaccountable corporate lobbying, undocumented private dinners and un-minuted meetings between politicians and media executives makes those instances of visibility particularly interesting.

Consider the annual meetings at Davos and of the Bilderberg Group that offer participants the opportunity to network, do deals and discuss issues 'off the record' as with any professional conference. The difference here is the level of power and influence that participants bring to the table. Bilderberg, for example, is divided into 'lobbies' – the banking and finance lobby, industry and energy, politics and of course the media – composed of those people who comfortably inhabit the Forbes 2000 list. The 2013 event, in the words of the organizers, allowed politicians to 'spend an intense 3 days in meetings with "newspaper and other media proprietors, senior editors and executives" of media companies. But without any press oversight or any public record of these meetings' (Bilderberg 2013). The fact that the organizers felt it necessary to make this information available supports Thompson's point that the spotlight of the media has made it harder for the powerful to hide but this does not obscure the fact that elites do meet together to debate and, in general, to offer confirmation that they exist.

But neither are these events simply a showcase for powerful interests. The annual Sun Valley conference in Idaho, hosted by investment bank Allen & Co., has long been a crucial place for media elites to meet privately – the communications version of an arms fair. In July 2013, the entire North American media establishment was present, including Rupert Murdoch and sons, Facebook's Mark Zuckerberg, Apple's Tim Cook, Microsoft's Bill Gates, Twitter's Jack Dorsey, Google's Eric Schmidt and even Warren Buffett and the Mexican president Enrique Peña Nieto. Unnoticed in the middle of this gathering were two meetings between Amazon founder Jeff Bezos and Donald Graham, CEO of the Washington Post Company, which culminated in the sale of the *Post* to Bezos within a month. This follows Comcast's purchase of NBC in 2009 and Disney's acquisition of ABC in 1996, both of which were initiated at Sun Valley. Indeed, the latter deal occurred, according to the *Los Angeles Times*, because Disney's Michael Eisner ' "bumped into" Cap Cities [owner of Disney] shareholder Warren Buffett in the bracing noontime air of the Idaho resort' (Hiltzik and Eller 1995). Thanks to the privacy of the encounter, the deal was negotiated in complete secrecy and wrapped up far more quickly than is usual for deals of that size and significance.

The club-like association of media involves far more than business deals, however, and extends well beyond the media itself to include other members of Mills' 'interlocking directorate'. Perhaps the most notorious of these in recent years has been the 'Chipping Norton set' (see Chapter 1), the group based around Prime Minister David Cameron in his Oxfordshire home and which counts, among its members, Rupert Murdoch's daughter Elisabeth, Google's head of communications and public policy Rachel Whetstone and her husband Steve Hilton, Cameron's former strategy director, as well as former News International CEO Rebekah Brooks. Again, it is not surprising (nor illegal) that such individuals would seek each other out for company and comfort but as one leading British commentator argues (Harris 2011), the 'Chipping Norton set' had become 'a hardened clique' that demonstrated the collusive impact of concentrated media power on British political culture. 'British politics was blurring into a mulch largely built around policies the Murdochs could endorse, and their company was apparently so gone on its own power that some of its staff obviously thought they were way beyond the law' (Harris 2011). The fact that Tony Blair is the godfather of Rupert Murdoch's youngest daughter Grace should, perhaps, be seen in this context.

The nature of this 'mulch' was evident only three days before the phone hacking crisis broke, when a party hosted by Elisabeth Murdoch at her Oxfordshire home was attended by an impressive range of government ministers, advisers, senior Labour politicians (including the recently defeated candidate for the leader of the party, David Miliband, the son of Ralph), journalists, musicians and PR gurus. This followed on from Rupert Murdoch's summer party some two weeks before, which was attended by the prime minister and his wife, the Labour leader Ed Miliband (and another son of Ralph) and, generally, the 'great and the good' of British journalism and politics. Interestingly, the opposition Labour Party was better represented, 'a reflection, perhaps, of Labour's continuing obsession with winning over Murdoch when they can, and trying to neutralise his titles' most venomous attacks when they fail' (Robinson 2011).

Further examples of the 'club' nature of media power elites include both the highly interconnected nature of board membership involving individuals with directorates spread across industry (see Castells 2009: 433–443) as well as the 'revolving door' phenomenon whereby representatives of one sector migrate seamlessly to another sector. While this latter activity is unlikely to involve proprietors and CEOs, it nevertheless serves to illustrate the porous nature of divisions between media, corporate and political spheres and is evidence, once again, of the 'interlocking' character of an elite system. One of the most popular journeys seems to be from the US Federal Communications Commission into the private sector including, in recent years, former FCC chair Michael Powell, who is now the cable industry's chief lobbyist, former commissioner Meredith Baker, who left the FCC to become a lobbyist for Comcast right after having voted to support the company's purchase of NBC and Edward Lazarus, the former FCC chair's chief of staff, who left the FCC to become general counsel at Tribune, previously in a dispute with the FCC over the agency's media ownership rules. According to Free Press' Craig Aaron, the 'corruption at the Agency is so entrenched that selling out is the new normal. Too many people go to work at the FCC with the expectation of cashing in on their public service' (Aaron 2013). Media and political elites are connected together not just through personal association but also through structural configurations of mutual interest. The result, according to Calabrese and Mihal, is 'a network of individuals, influence, power and money that bears on matters of public policy' (2011: 238). Nowhere are these issues more evident than in patterns of ownership and their relationship to media power.

Ownership and media power

The question of who owns the media has long been asked in relation to the overall purpose and political impact of the media. Some of the founding scholars of communications and cultural studies identified diversified ownership as central to the ability of media to pursue an independent and critical role in public life. Back in 1948, Lazarsfeld and Merton noted the importance of investigating mass media in relation to the specific economic structures in which they operated and argued that 'the social effects of the media will vary as the system of ownership and control varies' (Lazarsfeld and Merton 2004: 236). Ownership, they insisted, was not a neutral social arrangement: 'Since the mass media are supported by great business concerns geared into the current social and economic system, the media contribute to the maintenance of this system' (2004: 236). In his book *Communications*, Raymond Williams highlighted the emergence of new forms of media ownership in the UK that were contributing to a growing commercialisation of audiences and content. He argued that even in a media economy that contained a significant not-for-profit, public service core, the 'methods and attitudes of capitalist business have established themselves near the centre of communications' (Williams 1968: 31). According to Vincent Mosco (2009: 113), ownership has also been a central issue for political economy researchers who have been 'especially concerned with the tendency for fewer and fewer companies that grow ever larger to control more of the media market than ever before'.

In Chapter 1, I raised the argument that democratic life is seen as compromised when the number of media outlets and range of distinctive voices is restricted as a result of highly concentrated ownership structures – when media plurality, in other words, is threatened. In these circumstances, media elites are all the more likely to 'use their power to advance their political agenda' (McChesney 2004: 224) which both undermines the possibility of a vigorous exchange of competing perspectives and weakens the media's ability to hold power to account. All around the world, claims are being made about the negative impact of this form of media power: against Clarin in Argentina, Televisa in Mexico, Mediaset in Italy, CCTV in China, Comcast in the US and News Corp in Britain and Australia. Media ownership has, therefore, become an increasingly significant proxy for media power and, in its concentrated form – whether in the hands of private corporations or the state – has emerged as a major threat to democracy.

To what extent can we draw a clear link between media concentration and diminished diversity and, indeed, is there an actual problem with concentration in major media markets? At one level these are empirical issues that, in the middle of often polarized debates about media ownership, require quantitative responses based on the analysis of 'evidence' and the gathering of 'data' in order to be mathematically precise about the problem. This fetishization of what has come to be known as 'media metrics', described by pro-liberalization campaigners as 'objective measures in contrast to subjective barometers' (Thierer and Eslkelsen 2008: 9) raises its own problems.

First, there is the fact that such data is far more likely to be demanded of and shaped by commercial organizations with their own vested interests. According to Philip and Karaganis (2007), policymakers generally tend to draw their data from a narrow range of elite sources. 'Today, communication policymakers rely heavily on the data sets developed by commercial data providers for their clients and the investment community, and, therefore, neglect their own substantial data collection capabilities and responsibilities' (2007: 56). Second, while a data-driven approach is designed theoretically to insulate media policymaking and regulatory domains from partisanship and bias, there is little to suggest that a call to 'objectivity' will necessarily undermine the use of selective facts and subjective judgements. Countervailing ideas can just as easily be marginalized, ignored or buried, as happened when FCC officials refused to distribute a piece of research that demonstrated a link between increased consolidation and decreased amount of local news (Associated Press 2006). Indeed, the heavily economistic Diversity Index employed by the FCC in 2003 to measure degrees of concentration in local markets was eventually discredited by the Appeals Court for relying too heavily on quantitative methods; for not paying enough attention to issues of content and the impact of different types of speech;

and for effectively treating all sources, irrespective of their size, as equally powerful (Freedman 2008: 111).

Nevertheless, there are sufficient indicators to make a good case that media plurality is insufficiently developed in countries across the globe. A quick journey around the world reveals that four groups account for 90 per cent of newspaper circulation in Chile and South Africa, 89 per cent of TV viewing in Argentina and 83 per cent of TV viewing in Chile (Berger and Masala 2012: 77, Mastrini and Becerra 2011); two groups hold 94 per cent of all private television frequencies in Mexico, with a single company dominating 69 per cent of free-to-air TV advertising (Gomez and Sosa-Plata 2011: 62, 84), but this is admittedly not quite as bad as in Malaysia, where one company dominates 90 per cent of free-to-air advertising (Ding and Koh 2013: 83); two groups account for 86 per cent of newspaper sales in Australia and 54 per cent in the UK (Flew 2013), while Hollywood still manages to dominate nearly two-thirds of world box office (Management Today 2013). This is to say nothing of the fact that Google has an effectively monopoly of search in many countries.

Of course, this is a tremendously uneven picture and one in which there is virtually no consensus on levels of concentration, their significance nor indeed on the methods for measuring plurality (see Hesmondhalgh 2013 for a very thorough overview). For example, for every industry-backed survey that shows that increased media consolidation has a negligible impact on minority and women ownership of broadcast stations – such as the report produced by the Minority Media and Telecommunications Council for the FCC's most recent ownership review that was based on a mere fourteen respondents (Eggerton 2013) – there is another that demonstrates that women and minority owned stations are far more likely to thrive in less concentrated markets and that the 'best way to ensure a diversity of owners on the public airwaves is to roll back media consolidation' (Turner 2007: 9). For every scholar that argues that the emerging media marketplace 'may be noted more for information overload and fragmentation than for concentration and scarcity' (Compaine and Gomery 2000: 578), there are plenty of others that argue just the opposite (Bagdikian 2000, McChesney 2004).

Media ownership and levels of concentration are not, however, solely empirical matters but ones that connect to more ideological questions about how, in neo-liberal circumstances, the market in particular is presented as the most desirable and efficient enabler of productive symbolic activity. Far from being a simple technical or administrative matter, attitudes towards ownership (and the systems that follow) are connected to values and priorities that are by no means natural or inevitable. Ownership structures have to be designed, created, institutionalized and legitimized. According to Ben Bagdikian, whose book *The Media Monopoly* was one of the first to combine data on media concentration with a sociological analysis of media influence, ownership is a mechanism for managing the exclusion of certain voices from political power. Concentrated media ownership, he argues, is connected to the ability 'to treat some subjects briefly and obscurely but others repetitively and in depth' (2000: 16), a seemingly 'normal and necessary' journalistic practice that skews public opinion in the interest of powerful corporations (2000: 16).

Noam Chomsky and Ed Herman most famously developed this line of argument in *Manufacturing Consent* (Herman and Chomsky 1988) where they provided a *structural* account of the distortion of news agendas to suit corporate and political elites. We expect this to be the case in authoritarian states where monopolistic control over the media constitutes one further instrument by which elites maintain their power and restrict opposition. Herman and Chomsky, however, are more interested in assessing how a similar operation takes place in formal 'democracies' with privately controlled media systems and outline what they describe as a 'propaganda model' that works systematically to skew coverage in the interests of the powerful. The first 'filter' that they identify is the 'size, ownership, and profit orientation' of the media (1988: 3) which, in a country like the US, involves a highly concentrated news market that is dominated by firms that are intimately connected to other sectors of the economy including finance, industry and the arms trade. After conducting a detailed analysis of the US elite media coverage of international affairs, they argue that the 'mass media of the United States are effective and powerful ideological institutions that carry out a system-supportive propaganda function by reliance on market forces, internalized assumptions, and self-censorship, and without significant overt coercion' (1988: 306). These conclusions have been borne out by other researchers in relation to the coverage of gender (Cockburn and Loach 1986), labour and union issues (Pilger 1999), the 'war on terror' (Dimaggio 2008) and environmentalism (Winter 2007) together with other issues including the role of spin (Miller and Dinan 2008) and the power of Hollywood (Alford 2009).

Private ownership is seen here as a form of social organization that, through its dependence on advertising, its allegiance to shareholders or investors, its imbrication in elite networks and its long-term stakes in a market economy, is likely to organize the representation of the world in its own image. It is no accident, according to this perspective, that Rupert Murdoch, hardly in tune with world's public opinion, was able to swing his 'worldwide media organisation behind George W. Bush's disastrous invasion of Iraq' (McKnight 2013: 9); why financial journalism largely celebrated the stock market boom and was complicit in the crash of 2008 (Chakravartty and Schiller 2010); and why immigrants are regularly stigmatized as a 'problem' in media coverage (Philo, Briant and Donald 2013). Ownership confers the right to set corporate priorities, develop an editorial agenda and to hire a team that will best execute the will of the owner. Publisher power, for example, is exercised less through direct coercion than 'from the top through selection of senior personnel, the recruitment of new staff, through incentives and criticism, and through the editorial tradition of a paper' (Curran 2012a). According to the former editor of the *Sun*, David Yelland:

> All Murdoch editors … go on a journey where they end up agreeing with everything Rupert says. But you don't admit to yourself that you're being influenced. Most Murdoch editors wake in the morning, switch on the radio, hear that something has happened and think, 'What would Rupert think about this'. It's like a mantra inside your head, It's like a prism. You look at the world through Rupert's eyes. (Cited in Groksop 2010)

Given that Murdoch has rarely been afraid to articulate or be associated with conservative and neo-liberal views (McKnight 2013, Wolff 2008) and that the opportunity to own or control a large media organization is not a capacity that is equally distributed throughout society, proprietorial power is therefore a significant tool for the promotion and circulation of elite views.

How else can we explain how Tony Blair managed to find time to have three telephone calls with Rupert Murdoch in the weeks before the invasion of Iraq in 2003 in which, according to his then communications director Alastair Campbell, Murdoch lobbied the prime minister not to delay the military action (Watt 2012)? Actually Blair himself provides a fairly stark picture of the balance of power between politicians and media elites:

> the relationship [between politicians and the media] is one in which you feel this – this pretty intense power and the need to try and deal with that. And I'm just being open about that and open about the fact, frankly, that I decided, as a political leader – and this was a strategic decision – that I was going to manage that and not confront it. (Blair 2012: 4)

Blair was far from the only British political leader to 'manage' the relationship with media moguls. Before he was elected prime minister, David Cameron held 1,404 meetings with journalists and proprietors (including a trip to the Greek island of Santorini to join Rupert Murdoch on a yacht) – an average of twenty-six meetings per month, a figure that has fallen to thirteen a month while in office (Grayson and Freedman 2013: 70). Yet, at the Leveson Inquiry, Murdoch famously claimed that, 'I've never asked a Prime Minister for anything' (Murdoch 2012: 15) and argued that interactions between politicians and proprietors were simply a vital part of the democratic process: 'it is only natural for politicians to reach out to editors and sometimes proprietors … to explain what they're doing and hoping that it makes an impression' (2012: 51). The owner of the *Independent* newspaper, Evgeny Lebedev, was rather more blunt in his evidence to the Leveson Inquiry: 'I do ... think it reasonable that those who invest millions of pounds in publishing enjoy one potential benefit of that investment, which is the chance to meet politicians' (Lebedev 2012). In fact, Lord Justice Leveson heard various allegations of proprietorial interventions, most notably by former prime minister John Major, who insisted that Murdoch had threatened to withdraw the support of his titles if the government did not change its policy on membership of the European Union (Hickman 2012). According to the conservative columnist Charles Moore, Murdoch's influence is 'an anti-social force' and his newspapers 'were tools for his power, not that of his readers' (Moore 2011). Ownership, particularly when it is concentrated and thus exerts a disproportionate influence over the public, is, therefore, a decisive factor in the dynamics of elite-dominated patterns of media power.

This suggests that we should treat with caution proposals that, given the newspaper crisis across the West, the most likely means of salvation for a declining industry lies with a 'Bezillionaire model' (Gitlin 2013) where wealthy entrepreneurs like Jeff Bezos acquire titles less for profit than for influence, nostalgia, public duty or even a sense of adventure. It is true that there are several philanthrophic foundations that support public interest journalism, like the Sandler Foundation which funds ProPublica or the Scott Trust which underwrites the losses of the *Guardian*, but it is also true that philanthropic ownership is neither a secure nor a viable prospect for the vast majority of newspapers. Private ownership, along the lines suggested by Gitlin, is even less secure and far from an innocent proposition given that the new owners of ailing titles will bring with them their existing dispositions which, as Gitlin notes in the case of Bezos, is an opposition to higher taxes for the wealthy and a commitment to take advantage of corporation tax loopholes.

Consider the case of former property developer and conservative activist Douglas Manchester, the new owner/saviour of the *San Diego Union Tribune* who, together with chief executive John Lynch, has sought to reorient the title's editorial positions and to lobby actively for a sports stadium in the city. Lynch told the *New York Times* that, while respecting the demarcation between news and opinion pieces, the new owners were doing 'what a newspaper ought to do, which is to take positions. We are very consistent – pro-conservative, pro-business, pro-military – and we are trying to make a newspaper that gets people excited about this city and its future' (Carr 2012). Others are not so confident that editorial integrity can be protected when there is an overt commitment to be pro-business and point to Manchester's continuing financial interest in real estate near to the proposed stadium as further evidence of the corruption and decline of the newspaper (Strupp 2012). As the *New York Times* points out in relation to Manchester, the newspaper 'often seems like a brochure for his various interests' (Carr 2012), a further illustration of the potential pitfalls of monopoly ownership and its close association with elite circles.

However, even if we agree that there are media elites either in local communities or spanning the globe who benefit – in terms of influence and profits – from concentrated media markets and a monopoly of the national or local 'conversation', there are still many people who doubt whether ownership is a sufficiently robust and expansive frame from which either to 'read off' or to solve problems of unaccountable media power. Craufurd-Smith and Tambini argue that ownership concentration 'is only one among a number of variables that can influence media power, journalistic quality and content diversity' (2012: 39) and insist that consumer preferences, journalistic traditions and proprietorial cultures may all have an impact on the levels of diversity and the ability of elites to influence public discourse and action. Manuel Castells notes the contradiction that 'in spite of the growing concentration of power, capital and production in the global communication system, the actual content and format of communication practices are increasingly diversified' (2009: 136). The rise of digital technologies and the emergence of a more autonomous form of 'mass self-communication' has allegedly diluted the significance of concentration as a major problem (a claim I return to in Chapter 4).

David Hesmondhalgh, a harsh critic of existing marketized social relations, also argues that some media producers enjoy sufficient autonomy so that they are under no obligation to follow meekly or consistently the dictates of owners and executives. Indeed, a commercial orientation is as likely to enable the production of challenging and alternative forms of content as it is to lead to the emergence of trivial and sensationalized material (Hesmondhalgh 2001). He warns that an emphasis on ownership alone may foster an instrumentalist approach that marginalizes more complex questions concerning the management of 'risk and uncertainty within the media business' (2001: 2). Furthermore, the emphasis on news and current affairs in many debates on ownership misses out on the role of other formats and genres and diminishes the importance of popular culture. Finally, the fact that there is 'no necessary link between oligopoly and reduced diversity' (2001: 3) – witness the explosion of niche musics presided over by both large and small corporations – suggests to Hesmondhalgh that 'there are other factors, besides ownership, at work in explaining media output' (2001: 3).

Hesmondhalgh, in particular, makes some very valuable points about the contradictions of media power but his argument that media ownership is not a decisive explanatory framework neglects some important points. Firstly, this is a view deliberately promulgated by proponents of ownership liberalization who wish to de-prioritize concentration as a controversial issue and, indeed, are keen to play down their own capacity to exercise power in the communication field. For Rupert Murdoch, it is not he but his readers who are in control:

'I'm held to account by the British people every day' he told the Leveson Inquiry in April 2012 when asked about the political influence of his titles. 'They can stop buying the paper. I stand for election every day ...' (Murdoch 2012: 55). Downplaying the significance of media ownership as a proxy for media power requires us also to acknowledge that this is a strategy adopted enthusiastically by the powerful. Secondly, it is not the case that those who focus on ownership claim that it explains everything about media performance. McChesney (2004: 208), for example, points out that there are many factors that shape media output apart from ownership but he argues nevertheless that a public policy emphasis on stimulating competition within media markets by curbing excessive concentration is needed precisely in order to facilitate diverse, creative, unexpected and antagonistic content. Thirdly, specific crises like the phone-hacking scandal or more general cracks in the neo-liberal project have highlighted the flaws of contemporary ownership arrangements – that they have produced media that are connected to, rather than be monitors of, elite power – and contributed to an atmosphere in which demands for reform of media ownership structures are part and parcel of calls for wider democratic change.

By recognizing that what are all too often seen as rather bureaucratic issues of market structure and behaviour are in fact systems of thought and action that, in the present climate, mobilize market-oriented values and that marginalize non-commercial objectives, debates concerning ownership can be seen as crucial analytical ciphers for contemporary neo-liberalism. A critical evaluation of media ownership ought to combine a focus on *structure* with an emphasis on whose *interests* are best represented by existing ownership arrangements. Far from scaling down campaigns for more democratic forms of media ownership, the current situation requires a renewed focus on mechanisms to foster plurality and diversity in media markets as a prerequisite for, if not the sole ingredient of, a more fundamental reorientation of media structures and media power.

Conclusion

Mills' work on power elites and Miliband's study of the capitalist state have been extremely influential in the development of a critical perspective that argues that the media's overall function is to reproduce and legitimize the narratives of vested interests in society. Both sought to interrogate the composition of and interconnections within the dominant strata, and both identified the media as a particularly important agency of social reproduction. Their emphasis on the 'interlocking' nature of elites – especially the multiple points of contact between state and market – reminds us that, whatever divisions may exist, there is an overriding common purpose and shared vision among those that populate the 'higher circles'. Although Mills has often been accused of underestimating the power of the Executive and exaggerating the power of the military, his notion of a defence establishment that commands significant influence over social life rings increasingly true in the years following 9/11. Indeed, Mills' focus on the military dimension of power presages later analyses of the relationship between the media and the state that we see in, for example, Herbert Schiller's notion of a 'military-industrial communications complex' (1969: 54) or the compliance of some of the world's largest communications companies with the activities of the National Security Agency in intercepting personal data (Guardian 2013a). The increased harassment of reporters on both sides of the Atlantic – witness the detention under the UK terrorism legislation of the partner of a journalist who helped to expose the US government's surveillance programme or the secret acquisition by the US Justice Department of telephone records of Associated Press staff – signals the creeping redefinition of investigative journalism as a terrorist activity (Jenkins 2013) as well as the continuing coercive power of the state.

Both Mills and Miliband have been extensively criticized of course. Conservative voices generally refute what they see as an empirically weak and overly conspiratorial approach that neglects the vitality and competition that marks the pluralist marketplace. More sympathetic voices chide them for marginalizing prospects for change, minimizing conflict and for pursuing accounts of society that ultimately reside in the behaviour of individuals rather than in the movement of classes or other social groups. Their conclusions, in other words, while provocative and urgent, tend towards the descriptive and lack the ability to explain underlying mechanisms of power. As Lukes puts it, elite theory refers to an instrumental version of power that cannot account for the 'power to extract, preserve and augment material power resources' (Lukes 2012).

Despite these points, both Mills and Miliband have nevertheless provided a rich frame with which we can productively examine the material coordination of social resources gathered inside the media, a central task of political economy approaches. Indeed, it may be that their ideas are all the more relevant today when a relatively small group of people have increased their share of the world's wealth and used the media as a constituent part of this process. *Neo-liberalism* remains a significant explanatory tool for understanding the conditions in which elites – whether constituted as a dominant class or as a set of highly specialized interests occupying the commanding heights of society – engage in the pursuit of 'extractive power'. Neo-liberal elites are now embedded inside the media and communications sector and are increasingly investing in networks and platforms that will provide them with economic rewards and ideological influence. In this context, media ownership patterns, while unable to reveal the full dynamics of how the media function, are one of the crucial elements in the reproduction of media power. Analysis of media ownership and control is not, as Stuart Hall points out, 'a sufficient explanation of the way the ideological universe is structured, but it is a necessary starting point. It gives the whole machinery of representation its fundamental orientation in the value-system of property and profit' (1986: 11). Media power is not reducible to the properties of elites alone but neither is it separate from the worlds they inhabit, the structures they preside over and the objectives they pursue.

3

Media Policy and Power

*I suggest that power is real and effective in a remarkable variety of
ways, some of them indirect and hidden, and that, indeed, it is at
its most effective when least accessible to observation.*

LUKES (2005: 64)

Policy activism in neo-liberal times

February 12, 2009 was supposed to have been an epic day in the history of
the broadcast media in the USA: the date on which television was originally
designated to switch off its analogue transmissions and firmly embrace a
digital future. The day did not go too well. Only about a third of all stations
actually turned off their analogue signals, and the regulator, the Federal
Communications Commission (FCC), was flooded with 70,000 complaints in
two days. With millions of Americans still unprepared for analogue switch-off
and with a waiting list of some 4.3 million people for the coupons designed
to offset the cost of a digital set-top box, the new administration of Barack
Obama was forced to delay the switchover date by four months. The problems
were perhaps best illustrated by the case of Walter Hoover, a 70-year-old
man from Joplin, Missouri, who, enraged when his new set-top box failed
to function and therefore deprived of access to his favourite programmes,
pulled out his high-powered hunting rifle and shot his TV set at least two
times before being captured by police. As one reporter concluded, 'Missouri
is known as the "show me state" and Walter just wanted to be shown his TV
shows' (Starr 2009).

Hoover's action demonstrates not simply the passion that many viewers
continue to hold for television but also the risks involved in such a decisive act
of government intervention. Digital switchover is far from the unambiguously
consumer-led or even market-led phenomenon it is sometimes portrayed to be;
instead, it is a course of action pursued vigorously by different administrations

with different interests but nevertheless wedded to the idea of the intrinsic desirability of a digital future (Freedman 2008, Galperin 2004). As such, it is a powerful example of *activist* public policy designed to transform our basic communications infrastructure. But surely such activism is out of step with what we usually expect from neo-liberal minded governments in relation to whole swathes of media policy where it is assumed that markets will work their magic, customers will assert their preferences, and particular media structures, platforms and practices will follow as a result? As befits their commitment to a neo-liberal conception of the state, many governments claim to be firmly adhering to a policy agenda that emphasizes the efficacy of markets to promote innovation, competition and consumer sovereignty, the need for government and the state to remain 'small', and for media policies to act, above all, as 'support mechanisms' for private economic activity in the communications field.

This relates to a conception of *negative policy*, of a form of non-intervention where media markets, institutions and sovereign individuals are left to govern themselves without outside interference. For policymaking bodies, this involves a reluctance to develop new rules and to secure fresh legislation affecting the media for fear of undermining innovation or of imposing bureaucratic restrictions on market activity. Where government intervention is necessary, it should – according to this perspective – be minimal and non-intrusive, as the business correspondent of the *Independent* newspaper argued in his response to the UK government's aggressive digital strategy: 'Public policy does have a role to play in business and industry, but it is the narrow one of ensuring fair play, establishing a level playing field, and putting in place equitable labour protections. Otherwise governments tend to serve business and the public best by merely staying out of their way' (Warner 2009: 37). This determination to 'stay out of the way' is exemplified by the passage of only *two* significant communication bills in seventy-five years of American history, the 1934 Communications Act and the 1996 Telecommunications Act. It finds an echo in the UK where, as Colin Seymour-Ure puts it (1991: 206), there was for many years a 'popular belief that they [governments] had no media policies at all'. Even in an area like broadcasting which has long been subject to detailed regulation, this is still characterized by principles of voluntarism and minimalism, that is, of the desirability of self-regulation and the brevity of acts of statute.

The most celebrated example of 'negative policy' is the First Amendment to the US Constitution that states that 'Congress shall make no law abridging the freedom of speech, or of the press'. This is the key political underpinning of the non-interventionist style and dates back to a post-Enlightenment, effectively libertarian, conception of freedom. In this view, the state is conceptualized as the main danger and state power viewed as potentially the main barrier to the unrestricted circulation of ideas. Freedom, here, involves the ability of the media to be free *from* state interference and control as well as the capacity to be free *to* challenge arguments proposed by representatives of the state and to monitor their activities. The emergence of 'free media' is the story of the titanic struggle against government licensing and control and the establishment of a system committed not to the exercise of power but to the service of individual readers, listeners and viewers. This is what James Curran describes as the 'liberal narrative' of media history, a persuasive account of the positive impact of firstly the press and latterly cinema, broadcasting and the internet on democratic life. It is 'a story of progress in which the media became free, switched their allegiance from government to the people, and served democracy' (Curran 2002: 7). In this uplifting narrative, 'negative policy' is seen as a more appropriate way to safeguard the public's freedom of expression and to secure a 'marketplace of ideas' than the micro-managing of the communications field by state 'do-gooders'.

Yet, 'micro-managing' and intervention is precisely what we are seeing at the moment as governments seek to recalibrate their communications systems in the light of the ongoing 'digital revolution'. This is particularly true in the area of broadband deployment where governments across the globe are scrambling to take advantage of the economic, political and social benefits of a high-speed network infrastructure. By 2012, 131 governments around the world had either adopted or were planning to adopt national broadband plans that specified targets for broadband rollout (International Telecommunication Union 2012: 37). This is a major component of public telecommunication investment which in 2011, according to the OECD (2013: 70), corresponded to some $87 billion in the Americas, $67 billion in Europe and $34 billion in the Asia/Pacific region. Most of this comes from the private sector but there are some significant exceptions. The Korean government, for example, has invested $24 billion in a public internet backbone while, in the US, $7.3 billion was allocated to broadband development as part of the 2009 American Recovery and Reinvestment Plan (Alcatel-Lucent 2009: 8). Meanwhile, in April 2009, the Australian government introduced a $35 billion public/private initiative to build a high-speed fibre-to-the-home network, a plan that is now likely to be scaled back somewhat following the election of a conservative prime minister in 2013 (Hopewell 2013). Even the cash-strapped UK administration of David Cameron has promised to invest £1.6 billion of public money to extend superfast broadband to 95 per cent of households by 2017 (DCMS 2013a: 7).

This activity is not confined to modernizing broadband infrastructure alone. The European Commission, for example, has initiated various investigations in relation to media pluralism, setting up a High Level Group to provide recommendations on how best to secure a more open and diverse media environment, published its own consultation paper on communications in April 2013 (European Commission 2013) and launched reviews of many other areas including copyright, net neutrality and online regulation. In the UK, the communications regulator Ofcom has carried out over 800 consultations since its birth in 2003, a hyper-activism that seems to be at odds with both the caricature of the media policymaking environment as lax and reactive and the view that the market, if left alone, will deliver the networks and services that are necessary for life in a digital age.

But these initiatives are all confined to *overt* acts of government, to the decision-making actions of policymaking bodies and to the consultative work of regulatory agencies – in other words to the public exercise of 'official' power. There is, however, an entirely different approach to the media policy process that takes its cue from debates in social and political science that emerged in the 1960s (for example Barach and Baratz 1962, Crenson 1971, Lukes 2005). These perspectives locate power in less visible arenas of decision-making and focus on examples of non-decision-making and policy neglect. Instead of dwelling on the evidence provided by key participants, the content of white papers and regulatory orders, the detail of draft bills and Congressional acts and the flavour of parliamentary debates, this approach examines the means by which alternative options are marginalized, conflicting values delegitimized and rival interests de-recognized. This flows from an understanding of decision-making as an ideological process structured by unequal access to power and where power itself 'is at its most effective when least observable' (Lukes 2005: 1).

So, in this chapter, I want to consider legislative and regulatory initiatives not in terms of policy noise but policy *silence*, not policy visibility but policy *opacity*, not decision-making but *non-decision-making*. I suggest that this approach is a valuable way of reflecting on an environment in which policies are developed on the basis of a limited palette of ideological values and preferences that further pre-empt the emergence of contrasting – and in a neo-liberal environment, that means public-facing – policy approaches. The chapter focuses in particular on policy debates concerning media plurality (referring back to the discussion of elites and ownership in the previous chapter) and net neutrality (looking ahead to the next chapter) in order to explore what appears to be a clear contradiction between policy intervention and non-intervention and to illuminate the dynamics of power as they relate to the media policy process. Instead of being swept along in the currents of visible policy activity, the chapter argues that we need to develop a more critical approach to media policy that challenges dominant frames and objectives by highlighting the exclusions, gaps and taken-for-granted agendas that mark ongoing policy debates.

Power, decision-making and the policy process

The ability to formulate and implement policy is a significant indicator of power in a pluralist society. Not surprisingly, therefore, mainstream policy analysts tend to focus on the people involved, the spaces they inhabit and the forms that policies take. We are likely to associate policymaking with parliaments, government departments and the offices of industry lobbyists and to highlight the significance of individual 'experts': technologists, economists, lawyers, executives, ministers, civil servants and lobbyists. We often see policies as tangible objects – as documents that contain the most up-to-date rules and regulations, laws and liabilities, commitments and constraints – rather than concentrating on the boundary-setting processes within which these rules, regulations and laws are devised and implemented. Media policies, despite their relationship to symbolic forms of production and different types of value, are just as likely to be viewed in this way: as rational, evidence-based and necessary prescriptions for the operation of competitive markets and public well-being. Media policy, as Thomas Streeter puts it (2013: 488), is regularly conceived as 'a technocratic field best left to the acronym-fluent with ambitions in government service'.

This is actually a highly contentious perspective on policy that, by privileging its administrative, consensual and visible components, marginalizes more critical accounts of policymaking that emphasize the ideological and discursive dimensions of the policy process (Fischer 2003, Lukes 2005, Streeter 2013). In relation to media policy, it is an approach that strips the process of its politicized and exclusionary features (Freedman 2008) in order to highlight the visible jostling for advantage among a multitude of actors that, according to its supporters, characterizes the transparent and competitive nature of contemporary policy debates. For pluralist theorists, power in the policymaking process is intimately related to decision-making authority and to the successful deployment of a capacity by one actor to induce another actor to do something that, in the words of Robert Dahl, they 'would not otherwise do' (cited in Lukes 2005: 16). Power, in this account, is something to be *exercised*, a property that is cemented in a decision-making situation rather than a characteristic of the resources – unequally distributed across society – that actors may bring to the situation. Liberal democracy in these circumstances is secured by observable transactions that take place in circumstances where power and effectiveness are determined less by 'fixed' notions of class or privilege than by the more subjective variables of status and insider knowledge. This takes us back to the consensus paradigm that we first identified in the opening chapter in which there is said to be a fierce struggle for power in modern plural societies among the many participants and yet no single or durable source of elite domination.

This is by no means a new debate and, indeed, the pluralist account of the dynamics of decision-making was criticized in a series of famous discussions that emerged in the US in the second half of the twentieth century (Bachrach and Baratz 1962, Domhoff 1967, Mills 1959). These critics accused their pluralist counterparts of exaggerating the openness of the bargaining process (and, by implication, the pluralism of American society itself) and of having a misplaced confidence in the competitive allocation of power. But, perhaps more fundamentally, they also challenged the pluralist account for focusing on only one, limited, 'face' of power: that of agreements struck in specific and visible instances of decision-making. According to Peter Bachrach and Morton Baratz, pluralists missed out on a 'second face of power': the promotion of particular interests through the selection of *non*-issues. 'Of course power is exercised when A participates in the making of decisions that affect B', they wrote, with reference to Dahl's initial conceptualization of power. 'But power is also exercised when A devotes his energies to creating or reinforcing social and political values and institutional practices that limit the scope of the political process to public consideration of only those issues which are comparatively innocuous to A' (Bachrach and Barataz 1962: 948).

Power ought to be understood not simply in terms of visible decisions but questions of influence. It is not about whether there are disagreements between participants (which pluralists admit is the case) but whether these disagreements are significant and in what ways their significance is allowed to structure the shape of the policymaking process. Power for Bachrach and Baratz is related to the exercise of interests and the ability to prevent 'potentially dangerous ideas from being raised' (1962: 952). In a later formulation, they argued that non-decision-making is a 'means by which demands for change in the existing allocation of benefits and privileges in the community can be suffocated before they are even voiced' (1970: 44). This capacity to silence 'dangerous' demands is not shared equally by all participants, undermining the pluralist view of public policy as a transparent and egalitarian process. Instead, power in the policy process is related to the ability for one set of interests to marginalize and dominate other sets of interests and to control the decision-making agenda in the pursuit of managing conflict: 'to the extent that a person or a group … creates or reinforces barriers to the public airing of public conflicts, that person or group has power' (1962: 949).

This has significant implications for the analyst of public policy. While pluralists, as Nelson Polsby argues (quoted in Lukes 2005: 17), 'should study actual behavior, either at first hand or by reconstructing behavior from documents, informants, newspapers, and other appropriate sources' in order to identify the victorious interests in a decision-making situation, critically-minded researchers need to dig a little deeper. Drawing on Schattschneider's notion that 'organization is the mobilization of bias' (1960: 71), Bachrach and Baratz insist that we ought not to take things like 'evidence' and 'participation' for granted and instead should investigate 'the dominant values and the political myths, rituals and institutions which tend to favor the vested interests of one or more groups, relative to others' (1962: 950) and, as a result, highly selectively, to classify some issues as 'problems' meriting policy action and others as not worthy of attention.

The invitation to investigate non-decision-making was taken up by Matthew Crenson in his very thoughtful study of urban responses to air pollution (Crenson 1971). Crenson sought to figure out why some American towns ignored their dirty air while others moved to regulate emissions, and why some places failed to identify pollution as a 'problem' while others treated it as a policy priority. He concluded that a number of variables had to be taken into consideration – for example, levels of industry lobbying, degree of party organization, traditions of community campaigning – in order to explain why rules on air pollution were introduced in East Chicago many years before action was taken in Gary, Indiana, a company town dominated by US Steel. His focus, however, was less on the action necessary to secure legislation than on the 'power of obstruction – of enforcing inaction and thereby maintaining the impenetrability of the political process' (1971: 21). Securing air pollution as a 'non-issue' required a mobilization of power at the local level that would not be immediately identifiable from studying the formal decision-making process. Indeed, in a direct challenge to pluralist faith in the competitive nature of bargaining, Crenson argued that 'a polity that is pluralistic in its decisionmaking can be unified in its non-decisionmaking' (1971: 179). The central task for policy critics is therefore to bring to light the 'seemingly important decisions that are never made, significant policies that are never formulated, and issues that never arise' (1971: 4) and, crucially, to identify the values and interests mobilized in the dynamics of 'non-decisionmaking'.

For Steven Lukes, author of the influential *Power: A Radical View* (2005), Crenson's work has played a significant role in developing our understanding of power. While Lukes welcomes Bachrach and Baratz's challenge to the pluralist definition of power as related to the control of visible instances of decision-making, he nevertheless criticizes their analysis for being too focused on the intentional behaviour of key policy actors as well as the 'association of power with actual observable conflict' (Lukes 2005: 26). Non-decision-making provides a valuable rejection of the pluralists' narrow and misleading emphasis on success in specific policy debates but it is still rooted, he argues, in a behavioural paradigm that leads them to examine only individual examples of purposeful activity. Crenson is important because he acknowledges that power is mobilized not only in actual decisions but also in *inaction*, in the ability, for example, of US Steel to prevent pollution from becoming an issue that required public action. When Crenson argues that the 'mere reputation for power, unsupported by acts of power, can be sufficient to restrict the scope of local decisionmaking' (1971: 177), this chimes with Lukes' conception of a third, ideological, face of power: 'a serious sociological and not merely personalized explanation of how political systems prevent political demands from becoming political issues or even from being made' (Lukes 2005: 40).

Power, according to this perspective, involves the capacity to mobilize one set of interests against another set of interests in the pursuit of the latter's yielding to the former's wishes. This need not involve visible acts of power – for example, military force or legal sanctions – but may consist of 'negative actions' as Lukes describes them, 'failures to act' (2005: 77) that demonstrate the power of one actor significantly to affect the interests of others in a situation of conflict (Lukes cites the US government's refusal to ratify the Kyoto Protocols on the control of greenhouse gases or non-participation in the International Criminal Court as examples of negative actions that continue to have major consequences). But for Lukes, 'the most effective and insidious use of power is to prevent such conflict from arising in the first place' (2005: 27), an encouragement for the student of power to concentrate on the ideological as well as material resources necessary for any actor to impose their interests on others.

Lukes' definition of power is at times awkward – he adopts a rather simplistic version of domination and he certainly underplays the contradictions and difficulties of securing compliance (an argument I shall return to in Chapter 5). This is particularly true in relation to the (admittedly few) references to the media as crucial vehicles of false consciousness and agenda formation that have both the 'power to affect your central and basic interests' (2005: 80–81) as well as the 'power to mislead' (2005: 149), a sensibility that seems to be at odds with his more subtle argument that 'three-dimensional power does not and cannot produce one-dimensional man' (2005: 150). Yet, Lukes' focus on the ideological dimensions of power, his analysis of the implications of 'inaction', his highlighting of that which is not immediately observable, and his insistence that power involves the capacity to mobilize and entrench particular interests (and does not simply refer to an exchange of differences) has much to recommend it to critical theorists of power and policy.

This is especially true given the emergence of what Frank Fischer has called a neopositivist policy paradigm (2003: 188) that privileges narrowly empirical methods, an unreflexive technical rationality and a commitment to 'truth' that hides the elite interests that underpin it. Such an approach 'deceptively offers an appearance of truth. It does so by assigning numbers to decision-making criteria and produces what can appear to be definitive answers to political questions' (2003: 13). While pluralist approaches to policy neglect the power of institutions and ideas, Fischer argues for a postempiricist method that sees policymaking as the strategic interventions, symbolic interactions and discursive practices that combine together in an effort to resolve socially constructed 'problems'. In this situation, rituals, language and 'even the design and décor of buildings' (2003: 60) can be significant in assessing the dynamics of policymaking. For Thomas Streeter, policy discourse does not merely structure, legitimate or even mystify the everyday operations of the media but is actually part of 'creating the conditions that make market relations possible' (2013: 495).

This is very helpful in terms of developing fresh approaches to media and communications policy, a field that I have previously argued has been characterized by a de-politicized, technologically determinist and administrative mindset (Freedman 2008). Naming the 'problem' is, as we shall see, a central feature of any policy process while a focus on the more informal spaces within which policy debates take place is also valuable, especially when we consider the importance to media policy of, for example, the private entrance to Downing Street (through which Rupert Murdoch has so often gone) together with the yachts, dinner parties and soirees which have regularly brought together lobbyists, politicians and executives. Bill Kirkpatrick talks of the importance of a 'vernacular' media policy that is the direct counterpart of dominant 'formal' practices. This refers to 'the vast range of unofficial sites at which media regulation occurs and the multiple levels, directions and modes of policy production and enforcement that operate beyond the contours of the official policy sphere' (Kirkpatrick 2013: 635–636). Referring back to the transition to digital television where we started this chapter, he gives an excellent example of how the $40 coupons provided by the government to offset the purchase of a digital set-top box were actually used by many consumers in more imaginative ways: 'some consumers, who already had television equipped with digital tuners realized that they could get the coupons, go down to Best Buy, buy two converter boxes that they didn't actually need, then return them the next day for $80 of store credit toward something they actually wanted' (2013: 641).

We should not, however, see policy simply as a discursive enterprise nor as a purely 'bottom-up' and creative phenomenon; nor indeed should we reject all forms of 'evidence' as intrinsically illegitimate. Instead, we need to conceptualize media policy as a conflict-ridden process in which rival interests struggle in order to shape the dynamics of the media environment and to lay the preconditions for the production, circulation and consumption of media experiences. This means that we need to look at ideologies as well as institutions, elites as well as evidence and certainly power as well as paperwork. We need a 'force of ideas approach' (Kunzler 2012) to think about how the various actors in the policy process conduct themselves, how they compete to structure the terms of debate, and how they negotiate the inclusion and exclusion of different actors, objectives and agendas.

In the context of the bursts of activity that we are increasingly witnessing in relation to emerging digital environments, how does this more ideological definition of media policy play out and, in particular, in what ways does an emphasis on non-decision-making and 'policy silences' help to illuminate the dynamics of contemporary policymaking? How has power inscribed itself into recent media policy debates and to what extent can we characterize the media policy approaches of existing administrations as being driven by a simultaneous determination to intervene and a conviction that market forces should be left alone to structure media markets?

Media policy silences

At first glance, an emphasis on *inaction* tells us very little about media policy approaches in the context of the current hyperactivity of governments, corporations, civil servants and regulators as they prepare to modernize their communications infrastructures and update their media systems and rules for a digital future. As I have already pointed out, governments around the world are producing reports and fashioning plans for broadband roll-out at a speed that far surpasses any 'organic' growth that the market is delivering. The preferred term for the policy role of the state in this context is 'industrial activism', defined in the UK government's *Digital Britain* (*DB*) report as 'about the considered application of Government resources and policy-making across the areas where public policy and the market meet' (BIS/DCMS 2009: 8). Despite neo-liberal rhetoric about shrinking states and the danger of 'big government', this is not a policy environment marked by sloth or by passivity and there are a vast number of media-related issues that are capturing the attention of administrations and elites across the globe.

It is worth emphasizing immediately that the 'liberal' narrative of non-intervention and the libertarian principles on which it is based have not disappeared among the multiple media policy initiatives launched by governments. It is present, for example, in the success in the US of *Citizens United*, the use of the First Amendment to protect commercial speech as opposed to individual self-expression (see Wu 2013) as well as the very strong arguments made by the British government and major internet players in opposition to the prospect of the regulation of on-demand services in negotiations on the European Union's 2010 Audiovisual Media Services Directive (for example Mandelson 2009).

A similar reluctance to intervene has long characterized the UK government's official response to demands for stronger regulation of the press in order to curb some of the worst excesses of tabloid behaviour:

The Government strongly believes that a free press is vital to the health of our democracy. There should be no laws that specifically seek to restrict that freedom and Government should not seek to intervene in any way in what a newspaper of magazine chooses to publish. (DCMS 2003)

The only reason that this language has now changed is because of the phone hacking crisis that led to Lord Justice Leveson's recommendations for an improved system of press self-regulation (Leveson 2012) that is, nevertheless, still based on a principle of non-intervention in editorial decision-making. This was not sufficient to ward off a vigorous industry lobby against *any* form of statutory intervention, even if that related only to the setting up of a body with oversight of the independent regulator and which had no remit whatsoever to demand changes to press content. Press barons, led by the *Daily Mail*'s editor, Paul Dacre, launched a vicious assault on Leveson's proposals (and the Royal Charter that was eventually set up to incorporate these proposals) arguing that they constituted the 'end of 300 years of press freedom' and would represent the ultimate triumph of politicians over the press (Freedman 2013). These arguments not only misrepresent the substance of Leveson's recommendations but also ignore the changed historical circumstances in that the most restrictive influence on journalists today is not the formal pre-publication censorship by the state that was evident in previous eras (and, of course, that still remains a common practice in some countries) so much as the commercial consideration to secure exclusives and increase circulation whatever the ethical consequences. Where journalists do face overt state intervention, for example in the *Guardian*'s coverage of the NSA's surveillance programme, other editors and proprietors (at least in the UK) have been quick to condemn the *Guardian* and to prioritize the 'national interest' over their version of 'press freedom' (Freedman 2013).

The liberal demand for non-intervention has, however, been most purely expressed by James Murdoch, who, when he was chief executive of BSkyB, called for the dissolution of all rules affecting the broadcast sector. In a speech to the European Broadcast convention, he declared that 'there is a long way to go before consumers enjoy the sovereignty that is their right. We don't need more controls to achieve that. We need a bonfire of controls. Then commerce will be free to drive out culture forward to the Golden Age of broadcasting' (quoted in Plunkett 2005).

This latter perspective, intimately linked to neo-liberal visions of economy and society that privilege the dynamism of market forces and relegate the state to a secondary role, is far from absent in contemporary media policy documents like *Digital Britain*, a document that is marked by its detailed policy prescriptions for a whole range of areas including digital radio and intellectual property. The opening of *DB*, however, makes it clear that meddling should be the exception and not the rule. In those cases where market forces are adequately serving customers, the 'simple position is that these sectors are working well and do not need commentary, intervention or unnecessary interference' (BIS/DCMS 2009: 9). Furthermore, the report argues that 'an excessive focus on the sector could chill operational negotiations and decisions while participants wait to see how it all pans out' (2009: 10). This is a line of argument that is frequently used against any regulatory interventions that may undermine long-term investment decisions or short-term profitability so that, for example, limits on media ownership are regularly described as likely to deter investment rather than to increase diversity and that they are punitive rather than creative. Non-intervention, in other words, is the safest option, generally the default position for neo-liberal governments for whom an activist public policy approach is only needed in those areas in which 'market failure' is likely to take place, for example, the provision of a universal broadband infrastructure or the delivery of regional and local news.

Now this sounds reasonable enough at first glance but, of course, it begs the question of what constitutes an example of 'market failure', who decides this, what values are brought to bear on the decision-making process, and what other options are considered in achieving the public policy objectives in relation to this particular area? The central question then concerns not the rights and wrongs of intervention *per se* (as neo-liberals claim) but the reasons for intervening in *this* area and *not* in another one. Why does a particular issue become a 'problem' that is worthy of public policy attention? Why does the building of a broadband infrastructure become a 'problem' for which senior government figures attempt to find a solution while the increasing concentration of ownership of radio stations and the closure of local newspapers does not? Why does music piracy become a central issue for legislators when the basic conditions under which musicians have to work is of limited interest? An exclusive emphasis on immediate and observable policy debates misses out on this deeper level of questioning: What are the presuppositions that govern the parameters of the media policy process and that shape what questions are asked as well as which ones are not? Who holds *definitional* as well as *organizational* power inside policymaking networks?

This is where a focus on non-decision-making can be highly productive in terms of identifying, as has already been quoted, the 'dominant values and the political myths, rituals and institutions' (Bachrach and Baratz 1962: 950) that structure access to power in policy contexts. For example, as we see in the UK government's most recent assessment of the legislative environment affecting communications, *Connectivity, Content and Consumers* (DCMS 2013a), major intervention is simply not necessary: 'Our discussions with industry and others demonstrated that the present framework is broadly working well, supporting economic growth and innovation, and the things that we value as a society:

high-quality news, radio and TV programmes' (2013a: 6). This is a contentious statement given that the Leveson Inquiry into press standards together with recent opinion polls about trust in journalists – a Eurobarometer poll in 2012 revealed that only 21 per cent of the UK public trust the press, the second lowest across the whole of Europe (European Commission 2012: 19) – show quite the opposite: that the framework is *not* working well and that it needs serious adjustment if it is to win back legitimacy. Even more illuminating, however, is the government's claim that discussions have taken place with industry and unnamed 'others' with growth and innovation simply assumed to be the main goals for communications policy. If these are accepted as the key values underpinning the policy process then it makes perfect sense to focus on how best to stimulate competition and efficiency and to marginalize issues of pluralism, diversity and digital inequalities.

We need, however, to go beyond instances of non-decision-making to identify not simply the priorities that dominate the visible policy process but rather the forces that are responsible for the silences that permeate media policy as a whole. This refers to an understanding of silence certainly not as an unconscious lapse or a momentary omission, nor even what some feminist scholars describe as a 'space of possibility' (Rowe and Malhotra 2013: 2) that may be used strategically by marginalized groups to highlight the suppression of their voices and to mark their refusal to represent themselves in the terms proposed by those who dominate them (Fleming 2013). However, while I would not want to equate silence merely with powerlessness and while I also recognize the significance of struggles for voice as attempts to challenge the instrumentalism of neo-liberal life (Couldry 2010), I see silence as a socially constructed phenomenon that reflects the unequal distribution of power in society. Media policy silences, according to this logic, are structuring forces that, as Sue Jansen argues in relation to the 'censorship' of media goods through market forces, attempt to 'render the system of control of industrial capitalism extremely resistant to criticism' (1991: 134).

Applied to media policy, this would involve an analysis of the terms on which the policy agenda is formulated and objectives are framed, which voices are privileged inside and which are frozen out of policy debates, how participation is invited or barriers erected, and from whom information (or 'evidence') is sought. It would focus on the ideological positions that are brought to bear in shaping policy questions and suggest that policymaking, far from being a simple administrative act, is instead a series of highly politicized transactions in which certain preferences are celebrated and others marginalized (Freedman 2008). As Sandra Braman notes (2004: 154):

How a policy issue area is identified is political because it determines who participates in decision-making, the rhetorical frames and operational definitions applied, the analytical techniques and modes of argument used, and the resources – and goals – considered pertinent.

Indeed, according to Bill Kirkpatrick, the assertion of authority inside the media policy process actually depends on 'validating some regulatory knowledges and practices while ruling others irrelevant, out of bounds, or criminal' (2013: 637).

Policy silence, in this context, does not mean 'doing nothing' and 'negative policy' does not suggest a lack of energy on the part of policymakers or a reluctance in principle to intervene. Rather it refers to a strategic decision taken by elites that the best way to promote hegemonic interests and to naturalize foundational values is through a *particular* role for the state: for example as enabler, patron or ideologue (Sparks 1986). In recent years, this has consisted of administrations assisting, often as quietly as possible, in fostering market conditions and embedding a neo-liberal logic in the media sector. In helping market forces to operate 'freely' and to extend their reach, public policy, in for example the US and the UK, has been crucial. From decisions on what constitutes an acceptable level of ownership concentration to their determination to secure analogue switch-off, and from their unyielding support for domestic rights holders to increase market opportunities in export ventures to their commitment to leverage existing copyright protections onto emerging distribution platforms, the British and American states have played a decisive role on behalf of key sections of their communication industries. Mainstream commentators may call it 'deregulation' and present this as evidence of 'small government' but others will identify it as re-regulation and as proof of a complex partnership between activist governments and private industry that is resonant of the neo-liberal state (Mirowski 2013).

This partnership is successful to the extent that it is able to legitimize its preferences and to use its policymaking power pre-emptively to smother any challenges (and the campaign in 2003 against the proposed relaxation of ownership rules in the US where the media reform movement certainly found its 'voice' shows that this is not a foregone conclusion). Policy silences, therefore, refer to the options that are *not* considered, to the questions are kept *off* the policy agenda, to the players who are *not* invited to the policy table, and to the values that are seen as unrealistic or undesirable by those best able to mobilize their policymaking power. For example, in current discussions concerning the allocation of spectrum released by digital switchover, why is it that principles of remuneration dominate and why is it that the idea of handing spectrum to community and public bodies is virtually ignored? When it comes to the future of news, why is it that the idea of introducing some sort of public subsidy is anathema to policymakers, ignoring the simple fact that news production has long been subsidized in different ways by the state (see McChesney and Nichols 2010 for a range of options for rescuing for US press)?

A focus on policy silences would also have consequences for study of the field itself. Methodologically, this would involve a more qualitative approach to policy analysis including interviews with a range of people beyond traditional 'insiders' in order to find out what different actors think about the relevance or openness of the policy process as well as consideration of the spaces outside of the official fora in which policies are seen to be devised and decided. It would require analysis of the submissions to consultations that are ignored as well as those that are cited together with discourse analysis of the agenda-setting documents that frame the policy process. Finally, on the basis that decision-making often involves 'private and mediated forms of communication' (Davis 2007: 11), it would need forensic work to uncover the 'hidden' channels – for example, the lobbying activities and sites of elite interaction – in which influence is applied and interests promoted.

This conception of media policy would help to illuminate the many revealing absences in the policy approach articulated in documents like *Digital Britain* and *Connectivity, Content and Consumers*. In their rush to embrace the digital 'revolution' and to develop a primarily industrial strategy to stimulate construction of a digital infrastructure, successive British governments (and they are far from alone) have emphasized highly consumerist notions of *choice*, *efficiency* and *value*. They have sought to naturalize these values as 'desirable' policy objectives but, by adopting a restricted approach to policymaking, have failed to engage the population in a discussion about how it could use digital platforms to develop meaningful forms of interactivity, to foster new forms of public and non-commercial media and to stimulate 'thick' forms of social interaction.

They have also failed seriously to consider alternatives to existing funding regimes. For example, given the crisis in local news in the UK, why is there absolutely no public discussion in official circles about the possibility of industry levies on content intermediaries, pay-TV operators and mobile phone companies to subsidize those programmes and genres that are rapidly disappearing but that have significant public value (as proposed by Barwise 2009, the Institute for Public Policy Research 2009 and the Media Reform Coalition 2012)? As the media economist Patrick Barwise argues (2009):

> I don't think you have to be a Marxist or a paranoid schizophrenic to note that the dominant pay-TV operator is controlled by Rupert Murdoch and that this might, at the margin, influence politicians' willingness to introduce a levy on pay TV, however small and however great the benefits for the British public and the creative industries.

Here is a clear case of power being deployed inside the policymaking process not to argue against the introduction of industry levies but, far more effectively, to prevent the proposal ever being raised as a 'serious' policy option in the first place. It is the conception of power raised by Lukes (2005: 1) as being especially effective precisely because of its invisibility. For all the consultations, reports, seminars, working parties, blogs, speeches and even legislation that populate the policy environment – in other words, for all the *noise* that is generated – what needs to be made visible are the questions that are not asked, the alternatives that are not considered and the agendas that are not posed. It is these silences that media policy activists need to highlight.

Silences in pluralism policy debates

A spectre is haunting the media policy environment and its name is pluralism: the commitment to develop a framework both to ensure the provision of a diversity of viewpoints and to prevent undue influence by dominant owners and voices over the political process (Ofcom 2012: 1). In Europe alone, there is the European Commission's High Level Group on Media Freedom and Pluralism, its associated Centre for Media Pluralism and Media Freedom, the Commission's Media Pluralism Monitor together with the many high-profile meetings, reports, working groups and regulatory initiatives all devoted to safeguarding and enhancing media pluralism in individual states. While pluralism should not be reduced to questions of structure alone – pluralism can also be secured through behavioural forms of regulation including public service interventions, adherence to journalistic codes of conduct and enforcement of obligations concerning editorial autonomy – diffuse media ownership is seen as a key determinant of a pluralistic environment. In the US, for example, the FCC presides over media ownership rules that are designed 'to ensure that diverse viewpoints and perspectives are available to the American people in the content they receive over the broadcast airwaves' (FCC 2011: 8).

   This devotion to media pluralism is hardly surprising. Who, after all, can be *against* media pluralism and thus presumably for media monotheism? It would be like being against citizenship or apple pie or oxygen. So we are all in favour of it and expect our policymakers to preside over guidelines and rules that will secure diversity and pluralism for all. This has been especially true in the UK where one of the reasons provided by the prime minister when setting up the public inquiry into the ethics and standards of the press that followed the phone hacking scandal in 2011 was precisely to investigate the relationship between media power and pluralism. This was a tacit acknowledgement of the fact that the phone hacking scandal arose precisely due to the reluctance of senior police and politicians to investigate allegations concerning criminal behaviour in some of the country's best-selling newspapers both because of institutional corruption and concerns that the largest news organizations would use their overwhelming influence on public opinion to destroy the reputations and electoral prospects of any politician who crossed them.

But even something as superficially benign as pluralism masks a series of different interpretations, most importantly between those who see it as deliverable through 'natural' cycles of market competition and those who see the need for more decisive forms of intervention in order actively to produce pluralistic media systems; between those who see the application of general competition law to the media sector as sufficient and those who call for more focused rules that deal with the special democratic role of the media in providing the information and forms of knowledge and entertainment that are essential to contemporary citizenship.

Contemporary neo-liberal policymakers are more than likely to equate aspirations towards pluralism and diversity with initiatives solely designed to maximize consumer choice and market penetration. Consider the accompanying paper to the Communications Review that was set up in 2011 to advise the British government on forthcoming communications legislation and which makes the following claim: 'As with markets more generally, media markets need to have a stable, robust and clear competition regime, aimed at driving growth, encouraging innovation, enterprise and investment and ultimately ensuring that consumers benefit through having a choice of content and services at competitive prices' (DCMS 2012: 1).

The first issue here is the assertion that media markets ought to be treated like any other part of the economy despite the contribution that media make to democracy, identity and knowledge. The second is that the document equates pluralism simply with maximizing customer choice at low cost. This quantitative account is both insufficient to foster meaningful diversity and totally misses out on the fact that the existing competition regime has failed to produce a genuinely competitive market in the first place. It is a major problem in news, as was implicitly recognized by the inclusion of pluralism in the remit of the Leveson Inquiry, given that Rupert Murdoch's newspapers like the *Sun* and the *Sun on Sunday* account for 34 per cent of daily circulation in the UK, that the *Daily Mail* has a further 21 per cent share and that it is generally acknowledged that these titles exert a very powerful influence on public life. But there is a further problem in that pluralism, as a policy objective meriting its own discussion, has effectively been absent from the official Communications Review *despite* the discussions taking place in full view of the public at the Leveson Inquiry.

The open letter that launched the Review (Hunt 2011), for example, makes no reference to the potential threat to plurality posed by the then highly controversial bid by News Corp to take full control of BSkyB (a bid that eventually collapsed in July 2012 following the phone hacking revelations), nor indeed to any proposals to secure plurality in an increasingly volatile environment. Instead, the emphasis is firmly on growth, innovation and deregulation at the expense of other socially and politically desirable objectives: while 'pluralism' is mentioned once, 'growth' is referred to twenty one times; while the 'public interest' merits a single mention, 'competition' or 'competitive' is referenced eight times.

The letter *assumes* that deregulation is the sole, or even preferred, route to ensuring growth and innovation when the picture is far more complex. For example, the government wishes to see British content thrive in export markets but the reason why British television has strong international appeal is that it is largely the product of a highly regulated, not deregulated, environment. It is especially revealing that the government's commitment to secure the future of the communications sector as a series of industries that are *both* engines of growth *and* mechanisms for delivering content in the public interest was predicated in advance on a desire further to shed rules that have helped to create strong organizations. Why is a deregulatory approach 'the aim' (Hunt 2011: 2) of the review as opposed to being one possible outcome? Why is 'economic growth' separated out from the role that the media plays more generally in equipping citizens with the resources they need fully to participate in contemporary life? Such absences and silences are highly revealing.

The omission of pluralism from the official policy debate was partially corrected when, during the summer of 2013, the government published two documents that revealed its plans for the media and communication sectors. The first is a 'strategy document' to which we have already referred, *Connectivity, Content and Consumers* (DCMS 2013a), effectively a white paper on digital Britain, which deals with issues including broadband roll-out, spectrum management and consumer safety. The second is a consultation 'that seeks views on the scope of a measurement framework for media plurality' (DCMS 2013b: 3) in line with Lord Justice Leveson's recommendations to consider similar issues.

By deciding to separate out the thorny question of who dominates the UK's media landscape from the less contentious 'four areas for action' (connectivity, content, consumers and costs) identified in the strategy document, the government was adopting a tactical response to a difficult situation. Despite the protracted and highly controversial attempt by News Corp to take full control of BSkyB in 2011–2012 and despite the overwhelming evidence provided to the Leveson Inquiry of the intimate relationships between powerful media moguls and top politicians, media ownership, the government ruled, is an area suitable for measurement, and not *action*, at this time. Indeed, the consultation's emphasis on measurement is deliberately designed to deflect demands for action to curb concentration. Of course, it is important to clarify what platforms and genres should be included in any review and what tools are necessary to measure plurality, but the consultation's remit was unnecessarily limited to a consideration of metrics that ignores proposals for remedies – many of which were put directly to the Leveson Inquiry.

The decision to keep plurality separate from its more general proposals for a digital infrastructure is understandable for a government that had little inclination to upset large media companies ahead of a general election. This was a case of putting political expediency ahead of the public interest. First, while it is true that Lord Justice Leveson did recommend that the government develop an appropriate measurement framework for plurality, he also mentioned both the 'menu of potential remedies' that needed to be considered and the 'levels of influence' that gave rise to concerns about media plurality (Leveson 2012: 45). There is no mention, however, in the government's consultation paper either of remedies or influence, the latter of which has been seen by some commentators (for example Grayson and Freedman 2013), as a problem of collusion between media and political elites and therefore a particularly compromising issue for the government.

Second, that this was a delaying tactic – designed to push awkward issues concerning ownership into the 'long grass' and to render them as invisible as possible – is evident in that many of the questions in the consultation on are precisely the same as those answered by Ofcom in its own report on media plurality (Ofcom 2012), a report which the government warmly welcomed and which it has done nothing to rebut. The government's response, therefore, has been far from a 'proportionate' response to the issues of media power and political transparency that were raised in the Leveson Inquiry and is instead a clear case of deploying its agenda-setting power to stifle certain problematic questions and to 'naturalize' more comfortable approaches.

We can also see this approach in relation to the consideration by the UK Competition Commission (CC) of potential anti-competitive behaviour in the British pay-TV sector. This is a good example of an ideological preference (that of market forces acting as regulating agents in their own right) circumscribing the way the 'problem' is defined. The issue here is not that the CC's analysis relied too heavily on metrics but that its use of the data was predicated on a belief in the self-correcting ability of the market that then places limits on its own capacity to secure unfettered competition. For example, despite noting 'the very high and stable level of concentration, the low level of switching between suppliers, the difficulty of large-scale entry/expansion as a traditional pay-TV retailer and the absence of countervailing buyer power in pay TV', the Competition Commission found that this 'did not of itself lead to the conclusion that there was an AEC [adverse effect on competition]' (2012: 8). The more sensible conclusion would be *not* that all is well with the pay-TV market but that contemporary competition law is unsuitable for dealing with bottlenecks and concentration inside that market.

A normative commitment to the equitable distribution of cultural resources, however, would have identified some significant problems in the pay-TV market where BSkyB has 'enclosed' highly valued content behind quite substantial paywalls. This is not the case simply for movies and sports, the subjects of two recent Competition Commission investigations into BSkyB's market power, but also in relation to original drama and entertainment. For example, BSkyB signed a deal with HBO in 2010 worth around £150 million over five years to have exclusive access to both first-run and archive HBO programmes (Robinson 2010). It also acquired the rights to AMC production *Mad Men* which resulted in its moving from BBC2, a free-to-air public service channel with a 7 per cent audience share, to Sky Atlantic, a pay channel with a 0.2 per cent share. BSkyB has now promised to spend £600 million on original UK material by the end of 2014 to go on channels like Sky One, with a 0.9 per cent share and the two Sky Arts channels, each of which, as of late 2013, had an average weekly viewing of one minute, with Sky Arts 1 registering a 0.1 audience share and Sky Arts 2 registering nothing at all. Of course, we should welcome any new investment into original programming but it ought to be a public policy issue if this output is locked into gated communities aimed thus far at a minority of people who happen to get the channels because, by and large, they are sports or film fans. Increasingly subsidized by lucrative subscription audiences, content markets in the mixed economy of the UK media are now even less likely to operate in a genuinely open and pluralistic fashion. This, however, is not an issue that has captured the attention of policymakers.

The problem is that the dominant public policy response is locked into an approach that remains fixated on questions of economic value and instrumental rationality and that either suppresses or undermines any alternative values and objectives. For example, Ofcom, while capturing very effectively why pluralism is important, rules out the possibility of plurality reviews being triggered either by sustained complaints or when a single company reaches a particular share of consumption. Mindful of the 'need to avoid triggering repeated reviews', Ofcom argues that such 'a process would be potentially wasteful and place a disproportionate burden on industry – both in terms of cost and uncertainty' (Ofcom 2012: 30). Instead it proposes that there should be periodic reviews every four or five years – a position that makes it potentially even more lax than the notoriously deregulatory FCC in the US. This demonstrates both exaggerated political caution and an overbearing concern with market stability that is out of step with the democratic necessity to tackle media concentration and increase pluralism.

Given this reluctance to face down large concentrations of media and political power, the public interest is subordinated instead to a commitment to protecting industry interests. This relates to an understanding of media policy as those interventions, or rather non-interventions, which are necessary to maximize the stability of the sector and to limit any undue volatility. The issue is not that industry viability is not significant but that this emphasis on profitability and predictability is unbalanced. This is a policy reaction that privileges 'practicability' and 'proportionality' above the need to take decisive action to unblock the media at a time when, partly thanks to events like the Leveson Inquiry, the consequences of unaccountable media power have been laid bare.

For example, during his appearance at the Leveson Inquiry, the leader of the opposition Labour Party, Ed Miliband, called for a cap on newspapers owning between 20 and 30 per cent of the news market in order that 'one organisation does not exert an overweening power'. Earlier the same day, former Conservative prime minister John Major argued that there should be a 'clear limit' to concentrated ownership capped at about 15 to 20 per cent of the media. Indeed, even the deputy prime minister Nick Clegg told Leveson that 'when concentrations of power or power as wielded unaccountably occurs, you need to try and find some remedies and safeguards against that' (Freedman 2012a). In his written submission, he argued for 'strong rules around media ownership that protect plurality in the market' (Clegg 2012). Leveson's response in his report was to sidestep any firm recommendations concerning market caps and to pass the initiative to a government that, as we have already seen, has refused to take any firm steps to clamp down on the market power of the largest media groups.

Radical demands for reform of media ownership, therefore, continue to be either ignored or dismissed as impractical. Proposals are rejected on the basis that 'setting absolute limits [on market share] leaves no room for flexibility' (Ofcom 2012: 34), that platform specific rules are harder to justify in a converged era, that nationally-based rules no longer apply in a global era, and that the constant threat of regulatory intervention makes it more difficult for companies to develop fixed, long-term plans because 'too much discretion would create market uncertainty and impair incentives to invest and innovate' (Ofcom 2012: 32). So even though many states continue to have at least some rules on media ownership and varying strategies concerning the protection of plurality, 'micro' regulation is seen in the same light as over-fishing: that it will unsettle the environment and ultimately deplete the stock of what is available for consumption.

For Thomas Streeter, media ownership policies (and the liberalized patterns of ownership they have generally helped to facilitate) serve to naturalize capitalist property relations and systems of thought (Streeter 1996) – to make certain outcomes 'desirable' and others 'unthinkable'. Ownership policy is, therefore, an ideological means both of enforcing the authority of corporate interests within the communications environment (and beyond) and of working through differences within elites: 'underlying all the (very real) disagreements and debates is a relatively constant structure of expectations that limit discussion, not by coercion, but by way of the subtle but profound power of interpretation' (1996: 117). We need to identify those elite interests that are most vociferously represented in ownership policies and to highlight the ideological, institutional and discursive mechanisms through which more radical perspectives on ownership are marginalized. Otherwise, pluralism, to the extent that is acknowledged as a 'problem' in the first place, simply becomes a lens through which the structural inequalities that are present within the media are further cemented through inaction and silence.

Silences in net neutrality debates

Silences can also occur in spaces that are undoubtedly noisy. The development of high-speed broadband networks is, as I have already pointed out, a policy priority for many administrations seeking to take advantage of the opportunities afforded by what they see as emerging forms of 'knowledge capitalism' (Burton-Jones 1999). This has led to frenzied activity in relation to infrastructural projects but a rather more ambiguous stance towards the regulation of the traffic that circulates across broadband networks. The key issue here is net neutrality: the requirements placed on broadband providers *not* to block, restrict or segregate the flow of online content whatever its provenance. As Lessig and McChesney (2006) argued ahead of the first Congressional vote on the issue, net neutrality means that 'all like Internet content must be treated alike and move at the same speed over the network. The owners of the Internet's wires cannot discriminate. This is the simple but brilliant "end-to-end" design of the Internet that has made it such a powerful force for economic and social good.'

Not surprisingly, there was huge controversy when the FCC eventually passed net neutrality rules at the end 2010 preventing internet providers from interfering with the flow of web traffic. Telecoms companies and neo-liberal commentators argued that this was a disastrous intervention into self-correcting markets and constituted a 'coup' by activist groups in which the real losers would be consumers 'who will see innovation and investment chilled by regulations that treat the internet like a public utility' (Fund 2010). Civil society groups, on the other hand, bemoaned the policy as 'Net Neutrality-lite', pointed to the loopholes and exclusions (most notably in relation to mobile devices) that littered the new rules and insisted that they represented a victory for corporate interests over ordinary users (Nichols 2010).

One of the reasons why the FCC engineered such an unstable compromise between different groups was simply that there is no agreement of what net neutrality refers to nor how it should be implemented. To this day, the Congressional Research Service insists that 'there is no single accepted definition of "net neutrality" ' and that 'consensus on the net neutrality issue has remained elusive' (Gilroy 2013: 1, 15). Far from being seen as an aspiration for equality that requires an active confrontation with powerful groups to secure unfettered access to public communication systems, net neutrality risks becoming a term that allows for multiple interpretations whose visibility and impact depend, as always, on the power to mobilize one interpretation at the expense of another. This is not to dismiss the importance of the issues themselves but to highlight the potential capture of the language involved (Lentz 2013).

A further reason for the current impasse concerns the very limited way in which policymakers have framed the whole debate on net neutrality: in terms that are heavily legalistic and economistic and that marginalize broader theories of the public interest, citizenship and, in particular, democracy. The FCC chairman that pushed through the rules in 2010, Julius Genachowski, spoke regularly of the importance of the internet – 'The Internet is the most transformational communications breakthrough of our time. It has become essential to the lives of Americans', he declared in a high-profile speech at the Brookings Institute (Genachowski 2009) – but proceeded to characterize net neutrality not in terms of a commitment to fairness or social justice but exclusively about the need to protect the internet's 'freedom' and 'openness' described as 'the ability to speak, innovate and engage in commerce without having to ask anyone's permission' (Genachowski 2010). The rules themselves were formally expressed not in a 'Net Neutrality' rulemaking but in the FCC'S *Open Internet Order*.

This rather *laissez-faire* approach to internet freedom was hardly new and indeed originated in the FCC's 2005 Internet Policy Statement (FCC 2005: 3) where it outlined four key regulatory principles that were all concerned with *consumer* entitlement:

- consumers are entitled to access the lawful Internet content of their choice

- consumers are entitled to run applications and services of their choice

- consumers are entitled to connect their choice of legal devices that do not harm the network

- consumers are entitled to competition among network providers, application and service providers, and content providers.

Net neutrality rules, therefore, were based on the safeguarding of customer choice through network competition using a language that permeated similar discussions elsewhere. In the UK, Ed Richards, the chair of Ofcom, insisted that net neutrality was scarcely relevant because of the existence of a competitive broadband market: 'Where competition thrives, the case for a highly interventionist net neutrality policy is harder to justify on the grounds of consumer protection' (Richards 2010). Neelie Kroes, the commissioner responsible for the digital agenda, introduced the European Commission's consultation on net neutrality by wondering whether 'regulation promoting more infrastructure competition [would] be reason enough to bring a lighter touch to net neutrality?' (Kroes 2010). The discussion rapidly started to coalesce around two further regulatory principles: non-discrimination, the prohibiting of service providers from favouring one form of content over another, and the transparency of network management for consumers. A policy debate that, at its core, is based on whether private companies have the right to determine the distribution of content via public communication systems, was limited to rather technical questions of 'traffic management'.

Curiously, at the same time that Genachowski and others were considering the implications of an 'open internet' for domestic regulation, former US secretary of state Hilary Clinton was making celebrated speeches extolling internet freedom as an engine of democracy in *other* countries. Promising that the US government was 'committed' to promoting internet freedom across the world and aiming her comments particularly at the Chinese government, Clinton provided a far more expansive account of the possibilities of the internet: 'We want to put these tools in the hands of people who will use them to advance democracy and human rights, to fight climate change and epidemics, to build global support for President Obama's goal of a world without nuclear weapons, to encourage sustainable economic development that lifts the people at the bottom up' (Clinton 2010). So while internet freedom was associated with tools of emancipation and democracy outside the US, domestic debate on internet freedom – as related to net neutrality – appeared to be stuck on questions of pricing and non-discrimination with questions of democratic rights firmly on the backburner.

Of course there have been exceptions, such as Lessig and McChesney (2006) describing net neutrality as a choice about whether the internet is to be 'a free and open technology fostering innovation, economic growth and democratic communication, or instead becomes the property of cable and phone companies that can put toll booths at every on-ramp and exit on the information superhighway'. On the whole, however, questions of democracy and control were largely absent from the official net neutrality policy debates. This was partly because of the traditionally de-politicized and administrative character of technology policy (Freedman 2008) but also because of the specific influence of telecoms and cable lobbyists who attempted to paint net neutrality as both unnecessary, given the existence of what was described as consumer choice, and counterproductive, in that further regulation would only deter infrastructure investment. Interestingly, democracy *did* become a major issue for corporate interests once the FCC rule had been passed in 2010 with Verizon, for example, appealing against the *Order* on the basis that it abused the constitutional rights of network owners.

It violates the First Amendment by stripping them of control over the transmission of speech on their networks. And it takes network owners' property without compensation by mandating that they turn over these networks for the occupation and use of others at a regulated rate of zero, undermining owners' multi-billion-dollar-backed expectations that they would be able to decide how best to employ their networks to serve consumers and deterring network investment. (Verizon 2012: 3–4)

Net neutrality, according to this perspective, involves the expropriation of network owners rather than a modest attempt to enshrine some protections in the relationship between owners and their customers. In a significant blow to any meaningful public control of the internet, in January 2014 a federal appeals court accepted these arguments and threw out the FCC's 2010 net neutrality rules (Wyatt 2014).

By arguing that the debate has been limited to 'traffic management' issues, I am not suggesting that there is no citizenship interest in or democratic flavour to issues of discrimination and transparency. Indeed online traffic management *ought* to be understood as a fundamentally democratic question of how society organizes the circulation of symbolic goods and questions of affordability are crucial, particularly at a time of austerity. We are, however, in danger of being swept away by metaphors that embody openness, clarity and visibility and that help to produce certain regulatory discourses and policy actions that are based on, and further legitimate, instrumental, market-based principles. Who, after all, could say that they are actively in favour of discrimination (even Verizon in the example quoted above would claim to be the victim, not the perpetrator, of discrimination)? Who could legitimately stand up and campaign *against* transparency given that, in itself, it is a rather opaque term. Do we understand transparency as 'open code' that, imposed consistently, is an essential check on government and corporate power (Lessig 2006: 328) or should we heed Onora O'Neill's warning that transparency by itself 'leaves many audiences unable to see the wood for the trees, unable to understand what is disclosed, unable to assess what they understand or to judge its accuracy, and ill-equipped to take an active and constructive part in democratic debate' (2004: 15)?

Instead, we should assert a vision of net neutrality that is based not on malleable metaphors but on the protection of the public interest in the face of an intensive corporate land grab. Net neutrality ought not to be indifferent to the power imbalance between network owners and citizens and is necessary to provide a minimal challenge to the concentrations of capital and influence that are likely to accrue in an online world (and that I discuss in the next chapter). This is even more essential given the striking down of the FCC's net neutrality rules if the promise of the internet to provide an egalitarian space for communicative activity is to be realized. This is not simply a question of how best to manage roads, traffic, channels, networks or pipes but about the needs of democracy: who controls which resources, in whose interests and for what purposes? By adopting a neo-liberal frame, as is still the instinct for many of our policymakers and regulators, and by silencing other narratives and approaches that place social justice at the heart of our communications environment, media policymaking remains a sphere that has been captured by elite interests.

Conclusion

The debates between pluralists and radicals on the dynamics of policymaking have focused on the control of the material and symbolic resources mobilized in decision-making, the extent to which power is a capacity distributed equally or not inside this process, and whether power can be characterized not just by the ability to make decisions but by the facility both to prevent alternative ones from emerging and to render this process entirely 'natural'. In this situation, it is essential to bring this process of exclusion to light, to challenge 'actually existing' policy frames, guiding assumptions, foundational principles and ideological presuppositions. Responding to consultations, serving on committees and acting as witnesses, attending expert seminars, providing evidence when asked – all of these are a necessary part of the policy activist's job but they are all predicated on existing assumptions about what we want from our media systems and based on a narrow range of instrumental values concerning the objectives of media policy. Borrowing from the language of formalism, we need to *de-familiarize* the comfortable structures and familiar market-led paradigms of the policy process, to introduce alternative frames and to ask tough questions about whose interests are best mobilized in existing policy contexts and whose perspectives are marginalized.

We need an approach to media policy that is ideological as opposed to administrative, interested as opposed to disinterested, and committed to delivering social justice instead of serving the interests of either state or private elites. When we think about questions of ownership or net neutrality or digital switchover or press freedom, policy should be understood both as an empirical fact and as an ideological tool. Indeed, media policy in particular is becoming increasingly fraught with tensions as the resources needed to govern and control become increasingly intertwined with mediated spaces both online and offline.

This is especially important because of the ongoing crisis of neo-liberalism and the resulting delegitimization of markets that have made pro-interventionist arguments much easier to make (and classic 'negative policy' approaches more difficult to justify). More and more people expect an activist approach to policy although *not* one that simply hands the initiative to unaccountable quangoes, unelected civil servants, partisan politicians or self-interested lobbyists. We need to propose imaginative interventions and fresh policies that relate to alternative ways of thinking about our communications systems – ones that value them for their democratic potential, for their contribution to the collective good, and as irreducible to private gain or state influence. These policies may initially be dismissed as being unrealizable, unwelcome, utopian or simply dangerous, but if we believe that our media systems are in crisis and that public policy has, thus far, failed to provide adequate solutions, then it is not enough simply to accept existing policy paradigms and therefore to reproduce the current terms of debate.

We need, first, to identify the powerful interests that are able to erect 'barriers to the public airing of public conflicts' (Bachrach and Baratz 1962: 949) and, second, to mobilize forces around a different policy agenda that puts the public interest at its heart. An analytical focus on policy silences, therefore, needs to be matched by a commitment to energetic campaigning.

4

Power Shifts and Social Media

Haven't you heard of the Internet? No one controls the media or will ever again.

RUPERT MURDOCH, TWEET, 20 OCTOBER 2012

A radical redistribution of power?

Power circulates in a messy rather than a controlled fashion according to the 'chaos paradigm', reflecting the more uncertain and contingent circumstances in which we live. For Brian McNair (2006: xviii), 'power in a globalised, mediated world has become more fluid and fragile, no longer monopolised by ruling classes whose dominance is pre-determined by structural advantage'. McNair conceived of 'cultural chaos' as a direct rebuttal of what he sees as functionalist and conspiratorial analyses of media and society that are rooted in political economy approaches. The latter, he argues, fail to appreciate the changing conditions in which power circulates and reproduces itself. At a time of ideological competition, elite dissensus, consumer activism, heightened expectations and global sensibilities, power is, in his account, no longer a capacity to be commandeered by one class at the expense of another and is instead in a state of flux and transition.

McNair is far from alone in trying to renegotiate the meaning of power in our contemporary world. For many theorists, the question of whom may be said to exercise it, to resist it, to dominate it or to embody it is an increasingly thorny one that coalesces around an agreement that power is *shifting*. According to Joseph Nye, the influential foreign policy commentator and advocate of 'soft' and 'smart' power as distinct from its 'hard', coercive variant, there are two power shifts taking place: 'a power transition among states and a power diffusion away from all states to nonstate actors' (2011: xv). For Moises Naim, former Venezuelan trade minister and executive director of the World Bank, 'power is shifting from brawn to brains, from north to south and west to east, from old corporate behemoths to agile start-ups, from entrenched dictators to people in town squares and cyberspace' (2013: 45). More importantly than this, however, power – wherever it is wielded – is decaying. So, while it may be true that we are seeing a reconfiguration of geopolitical dynamics with the BRIC countries (Brazil, Russia, India and China) playing a more central role, power in those contexts is likely to be just as elusive and unpredictable as it was in the incumbent hegemonic empires. No matter who or where you are, power 'no longer buys as much as it did in the past' (2013: 45) – a source for Naim of both optimism, as new social movements (like Occupy and the *Indignados*) emerge to voice democratic demands, and concern if it means that power can be wielded by groups without an established democratic mandate.

While McNair, Nye and Naim all attribute a range of social, political and economic factors to these transformations, some of the noisiest and most high-profile discussions of power shifts are focused on the impact of information technology and, more specifically, on the 'revolutionary' consequences for power of digital technologies. In *The New Digital Age*, penned by the perfect editorial confluence of state and market, Eric Schmidt and Jared Cohen (respectively the CEO of Google and the State Department official who developed the concept of 'twenty-first-century statecraft' in which social media were to be deployed as key tools of diplomacy and democracy), write that 'the most significant impact of the spread of communication technologies will be the way they help reallocate the concentration of power away from states and institutions and transfer it to individuals' (2013: 6). This point is made repeatedly in the scores of texts that attempt to chronicle the impact of social media on our lives so that Nicco Mele, for example, is able to insist that '[r]adical connectivity is altering the exercise of power faster than we can understand it' and that this involves a 'radical redistribution of power' (2013: 5). For Jeff Jarvis, Google has inspired a grass roots revolution in business and entertainment that is based on creativity, participation and openness: 'That is what we mean when we talk about power shifting to the edge, no longer centralized' (2009: 238). According to Tapscott and Williams, the chroniclers of 'wikinomics', the web is facilitating 'powerful new models of production based on community, collaboration, and self-organization rather than on hierarchy and control' (2008: 1), while for Chris Anderson (2009), digital distribution of content has produced a plethora of shifts in the balance of power: from music companies to fans, from labels to bands, from mass to niche and from top down to bottom up. There are many more such examples that painstakingly detail the means through which digital devices are recalibrating the relationships between individuals and corporations and between networks and hierarchies in such a way that power relations may be seen to be in flux.

Indeed, such is the impact of information technology on power relations that we are seeing not simply a shift in the balance of power, in other words in who might be said to 'hold' it or the direction of its flow, but in the very composition and texture of power itself. As Alvin Toffler, the prodigious and influential futurologist, argued in his analysis of technology as a determining force, a ' "power shift" does not merely transfer power. It transforms it' (1990: 4). Toffler defines power as 'the use of violence, wealth and knowledge (in the broadest sense) to make people perform in a given way' (1990: 14) and given the increased salience of knowledge and information in the contemporary world, that triad is disrupted and reconstituted resulting in a 'revolution in the very nature of power' (1990: 4). This is not a shift of power from person to another or from one state to another but a change in the underlying relationships between knowledge, violence and wealth that repositions power at the heart of our communications environment or, perhaps more accurately, repositions communications at the heart of power. 'In a knowledge-based economy the most important domestic political issue is no longer the distribution (or redistribution) of wealth, but of the information and media that produce wealth' (1990: 368).

This is an approach to power that finds an expression in more recent accounts of the role of high-speed digital networks and the significance of programming and code (Toffler, after all, was writing before the web and social media). As we saw in Chapter 1, Manuel Castells, in his comprehensive analysis of power in a digital world (Castells 2009), argues that information networks now provide the infrastructure for both the exercise of and the resistance to power. The capacity to exercise influence in any sphere of life has been informatized to the extent that power relationships are programmed inside, and not as an adjunct to, communications systems: 'Power in the network society is communication power' (2009: 53). Unlike Naim, Castells is not arguing that we are seeing the 'end' of power but instead its redefinition and relocation inside information systems. The key agents of power in this situation are therefore those people who are able to control specific networks, defined by Castells as the 'communicative structures' (2009: 20) that are the building blocks of social life, as well as to connect together different networks. Castells calls this 'switching power' (2009: 427) and describes Rupert Murdoch as the archetypal 'switcher' given his unprecedented ability both to hegemonize media networks, a key source of power in itself, and also to transfer resources between a series of other networks (for example political, financial, industrial and cultural spheres). So, while coercion remains a major instrument of state power, it is ultimately the capacity to command this 'switching' process and to dominate 'meaning making' – itself the result of a contest that takes place in and through networked activities – that is the source of power today.

If 'programmers and switchers are the holders of power in the network society' (Castells 2009: 429), then this certainly represents a challenge to traditional accounts of power that are rooted in the ability to exert control via established patterns of privilege and material advantage. In this new account, power has shifted from palaces to pipes and from armies to algorithms; 'distributed power' (Galloway 2004) facilitates new social relations, and for some, a whole 'new mode of production' (Tapscott and Williams 2008: ix). Given the realignment of power in a shift from capitalism to 'informationalism' (Bard and Soderqvist 2002), there are likely to be new protagonists of power – not least organizations like the hacktivist group Anonymous and the whistleblowing site WikiLeaks, which, in 2010, famously released many thousands of US State Department diplomatic 'cables' – as well as new capacities for human emancipation. As Diamandis and Kotler put it in their paean to the virtues of digital plenitude, power should no longer be feared: 'abundance is about creating a world of possibility: a world where everyone's days are spent dreaming and doing, not scrapping and scraping' (2012: 13).

There is, however, a growing literature devoted to critiquing the notion of a 'power shift' and, in particular, to challenging assertions that digital technologies are reliable and incontrovertible tools for equality, liberation and personal fulfilment. Indeed inequality, atomization and exploitation remain a persistent feature of the digital environment as evidenced by studies on, for example, identity (Miller 2011, Turkle 2011), digital labour (Burston, Dyer-Witherford and Hearn 2010, Fuchs 2013), political struggle (Fenton 2012, Morozov 2011) and commodification (Caraway 2011, Freedman 2012b). However, there are two claims that are made in relation to this world of possibility that are particularly relevant to this study: that incumbent centres of power are fragmenting given the decentralizing logic of networked communications and that social media platforms have enabled those previously without a voice to link to each other without the need for intermediaries. This chapter, therefore, examines these key features of the power shifts that are alleged to have taken place in the digital world – decentralization and disintermediation – and casts a very critical eye over these claims. This is not because they are unfounded but because, all too often, they lack context, specifically of the underlying dynamics of capitalism that, if they are acknowledged at all, are often seen only as part of the 'background scenery' (McChesney 2013: 13). For this, I will be called a curmudgeon and a pessimist, wilfully challenging any narratives about 'progress', 'participation' and 'empowerment' as long as they are associated with the internet. This is a million miles away from my intention. The point is *not* that digital technologies have made no difference to the way we live our lives or that power relations remain unaffected by social media but that the only way effectively to assess their impact is to consider them in the light of the social system from which they emerged and which they continue to shape.

If we fail to adopt this approach, to contextualize such crucial developments in relation to capitalism's operating principles, we face two risks. First, there is the dangerous allure of a technologically deterministic version of history in which social outcomes are read off against the specific attributes of technological systems (see Morozov 2013 for a critique of deterministic approaches) so that, for example, the internet is viewed as inherently democratizing and social media intrinsically equalizing. As James Curran puts it, simplistic (though widespread) predictions about the revolutionary political, economic and cultural consequences of the internet 'were wrong because they inferred the impact of the internet from its technology and failed to grasp that the internet's influence is filtered through the structures and processes of society' (Curran, Freedman and Fenton 2012: 180). Second, we face the prospect of reproducing a playground version of internet studies where 'digital optimists' line up against their critics and hurl binary abuse at each other. McNair (2006: 199) helpfully provides a list of the counterposed terms that are often used as ammunition for one side or another in this redundant parlour game – 'control/chaos; scarcity/abundance; sealed/leaky; opacity/transparency; exclusivity/accessibility; homogeneity/heterogeneity; hierarchy/network; passivity/(inter)activity; dominance/competition' – while Moore (2011: 86) sketches out an even longer 'versus' model which includes 'open platforms vs. walled gardens', 'cooperation vs. coordination', 'engagement vs. interruption' and 'bottom-up vs. top-down'.

Given that all these tensions are relevant to our understanding of digital possibilities, how do we 'rise above the optimist-pessimist, utopian-dystopian dichotomies that characterize our current discussions about the Internet' and 'transcend this sterile shouting match' (Naughton 2012: 294)? Naughton recommends that we embrace the concept of 'creative destruction', developed by the German economist Joseph Schumpeter (1994), wherein capitalism reproduces itself through cyclical waves of innovation and annihilation. However, I would suggest returning to the analysis, originally developed by Marx, of capitalism as a profoundly contradictory system that sees binary opposites not as a puzzling schism but as countervailing forces that are at the core of its personality. Let me be clear that this is not an understanding of contradiction as the holding of views that, taken together, somehow do not quite make sense. When David Weinberger argues in his book on knowledge in the digital age that 'we are a bundle of contradictions these days' (2011: 69) because we adopt an 'on the one hand ... on the other hand' attitude towards the internet, he is illustrating our *subjective* ambivalence and confusion in relation to an emerging information environment. It is about our personal strategies in relation to knowledge rather than a systemic feature. Neither is it an understanding of contradiction that reduces it merely to inconsistent behaviour, for example, publishing a book that discusses the end of traditional publishing via a traditional publisher ('I confess', writes Jeff Jarvis in *What Would Google Do?*, 'I'm a hypocrite' [2009: 136]) or publishing a book entitled

The End of Big (Mele 2013) with St Martins Press, part of a global conglomerate with revenue of over two billion euros.

We hold contradictory ideas not because we are confused (although we may be) but because the world is a contradictory place and because, in particular, the dominant social system of capitalism is structurally riddled with contradictions that cannot be wished away. 'Real contradictions exist', wrote Marx, 'and cannot be exorcized by imagination' (Marx 1976b: 148). As we saw in Chapter 1, Marx identified capitalism as a revolutionary and dynamic system but also one that undermined its own purpose and stability through its relentless drive towards accumulation and exploitation. Commodities are produced and innovations unleashed not for the collective good and individual fulfilment of the public (what Marx called 'use value') but so long as they can be sold for a surplus ('exchange value'). Marx speaks of an underlying tension between the productive forces of capitalism, the technologies and skills that are available at any time (and that obviously now include digital tools), and the social relations of capitalism, in other words the ends to which these technologies and skills are put: profit and the private appropriation of capital.

> The real barrier of capitalist production is capital itself...The means – unconditional development of the productive forces of society – comes continually into conflict with the limited purpose, the self-expansion of the existing capital. The capitalist mode of production is, for this reason, a historical means of developing the material forces of production and creating an appropriate world-market and is, at the same time, a continual conflict between this, its historical task, and its own corresponding relations of production. (Marx 1909: 293)

In more simple terms, as Ralph Miliband puts it, there is a 'supreme contradiction' between capitalism's 'ever more *social* character and its enduringly *private* purpose' (1969: 34).

These contradictions – between use value and exchange value, forces and relations of production and, in particular, between the social character of production and its private appropriation – are, therefore, central to the analysis of any technological or symbolic system developed and operating under capitalist conditions. Going back to the 'sterile debate' between digital optimists and pessimists about the extent to which digital platforms facilitate opacity *or* transparency, scarcity *or* abundance and indeed distributed *or* concentrated power, the point is that an emphasis on contradiction allows us to understand that it is not a question of choosing one or the other but of appreciating the tensions and constraints that shape the dynamics of the digital world. Indeed, it is entirely possible that social media can be tools of empowerment *and* control, that the internet is subject to centrifugal *and* centripetal pressures and that the web both encourages new voices *and* consolidates existing ones. By accentuating a materialist approach that acknowledges the contradictions of capitalist development (Fuchs 2009, McChesney 2013), we can avoid the pitfalls of a binary approach and reject the determinism of those who fetishize technology above all else.

Let me illustrate this point with a brief discussion of the contradictions of Twitter, one of the most dynamic and vigorous social media platforms that, in its short life, has been associated with radical transformations in journalism (Hermida 2010, Schmidt and Cohen 2013), social interaction (Murthy 2013) and, of course, with democratic change following the emergence of the notion of the 'Twitter Revolution' applied to both the Iranian election of 2009 and the Arab Spring of 2011 following which a celebrated *Foreign Policy* article was headlined 'The Revolution Will Be Tweeted' (Hounshell 2011). In his passionate account of the rise of global protest in 2009 to 2011, *Why It's Kicking Off Everywhere*, the British journalist Paul Mason also highlights the progressive role of new technologies for opposition movements. Distributed platforms like Twitter, Facebook, YouTube and Flickr, together with mobile phones and accessible blogging tools, have been essential, he argues, in mobilizing publics to contest existing power elites. According to Mason, there is a 'technological fact that underpins the social and political aspects of what's happened – a network can usually defeat a hierarchy' (Mason 2012: 76–77). A year later, however, and Mason was in despair about Twitter. After a series of rape and death threats were tweeted to feminist campaigners, Mason argued that Twitter had become 'morally depopulated' and that he was now considering leaving the microblogging site (Mason 2013).

What is the issue here? Certainly not Mason's outrage which was entirely justified and proportionate nor his solution which was to encourage Twitter users themselves, and not an unaccountable 'third party', to take action against the 'trolls' by exposing and blocking their messages. The issue is more that Mason was surprised that in a world marked by violence and discrimination against women (as well as against many other social groups), this kind of bigotry would make its way into the 'Twittersphere'. When Mason writes that 'it will be a disaster if Twitter becomes dysfunctional' (Mason 2013), this assumes that Twitter – or any another social media platform – can ever be fully 'functional' in the sense of maintaining only polite, respectful and rational dialogue in contrast, perhaps, to the vulgar 'shock jock culture' of much of US talk radio. When Mason argues that there has been 'a rise in the organised trolling of political opponents on Twitter', this is largely because there has been a steep rise in the number of Twitter users, not that sexists and homophobes have suddenly and consistently stepped up their activity (at least there is no evidence that this is the case). For as long as we have had social media and, in particular, the opportunity to abuse the anonymity offered by digital interactions to circulate hateful messages, we have had 'trolls'. As an early post on the problem indicated, trolling 'is an inevitable hazard of using the net. As the saying goes, "You can't have a picnic without ants" ' (Campbell 2001). Why would we expect even the most horrific offline behaviour *not* to be replicated online?

Twitter reflects, therefore, both the possibilities of democratic exchange and the serious problems of the world in which it is located. Yes, Twitter lowers the cost of entry for people to communicate with each other but not everyone brings with them the same level of resources and influence: some 0.05 per cent of all users attract almost 50 per cent of all attention on the network (Wu et al. 2011: 5); while Mason talks about the 'democracy of retweeting' (2012: 75), 71 per cent of tweets get no reaction at all, with 85 per cent of tweets getting a single response (brandongaille.com 2013). Yes, Twitter is a global phenomenon although just two countries (the UK and the US) account for more than two-thirds of all the world's users (Beevolve 2012); yes, Twitter is a tool that can be used to organize politically but, overwhelmingly, that is not the purpose to which it is put with personal and work updates leading the way (brandongaille.com 2013); and yes, Twitter is a platform that allows users to broaden their social networks and allows marginal voices to gain a following although it is also true that 75 per cent of users follow less than fifty people with 10 per cent not following anyone (Beevolve 2012). Indeed, while Twitter is a stimulus for activism and participation, it is the case that nearly 50 per cent of users check in either every few weeks or less including 21 per cent who never check their accounts at all (brandongaille.com 2013). In fact, while 177 million tweets are sent every day, 40 per cent of registered Twitter users have never sent a single tweet and prefer to sit back and watch what others do (Stadd 2013).

In other words, the inequalities and disparities that we see in non-mediated environments are reproduced in social media platforms where existing patterns of behaviour (whether enlightened or reactionary) find an expression just as we might expect. As Natalie Fenton concludes (2012: 143), social media 'are not first and foremost about social good or political engagement; their primary function is expressive and, as such, they are best understood in terms of their potential for articulating the (often contradictory) dynamics of political environments rather than recasting or regenerating the structures that uphold them'. Twitter is not being 'dysfunctional' when it carries hate speech but simply reflecting the scars and tensions of the 'dysfunctional' environment from which it has emerged. An understanding of these contradictions is therefore essential if we are to take advantage of the possibilities as well as to deal with the challenges posed by new media technologies.

Decentralization: The rise of the 'power mosaic'

In a book that topped the Swedish non-fiction charts for some months at the turn of the millennium, two digital pioneers wrote about what they saw as the revolutionary transformations associated with an emerging 'informationalist paradigm'. Power, argued Alexander Bard and Jan Soderqvist (2002) is changing shape, becoming more unstable and abstract and, crucially, freeing itself from any central point of control. Power, in this context, is far more likely to circulate through 'network pyramids', mobile and fluid structures which are difficult to monopolize and secure. Just as new qualities of 'vision' and 'knowledge', not wealth and status, are needed to thrive in these spaces, '[c]apitalism's perception of power structures – that all valuable human activity stems from and is controlled from a central core – has also become obsolete' (2002: 198). The notion that power has become more dispersed and fractured is partly an expression of Foucault's insistence that power refers to a generative process that cannot be 'localized in a particular type of institution' (1979: 26) but, perhaps more significantly, an endorsement of the idea that networks, not hierarchies, have become the dominant form of social organization.

This is similar to the prediction of Alvin Toffler, a decade earlier, that thanks to developments in microelectronics and information technology, power was shifting 'downwards' to programmers and systems operators to the extent that 'instead of a power-concentrating hierarchy, dominated by a few central organizations, we move towards a multi-dimensional mosaic form of power' (1990: 221). While we have already seen that these power shifts have been explained in relation to a range of social, political and economic factors, there is, however, a precise technological logic to this development given that networks are seen to be *structurally* predisposed to decentralizing pressures. According to Castells (2009: 23), networks are defined by three factors: their *flexibility* in adapting to changing environments, their *scalability* in being able to change in size to meet new challenges, and their *survivability*, their capacity to withstand attack precisely because they have no single, identifiable centre. A decentralizing urge, in other words, is neither extraneous nor accidental but a necessary and core characteristic of networks that explains their productivity, efficiency and collaborative potential.

This is particularly the case when applied to digital media developments in what Toffler calls 'the super symbolic economy' (1990: 226). So, while Leadbeater talks of the web's 'underlying culture of sharing, decentralisation and democracy' (2008: 7), Jarvis also insists that '[d]ecentralization is what makes the internet the internet' (2011: 214). In conditions of online 'abundance' (Diamandis and Kotler 2012) and digital 'velocity' (Ahmed and Olander 2012), we now have the prospect of a far more diverse and deconcentrated media market in the shape of the 'long tail': a potentially limitless back catalogue of cultural goods that defies the industry's traditional obsession with making a handful of hits (Anderson 2009) and with discarding products with more limited appeal. According to Anderson, we are witnessing the death of blockbuster power where 'big cultural buckets' are now in competition with a 'market of multitudes' in a 'mass of niches' (2009: 5). As Jarvis puts it, 'the mass market is dead. It committed suicide. Google just handed it the gun' (2009: 67). All these accounts suggest that digital technologies have contributed to a democratization of media production and consumption as power seeps away from a central core of producers and distributors to a far more dispersed collection of active media users who are able to blog, film, record, remix, upload and share in ways that were previously unthinkable (see Gauntlett 2011, Jenkins 2006 and Lessig 2008 for some of the best narratives that illuminate this creative potential).

The contention of this chapter, however, is that there is a fundamental contradiction between the possibilities offered by these technologies and the constraints of the system in which we live – between the forces and relations of production to use the terms referred to in the previous section. Consider the example of news gathering where, according to Erik Qualman in his account of 'socialnomics', we have 'shifted from a world where the information and news was held by a few and distributed to millions, to a world where the information is held by millions and distributed to a few (niche markets)' (2009: 14–15). News gathering has indeed been disrupted by social media platforms like Twitter and Facebook and the rise of user-generated content, WikiLeaks and 'networked journalism' (Beckett 2008, 2012) together with the flight of classified advertising from the print press to dedicated online intermediaries that has led to a crisis inside the newspaper industry. Yet, are these developments enough to transform entirely the power relations of a highly centralized news industry where a handful of wholesalers and retailers have long dominated and to empower instead a new layer of dispersed users and sources?

First, it remains the case that television, by and large a highly centralized form of cultural activity, remains the most popular source of news for citizens across large parts of the world. In the US, where online consumption is very advanced, 55 per cent of the population continue to turn to TV as compared to 39 per cent who use online and mobile devices to access news (Pew 2012a: 1); in the UK the domination of television is even more stark with 78 per cent of people claiming that television is their preferred source of news in contrast to 32 per cent who rely on online platforms, less than the number for radio and newspapers (Ofcom 2013: 107). These patterns are repeated when it comes to *time* spent on specific platforms. Research from McKinsey shows that 41 per cent of news consumption in the US lies with television, 35 per cent with newspapers and magazines, only 4 per cent with computers and 2 per cent with mobile phones and tablets respectively (Edmonds 2013). Of course, these numbers are set to change in the coming years with more people likely to access news via digital devices, but in what way will this automatically shift power away from news incumbents towards individual citizens? The Pew Centre's figures (2012a: 19) shows that online news in the US is dominated either by traditional news organizations (such as CNN, MSN, Fox and the *New York Times*) or by aggregators who produce no original news of their own but usually have a relationship with an established news provider (such as Yahoo's deal with ABC). The most popular online source that does produce original news is the Huffington Post, which comes tenth in the list and is preferred as their main source by only 4 per cent of online users. In the UK, a single television channel, BBC One, has by far the biggest reach of any source for news – some 57 per cent of the population. Once again, the list is dominated by traditional news providers consisting not only of the BBC but also of commercial television news and the leading national newspapers (Ofcom 2013: 108). The BBC dominates even the share of use for those who consume their news online – 52 per cent turn to the BBC as against 25 per cent for aggregators, 23 per cent for social media and 16 per cent for search engines (2013: 114) although, of course, the latter platforms are still likely to lead news consumers back to more traditional news sources.

A nine-country study of leading news websites (Curran et al. 2013) attempted to investigate the extent to which online news may be able to expand news agendas, offer a more international perspective and amplify the voices of the public. While it found that there were discrepancies between the different countries in relation, for example, to the use of experts or the existence of an outward-looking perspective, the researchers attribute them less to technological characteristics than to already existing national and cultural differences. Overall, however, they conclude that 'leading websites around the world reproduce the same kind of news as legacy media. These websites favour the voices of authority and expertises over those of campaigning organisations and the ordinary citizen' (2013: 887). Crucially, they argue that this is 'largely the consequence of the incumbent economic power of leading media conglomerates and the influence exerted by the wider context of society across news media' (2013: 893). Distributed technologies may be able radically to disrupt the conditions in which journalism takes place – just as they may change the architecture of media markets and improve possibilities for dispersed production – but this does not necessarily imply a transformation of underlying patterns of control.

Indeed, despite the rhetoric about unfettered competition and the triumph of the 'long tail', the structure of the digital media economy looks a lot like the structure of the analogue economy and is marked by dominant players in all its main sectors. This is by no means an accident as there is an in-built advantage in a networked environment for those companies that move first given that the value of the network increases exponentially the more people join it. This 'network effect' means that, despite the radical differences attributed to it, there is little reason to expect an internet economy to develop differently from any other industry that is based around networks. According to Tim Wu, 'For all its supposed singularity, the Internet shows itself, like any network, to be subject to network economics, with efficiencies naturally arising from central control. Economies of scale, a leading story of the twentieth century, is playing out in this century already' (2010: 318).

The upshot of this is monopolistic (and sometimes oligopolistic) control of key areas of the online economy. Despite Microsoft having invested billions of dollars into its Bing search engine and despite the increasing importance of the Chinese internet economy, Google continues to dominate the world market for search with a two-thirds share, in contrast to Baidu, with 8.8 per cent, and Microsoft, with a mere 2.5 per cent (Meyer 2013), and it has a 90 per cent share of search on mobiles and tablets (netmarketshare 2013). It is true that there are significant national differences (Yandex in Russia and Baidu in China both have a dominant share in their respective countries) but Google's hegemony is a perfect illustration of network effects operating inside apparently competitive markets: it accounted for 91 per cent of the UK search market at the end of 2012 as against 4 per cent for Bing (comScore 2013) and has a 67 per cent share in the US next to Bing's 18 per cent. Similarly, online book publishing may be growing rapidly but this has not led to a plurality of providers: Amazon has a 60 per cent share of the US e-book market and an astonishing 90 per cent in the UK (Cookson 2012), positioning itself as a gatekeeper that is far more powerful than any previous single publisher with implications that are discussed later in this chapter.

When it comes to digital downloads, the original inspiration for Anderson's 'long tail' thesis, there may be millions of songs and apps available but there is little evidence that this has resulted in reduced demand for blockbusters. Elberse (2008) found that the top 10 per cent of titles on the online music service Rhapsody accounted for 78 per cent of all plays, a result that 'demonstrates a high level of concentration' (2008: 2), while Tan and Netessine's study of Netflix concluded that 'hits still drive some markets, and may even become more popular over time, whereas the rising demand for niches is, at best, overestimated' (2009: 3). Meanwhile, Apple's iTunes controls 63 per cent of the US download market (and even more when it comes to individual tracks), with Amazon's share at 22 per cent – two companies therefore account for 85 per cent of all units sold (Pham 2013). App production is certainly more of a 'cottage industry' but even here, a handful of companies dominate with just twenty-five developers generating half of all mobile app revenue (Kerr 2013).

According to the *Wall Street Journal*, around 2 per cent of the top 250 app publishers are 'newcomers', with most app makers having a 'difficult time breaking into a business dominated by incumbents' (Lessin and Ante 2013). The 'long tail' structure of the app market is further undermined by the fact that some two-thirds of apps in the Apple Store are 'zombies', apps which are rarely, if ever, downloaded by consumers (Lee 2013).

All this rather challenges the claims that digital networks have decisively shifted power from the centre to the periphery and from elites to ordinary users and creators. Despite the fact that digital technology creates the conditions for a plurality of voices and organizations to flourish, the material ways in which networks operate in a free market economy constrains that process and privileges accumulation strategies that are designed to reward corporate interests more than to empower individual actors. Indeed, far from hierarchies being overwhelmed by networks or bureaucratic conglomerates being made powerless in the face of nimble start-ups, the reaction of the former is often simply to buy up the latter. Google, for example, has spent over $20 billion in acquiring (at the time of writing) some 127 companies; Facebook, Apple and Twitter have embarked on a similar buying spree. This is evidence, in digital circumstances, both of the innovation of the many as well as the economic power of the few. In this situation, Robert McChesney argues for the relevance of imperialism-related metaphors when trying to describe the online world: 'The best way to imagine the Internet is as a planet where Google, Facebook, Apple, Amazon, Microsoft, and the ISP cartel members each occupy a continent that represents their monopoly base camp … The goal of each empire is to conquer the world and prevent getting conquered by someone else' (McChesney 2013: 137).

Corporate domination of individual sectors (search, apps, e-publishing, etc.) is, therefore, complemented by a growing antagonism as these behemoths seek to ward off future competitors and to protect their revenue streams. Some of the fiercest competition takes place in relation to online advertising markets where the *Financial Times* now speaks of a 'turf war' between companies with very different functions but a common need to extract as much money as possible from their users (Bradshaw and Dembosky 2012). So, while the largest social media companies have quite distinctive remits, they are nevertheless competing for the same pot of advertising revenue. They are both accomplices in the emerging online world (Google, for example, is expected to pay $1 billion to Apple in 2014 to ensure that it remains the default search engine on Apple devices) and fierce rivals. 'As competition grows, a once collaborative energy among the top social networks is fizzling out as they each compete to maintain their own slice of the internet landscape' (Bradshaw and Dembosky 2012).

The collective benefits of emerging technological forces are reined in by the limitations of the actual social relations of production. As with other sectors of the capitalist economy, decisions concerning how best to exploit labour (whether paid at the point of production of 'free' in the form of user-generated material) and to maintain a 'competitive edge' swamp any commitment to producing goods and services that are socially useful and accessible irrespective of considerations of profit and loss. What were once dynamic and flexible start-ups have now constantly to look over their shoulders to meet the competition both of powerful rivals and the next generation of energetic innovators as well as to respond to technological challenges, for example the growing popularity of mobile platforms, a failure that cost Facebook dearly in 2012 before it made the necessary changes to adapt to the popularity of smartphones and tablets. The *Economist* describes this battle between Google, Facebook, Apple and Amazon as 'an epic story of warring factions in a strange and changing landscape, a tale of incursions and sieges, of plots and betrayals, of battlefield brilliance and of cunning with coin'. And in this high-tech version of the 'game of thrones' (Economist 2012), the focus is firmly on the barons, never the serfs.

There is, however, one further contradiction in relation to the discussion of 'power shifts': that those networks which have been endowed with such destabilizing and decentralizing properties are themselves the creation of highly centralized forces, most often those concentrated in the state. As is well known, the internet depended on military funding for its original development in the shape of the ARPANET and was only effectively privatized in 1995 when the commercial possibilities of the web became apparent (Curran 2012b). According to the economist William Janeway (2012), this is similar to many major transportation and communication infrastructural projects, the core elements of what he calls the 'innovation economy', which have had to rely on public support because the private sector has not always been willing to invest in areas where the potential rewards are unclear. As Janeway puts it (2012: 1), the innovation economy 'depends on sources of funding that are decoupled from concern for economic return'. This is a rather polite way of saying that market forces are usually inimical to the risks involved in large-scale innovation and that only the state, with its command of resources and its ability to plan ahead, has shown itself capable of initiating major developments. There are exceptions of course like the British railway industry and the US telegraph system but, even here, the state played a central role in their evolution and, in the case of the British railways, their operation.

This is far from a dry historical lesson as, despite the claims of political theorists like Kenichi Ohmae (1995) and technologists like Schmidt and Cohen (2013), the state has stubbornly refused to disappear under the impact of digital networks and, through its control of military, political and economic resources, it continues to fund, coordinate and deploy precisely those networks that were said to undermine its very existence. Nowhere is this more clear than in the existence, revealed by former National Security Agency (NSA) operative Edward Snowden in 2013, of government surveillance networks that expose the private communications data of ordinary citizens to official scrutiny. Programmes like PRISM in the US and Tempora in the UK are vast, sophisticated and centralized systems for eavesdropping into telephone conversations, emails and social media for the purposes of national security and demonstrate the tension inside any large-scale technological system between de-centred communicative practices and strategic oversight of the data generated. The fact that some previously resource-poor groups may be 'empowered' by digital technologies does not at all mean that traditional power holders will be marginalized by the same technologies. Joseph Nye's observation that NGOs and terrorists will be emboldened by the internet is therefore far less useful than his reminder that

> economies of scale remain in some of the aspects of power that are related to information. Although a hacker and a government can both create information and exploit the Internet, it matters for many purposes that large governments can deploy tens of thousands of trained people and have vast computing power to crack codes or intrude into other organizations. (Nye 2011: 117)

Without an acknowledgement of the power imbalance between states and those who oppose them, simple paeans to the internet's decentralizing instincts become meaningless. Indeed, Morozov makes the point that precisely because of the state's continuing power, it may be better placed to take advantage of the internet's centrifugal tendencies. 'Decentralization, if anything, creates more points of leverage over the public discourse which ... can make it easier and cheaper [for the state] to implant desired ideas into the national conversation' (2011: 136). Scale still matters and size still counts.

The state, however, has not acted alone to set up and operate its surveillance networks as it has required the complicity and silence, under legal threat, of some of the world's largest communications providers. According to the *Wall Street Journal*, the NSA's surveillance system 'is built on relationships with telecommunications carriers that together cover about 75% of U.S. Internet communications' (Gorman and Valentino-Devries 2013), companies like AT&T and Verizon as well as technology companies like Google, Facebook, Microsoft and Cisco Systems. In the UK, major telecoms companies like BT and Vodafone have also been accused of 'secretly collaborating with Britain's spy agency GCHQ' with each company given a secret codename in order to maintain confidentiality (Ball, Harding and Garside 2013). Perhaps most extraordinary of all, these very same private companies – most of whom have denied joining any government surveillance programmes – have actually been compensated by the NSA for costs incurred in providing the agency with the relevant data, a figure that has now run into many millions of dollars (MacAskill 2013).

The power relationships involved in Mills' identification more than fifty years ago of a nexus between military, political and economic interests and Schiller's description of a 'military-industrial communications complex' (see Chapter 2) have been resuscitated in what McChesney calls a 'military digital complex' (2013: 158), a comprehensive intelligence and information system underpinned by the government and largely welcomed by the major corporate interests in the digital sphere. While the internet has disrupted many traditional business models in ways that may one day facilitate the emergence of dispersed and networked forms of communication, it is simply not true that we have seen the replacement of concentrated power with a series of 'power mosaics' that are more democratic and egalitarian in spirit. Indeed, because of the continuing inequality in the distribution of resources that underpin media power, we may be seeing the opposite: a form of information distribution that is strengthening the centre. 'Instead of information reciprocity, what we may witness is an ensuing redistribution of information power from the powerless to the powerful – or to put in the information privacy context from the surveyed to the surveillant – that often takes place without the explicit consent (or even knowledge) of those from which power is taken' (Meyer-Schonberger 2009: 107). What we are most likely seeing is a simultaneous interplay of both forces – centrifugal and centripetal – that demonstrates both the possibilities and the dangers inherent to the current communications environment.

Disintermediation: Power to the people?

If we are to believe some popular titles, new information and communication technologies are the gravediggers of major elements of power, responsible for the 'death of distance' (Cairncross 1997), the 'end of the nation state' (Ohmae 1996), the 'end of work' (Rifkin 2000), the 'end of politics' (Carswell 2012) and the 'end of big' (Mele 2013). A further and particularly important quality of distributed networks that follows on from their structural urge to decentralize is their ability to facilitate direct connections between dispersed users without the need for mediating bodies. This process of 'distintermediation' has allowed bands to sell (or give) music to fans without the need for labels, for advertisers to communicate with consumers without the need for classified ads in newspapers, for film buffs to exchange opinions with other film buffs without the need for professional critics and for authors to reach readers without the need for publishers. Disintermediation, according to this logic, has severely disrupted the business models of the newspaper, publishing and music industries and has undermined the authority of elites and equalized the balance of power between what were previously seen as distinct 'producers' and 'consumers', 'professionals' and 'amateurs'. There are two aspects of disintermediation that I wish to examine in this section: the decline of intermediaries and the empowerment of publics that is seen to result from this.

On a technical level, disintermediation is a fundamental property of digital networks where, according to Alex Galloway (2004: 10–11), 'each node in a distributed network may establish direct communication with another node, without having to appeal to a hierarchical intermediary'. As always, Jeff Jarvis poses the problem in much starker terms: 'middlemen are doomed' (2009: 73). In a world of bits and not atoms, of abundance and not scarcity, there is no real need for intermediaries whether they are real-estate agents, literary agents or indeed advertising agencies. They represent an unnecessary additional layer between sellers and buyers and, as such, Jarvis sees them as 'the proprietors of inefficient marketplaces' (2009: 76). Far better to have direct transactions between those who have an immediate interest in the outcome as opposed to those who merely have a stake in seeing a deal go through. This has already had a huge impact in politics where social media platforms can facilitate communication between candidates and voters without the intervention of political correspondents and expensive TV commercials. Erik Qualman, for example, attributes Obama's success in his 2008 contest with Hilary Clinton for the Democratic Party presidential nomination to his ability to mobilize millions of direct recommendations (in what he calls the 'social graph') as opposed to relying on traditional middlemen (2009: 133). In the area of international news, specialist foreign correspondents are increasingly threatened not simply by editorial cuts but by competition with both international NGOs as well as celebrities. For Schmidt and Cohen, disintermediation could herald the emergence of 'Brangelina news' (2013: 50) where celebrities communicate directly with their fans about matters of interest to themselves, including ethnic conflicts as well as stories about their own brand. Celebrities, in a disintermediated news environment, could become 'the ultimate source of information and news on the conflict because they both are highly visible and have built up enough credibility in their work that they can be taken seriously' (2013: 50).

Yet, it is not simply celebrities who are set to take advantage of the 'death of middlemen', as the key beneficiaries of this rebalancing of power are set to be individual members of the public, empowered and energized by increasingly ubiquitous social media tools. Once again, there is a technical basis to this enhanced communicative ability as a distributed architecture and lower entry costs have, according to Yochai Benkler (2006: 212), 'fundamentally altered the capacity of individuals, acting alone or with others, to be active participants in the public sphere as opposed to its passive readers, listeners or viewers'. Whether this is on the streets of Cairo, the campaign trail in the US or in creative practices and business transactions anywhere in the world, disintermediation has not simply disrupted the hegemony of the middleman but has contributed to an increased sense of agency on the part of ordinary citizens. As a result, some very grand claims have been made in relation to digital innovation. 'Never before in history have so many people, from so many places, had so much power at their fingertips', write Schmidt and Cohen (2013: 4), while Tapscott and Williams insist that the consequences for individuals of the digital revolution are on a par with the Italian renaissance and the rise of Athenian democracy: 'A new economic democracy is emerging in which we all have a lead role' (2008: 15).

The key features of this democratic vision are the possibilities of collaboration and participation facilitated by digital technologies – the 'We-Think' described by Leadbeater (2008) or the 'wikinomics' promoted by Tapscott and Williams (2008). These types of grass-roots cultural production and economic activity have, according to Jeff Jarvis (2011), given the public a renewed sense of its purpose and power. Developments like the internet have not only undermined the power of traditional gatekeepers but have put in their place a 'public society' to which there can be no meaningful resistance: 'Publicness is a sign of our empowerment at their expense. Dictators and politicians, media moguls and marketers try to tell us what to think and say. But now in a truly public society, they must listen to what we say' (2011: 11). Social media platforms have amplified the voice of the public to such an extent that not only must the 'powerful' listen to their publics but their power is actually diminished by the force and vitality of an engaged and active public. This creative frenzy paid off in 2006 when the public received a major accolade, *Time* magazine's 'Person of the Year' award bestowed on 'you' for 'seizing the reins of the global media, for founding and framing the new digital democracy, for working for nothing and beating the pros at their own game' (Grossman 2006). While the public was distracted in subsequent years by the battles between Facebook and Google and between tablets and iPhones, 'you' made a significant comeback earning the top spot in the *Media Guardian 100* list in September 2013. 'You' beat off the chief executives of all the major social media companies as well as the director general of the BBC in order 'to reflect the extent to which the individual had become empowered in the online age' (Guardian 2013b: 31).

As with the theories concerning decentralization, there are important lessons to be learned from these accounts of public participation, collaboration and engagement. The sheer number of YouTube clips, tweets, blog comments, Flickr photographs and Facebook posts demonstrates that a vast amount of labour is performed by ordinary users in their attempts to communicate with their peers (and sometimes to organize themselves as publics). But what is less frequently analysed is the extent to which the disintermediating properties of digital technologies can be said automatically to lead to the disappearance of influential intermediaries in a manner that would suggest a meaningful transition of power from elites to publics. How are the possibilities of creative and political agency afforded by digital technologies intensified or constrained by present circumstances? For Manuel Castells, this is a crucial question as the digital age has delivered radical new forms of 'mass self-communication' that has stimulated 'unprecedented autonomy for communicative subjects to communicate at large' (2009: 135). However, he also argues that 'this potential for autonomy is shaped, controlled and curtailed by the growing concentration and interlocking of corporate media and network operators around the world' (2009: 135). Far from diminishing the importance of media moguls and tech giants, announcing the death of gatekeepers or lauding the autonomy of the public, we should be investigating the ways in which their power is being reconstituted inside a digital landscape.

There is little doubt that disintermediation has disrupted the media market as a whole, especially with the migration online of whole sections of print advertising. The internet is now second only to television in terms of advertising revenue in the US, virtually double that of the newspaper industry, and increased its revenue by over 15 per cent in 2012 alone (Interactive Advertising Bureau 2012). Given that search accounts for some 45 per cent of all online advertising and that Google dominates search, this puts Google in a particularly powerful position. This is even more the case given that the company is increasingly able to deal directly with clients without the need for dedicated ad agencies. 'Google is an incredibly efficient system for placing ads', writes Michael Wolff (2012). 'In a disintermediated advertising market, the company has turned itself into the last and ultimate middleman.' We have already identified the oligopolistic structure of other emerging media markets where large companies continue to interject themselves between the buyer and the seller, for example Apple in relation to apps and music downloads and Amazon in relation to e-publishing, and to assume a prominent gatekeeping role. Power may be shifting but it appears to be displacing previously dominant distributors (like book publishers or music companies) in favour of new corporate intermediaries rather than automatically empowering the public itself.

Consider the recent evolution of the e-publishing market. This is a sector dominated by Amazon, whose founder, Jeff Bezos (the current proprietor of the *Washington Post*, see Chapter 2), attributes the company's success to its 'self-service' approach that frees customers from the tyranny of middlemen. As he wrote to Amazon shareholders, 'even well-meaning gatekeepers slow innovation', whereas Amazon simply empowers '*others* to unleash *their* creativity – to pursue *their* dreams' (Bezos 2012). This has worked very well for Amazon which, as we have seen, now has some 60 per cent of the market share for e-books and a growing share of the market for physical books. While this might suggest to some that Amazon has assumed a gatekeeping role more decisive than any traditional bookstore or publisher, for Bezos this provides evidence simply of its commitment to encourage self-publishing and maximize customer choice. Strangely, given Amazon's dominance of the sector, in 2012 the US Department of Justice decided to file an antitrust suit not against Amazon but against Apple and five major publishers for alleged collusion in fixing e-book prices. Apple, somewhat ironically given its control of the apps and music download markets, argued in response that it was only trying to introduce competition into a sector dominated by Amazon and, unlike the publishers whose pockets were not quite as deep, it refused to settle the suit. In the summer of 2013, a judge ruled against Apple, a decision that is likely only to cement Amazon's position as the major powerhouse in the publishing industry, assuming the role, as the *New York Times* points out, that Penguin and Random House played when they turned publishing upside down in the 1940s and 1950s with the development of the paperback (Streitfeld 2013).

Gatekeeping, however, is not simply a matter of economic control but also of organizations and individuals being able to interject themselves at key stages of the communications process in ways that influence its output. Blogging, posting and uploading, for example, may appear to be highly disintermediated activities but they are, of course, all subject to process of moderation and surveillance undertaken by both humans and computers. In 2008, Jeffrey Rosen spent time researching an article on this topic for the *New York Times* with Nicole Wong, the deputy general counsel of Google whose responsibility it was to decide on what material was appropriate or not for Google's many services across the world. Reflecting on the values and beliefs that Wong brought to bear on very complex decisions concerning the balance between free speech and the avoidance of harm, Rosen concluded that 'Wong and her team arguably have more influence over the contours of online expression than anyone else on the planet' (Rosen 2008). Decisions on whether YouTube should allow jihadist videos, whether Google should permit searches about 'Tiananmen' in China and whether Orkut, its social networking site, should tolerate attacks on a hard-line nationalist party in India were based on a combination of political pragmatism, economic considerations and cultural norms concerning speech rights. The team led by Wong, who went on to be legal director of Twitter and then chief privacy officer at the White House, was known as 'the Deciders' (Rosen 2008) and there continue to be 'deciders' at all the major social media companies who are faced with similar decisions about how best to manage content, deal with hate speech and protect freedom of expression.

In a follow-up article on the work of the 'deciders', Rosen discusses how some internet companies are exploring the possibility of an algorithmic approach to content screening in order to minimize subjective bias and describes this as 'an engineer's response to a thorny historical and legal problem – a very Silicon Valley approach' (Rosen 2013). First, this will do little to ensure objectivity as algorithms are as susceptible to bias as the human decisions that are embedded within them. A report for the Nieman Journalism Lab provides a fascinating account of how news aggregators and summarizers that rely on a series of ranking, optimization and personalization algorithms are dependent on the data fed into them as well as the 'criteria used to help them make inclusion, exclusion, and emphasizing decisions' (Diakopoulos 2012). Second, algorithms do nothing to change the fact that what is allegedly disintermediated speech is subject to filtering systems at so many different levels. Morozov (2012) reveals how some of the most popular 'grass roots' blogs, like Tumblr and WordPress, run their comments through third-party controlled algorithms that check for spam, malware and harmful content without making it clear what the algorithms are based on and therefore what they understand, for example, to constitute hate speech. This lack of transparency is compounded by the extra layers that are being added to speech acts that are celebrated as evidence of a more open and dispersed form of communication. In fact, argues Morozov, it is 'the proliferation – not elimination – of intermediaries that has made blogging so widespread. The right term here is "hyperintermediation", not disintermediation' (Morozov 2012).

Networked communication, therefore, neither makes gatekeepers redundant nor eviscerates the need for what Schmidt and Cohen call 'discretionary power' in relation to who gets to decide on what information is released or redacted (2013: 42). Their example of discretionary power actually happens to relate to Julian Assange, the founder of WikiLeaks, but he is the exception: most of the time, the ability to stand between the public and the information and communication to which it is entitled is hegemonized by leading state and corporate actors with huge resources at their disposal. Despite the opportunities for distributed communication that connects together independent members of the public for pleasure, politics or education, there are all too often new 'choke points' (Gillmor 2011) that mediate this process. This is precisely the point made by Castells that, although we have seen a huge increase in socialized communication, 'government control over the Internet and the attempts of corporate business to enclose telecommunication networks in their privately-owned "walled gardens" show the persistence of networking power in the hands of the gatekeepers' (2009: 419). This is particularly true of electoral communications where, despite the predictions that direct communication between candidates and voters that undermine traditional intermediaries, established means of promotion remain dominant. According to Nichols and McChesney (2013), around $10 billion was spent on the 2011–2012 election cycle in the US, the vast majority of which was eaten up by local television advertising (2013: 130). Far from social media being able to remove the influence of power and wealth from the political process, the lesson for Nichols and McChesney is clear. 'This is the truth of 2012: money beat money' (2013: 5).

These examples show that disintermediation is an extremely uneven process – that it has radically disrupted some sectors more than others, for example newspapers and publishing – and that, frequently, what has been described as the 'death of middlemen' is little more than a sectoral restructuring that sees new gatekeepers emerging to take the place of older ones. This is extraordinarily unsettling for the media industry but is not evidence of a transformation that directly empowers publics at the expense of intermediaries. Indeed, if the democratizing impact of disintermediation has been exaggerated, it is possible that so too have the possibilities of forms of autonomous participation that have helped to realize the old slogan: 'Power to the People' (Qualman 2009: 192). As I have already made clear, there is no room in this chapter to examine the claims that social media have acted as reliable tools of political emancipation for ordinary citizens – others have done this very well (Bennett 2003, Fenton 2012, Morozov 2011, Sreberny and Khiabany 2010) – but a look at the everyday uses of digital technologies nevertheless reveals some interesting, if rather predictable, conclusions.

First, the activities that are most closely based on the opportunities afforded by digital technologies for content creation, collaboration and peer participation are undertaken by only a minority of the online population. Less than one third of the US adults share original content online or post comments to a blog or photo site while 14 per cent create or work on their own webpage or blog (Pew 2013); the figures are a little higher for teenagers, where some 38 per cent share original content and 21 per cent remix 'found' material into their own versions (Pew 2012b). In the UK, 13 per cent of the population aged above sixteen years old regularly upload content, 8 per cent comment on news-related sites, while only 4 per cent post their own news-related clips (Ofcom 2013: 291, 116). Given the size of the online population these are certainly significant numbers, and the impact of these creative and engaged acts will help shape evolving media and political cultures but they nevertheless represent *minority* behaviour. Second, by far the most popular activities remain either those which closely resemble the uses of information and communications in legacy media environments – for example, searching for information, checking the weather and enjoying other people's content – or general browsing, shopping and using a social networking site which, while distinct to the digital era, are hardly consistent examples of emancipatory behaviour.

Social media, the web and other digital platforms may have allowed greater numbers of individual citizens to create and exchange a wider variety of material, but this has not been done at the expense of powerful media and tech organizations who continue to structure, mediate and exploit the growing appetite and capacity for interactive communication. The conditions under which people use social media to self-organize, to create and to collaborate are not separate from the inequalities and disparities that mark social life more generally and, in this context, the decision of both *Time* magazine and the *Guardian* to equate the power of 'you' with the power of the captains of the media and technology industries is, at best, disingenuous. Actually, in the small print of their articles, both titles recognize the tensions in their claims: while *Time* acknowledges that 'Web 2.0 harnesses the stupidity of crowds as well as its wisdom' (Grossman 2006), one member of the *Guardian* panel also admitted that the situation was not quite so straightforward and that the 'power of them, versus the power of all of us, will be the [dominant] narrative' (quoted in Guardian 2013b: 31). Despite the lure of disintermediating technologies, we still appear to find ourselves in a rather old-fashioned struggle over resources and power.

Conclusion: 'It's called capitalism'

Robin Mansell is absolutely right to argue that any assessment of the impact of digital media needs to be firmly focused on the issue of power. 'Without research that gives a central place to power as a "headline" issue in new media studies, we can only speculate about how inequality may be reproduced and then seen as the "natural" outcome of innovations in new media technologies' (Mansell 2004: 98). This chapter has examined how new media technologies have both shaped *and* have been shaped by contemporary power relations. It has explored claims that digital technologies have dispersed power and control from a handful of dominant providers to a multitude of users and creators and that individual citizens have been 'empowered' by their appropriation of social media platforms that facilitate autonomous forms of communication. It has also provided a counterpoint to these arguments: that power, understood as the relationships that facilitate the capacity to dominate social situations, is not collapsing, declining or disintermediating so much as 'rebalancing' given the challenge digital technologies.

The chapter has also argued that the very real ways in which digital networks have helped to shake up the dynamics of existing media markets and patterns of behaviour need to be understood in the context of capitalist relations of production. This leads to some interesting ironies, if not full-blooded contradictions. 'Fast is better than slow' boasts Google's mission statement

(Google n.d.) and, indeed, the significance of speed was borne out towards the end of 2012 when information about a disappointing earnings report was accidentally released ahead of time, wiping $24 billion (£15 billion) off Google's value in just *eight* minutes, some $45 million per second (Gye and Boyle 2012). This was the largest single drop in stock market history, caused partly by the speed at which financial information flows across digital networks. Openness is another key characteristic attributed to digital technologies, not least for the online coupon company Groupon that boasts, in its own mission statement, that it has no time for 'BS [bullshit] … We want each Groupon purchase to feel too good to be true' (Groupon n.d.). This commitment to honesty is admirable but rather hard to deliver in the cut-throat environment of online start-ups as the company found out to its cost when it was forced by the US regulators, ahead of its initial public offering (IPO) in 2011, to admit that the way it counted its revenue was not entirely accurate. Following the intervention of the Securities and Exchange Commission, it reduced its stated revenue in 2010 from $713 million to $313 million (Davidoff 2011), a major embarrassment in the run-up to the IPO and a likely cause of its later plunging share price.

Transparency is a further feature said to be facilitated by digital interactions. According to its own founding principles, 'Facebook should publicly make available information about its purpose, plans, policies and operations' (Facebook 2014). This proved to be particularly important in relation to its own IPO in May 2012. If ever there was a case for the triumph of the new digital economy, the day that Facebook went public was destined to be it. A company with unparalleled access to the personal data of its over one billion users, that has reinvented networked sociality and that is the epitome of social media dynamism, was set to be floated and, of course, on the high-tech NASDAQ and not on the more traditional New York Stock Exchange. According to the Associated Press, the IPO was 'highly anticipated and was supposed to offer proof that social media is a viable business and more than a passing fad' (Associated Press 2012). Yet it proved to be a disaster, not just because of the technical problems on the day of the IPO and not just because the share price fell so dramatically (falling to half its original price after six months before climbing back up its original level) but because of a more fundamental problem with its lack of transparency. It emerged soon after the IPO that Facebook's bank, Morgan Stanley, had briefed only a minority of investors about private concerns about the share offering, that the company and its underwriters effectively hid reduced growth forecasts from would-be buyers, that the bank set the share price too high with a price-to-earnings ratio of over fifty (in contrast to Google's twelve) and that the bank was forced to intervene to protect the share price (Chon, Strasburg and Das 2012). The deal has since faced a number of official investigations with Morgan Stanley fined

$5 million by the financial authorities with other banks set to follow (Alloway and Massoudi 2012). This kind of 'selective disclosure', secrecy, greed and hype sounds resembles not the discourse of a shiny new capitalism but 'old economy' IPOs and deals in which transparency and openness were abandoned in the rush for profits.

Facebook is now in danger not simply of further undermining its own brand reputation through its lack of transparency but, along with other companies, of jeopardizing prospects for the wider new media environment by saturating the market for advertising, driving down costs and therefore potentially undermining the revenue it can earn per customer. Facebook faces a problem: it has a huge user base but an uncertain business model. Media commentator Michael Wolff (2012) describes this as a 'juxtaposition of realities' in which Facebook operates on a vast scale but 'is mired in the same relentless downward pressure of falling per-user revenues as the rest of Web-based media'. The same 'juxtaposition' can even be applied to Google, which, while continuing to show impressive profits, saw a 6 per cent year-on-year decline in 2013 in its 'cost per click', the amount of money it can charge advertisers on average (Ray 2013). The logic of market competition is such that Google is likely to continue to lower its per-user costs in order to retain its monopoly position leading either to an old-fashioned crash (which Wolff predicts) or to the crushing and silencing of its rivals. Neither solution particularly lends weight to assertions that the internet has abolished scarcity and decisively shifted power from the centre to the edge.

Why on earth would we expect any other outcome? After all, this is how capital – whether in the shape of the car industry, oil, pharmaceutical or even social media – operates. The digital economy, just like the 'analogue' one with which it is intimately connected, is marked by the same tendencies towards concentration and consolidation, towards enclosing and protecting private property. It could be argued, however, that digital technologies accentuate the tension between socialized production and private appropriation in an especially stark manner so that for every open-access journal there is increasingly a paywall; for every Creative Commons, there is an Apple that 'tethers' (Zittrain 2008) its users to its own proprietary goods and services; for every instance of citizen reporting, there is the exploitation of user-generated content by new intermediaries. The 'dynamism' of the online world cannot be insulated from the uncertainties and priorities of the world it is alleged to be replacing.

Despite utopian promises about the dispersion of new media power, we have seen that the digital media environment is often even more concentrated than its offline counterpart and that market imperatives are undermining the capacity of the internet to meet the needs of all citizens independent of their purchasing power. Indeed, one simple illustration of the extent to which social media companies are beholden to the power of profits above the interests of the public is their determination to pay a minimal amount of taxes. In 2012, Facebook paid £2.9 million in tax on profits of more than £800 million earned outside the US (Neate 2012), while Amazon paid £2.5 million tax on the UK sales of £4.3 billion (Sky 2013), with Microsoft paying no tax at all on revenue of £1.7 billion in the UK (Webb 2012). There is a simple explanation for this. Google chairman Eric Schmidt, reflecting on why his company channelled over £6 billion of revenue from international subsidiaries into Bermuda in order to halve its tax liability, stated that this was done purely 'based on the incentives that the governments offered us to operate. It's called capitalism. We are proudly capitalistic. I'm not confused about this' (quoted in *Telegraph* 2012).

So, companies and platforms that are said to be dispersing concentrations of power are determined to accrue more wealth and power along the lines of the neo-liberal values that I explored in Chapter 2. For some people, this is less of a puzzle that we might expect. According to internet pioneer Jaron Lanier (2013), power is increasingly vested in those people who control our digital networks – the programmers and 'switchers' discussed by Castells (2009) – and so any idea that power has somehow fragmented in the digital age is simply wishful thinking. 'The disruption and decentralization of power coincides with an intense and seemingly unbounded concentration of power. What at first glance looks like a contradiction makes perfect sense once one understands the nature of modern power' (Lanier 2013). Lanier may well be correct about the dynamics of contemporary power but there is nevertheless a productive tension between the opposing forces and capacities that this chapter has sought to grasp: between, for example, public and private, autonomy and control, socialization and atomization, networks and hierarchies.

We need therefore to take very seriously the arguments of those theorists who insist that power now flows benignly from the periphery and that concentrated ownership is a mere historical memory in the digital age and to integrate these claims into a perspective that acknowledges the contradictory development of social relations. While the internet has certainly facilitated the *possibility* of the broader circulation of marginal voices and the reconstitution of publicness, the claims described above are overstated, lack context and are, at times, simply wrong about the transformation of power these writers see as structurally attached to the embedding of digital technologies in daily life. Instead, this chapter has focused on a few examples that illustrate that corporate power, far from disappearing in recent years, is flourishing and has adapted itself to meet the challenges of the digital economy. Distributed technologies have led to the abolition neither of the laws nor the contradictions of capitalism but have offered a range of both existing and new organizations the capacity to secure customers for their goods and services. Capitalism has not dispersed; social media have simply helped it to develop a far more effective way of market dispersion.

5

Challenging Media Power

The will of the capitalist is certainly to take as much as possible.
What we have to do is not to talk about his will, but to enquire
about his power, the limits of that power, and the character of
those limits.

MARX (1969: 6)

Media, contradiction and resistance

A recent opinion poll in Britain was reported in the *Independent* newspaper
under the headline: 'British public wrong about nearly everything' (Paige
2013). On average, the public believes that immigrants make up 31 per cent
of the UK population when in fact the real figure is closer to 13 per cent; that
24 per cent of the country are Muslim as opposed to the real figure of only
5 per cent; that £24 of every £100 of benefits are fraudulently claimed when the
real figure is around seventy pence; and that 15 per cent of girls under sixteen
fall pregnant every year when the real figure is actually 0.6 per cent. Some 58
per cent of people do *not* believe that crime is falling when official statistics
show that crime has fallen by 53 per cent since 1995 while 26 per cent of the
public are convinced that foreign aid is among the top three areas of government
expenditure when in reality it accounts for a mere 1.1 per cent of the total
budget (Paige 2013). The survey, in other words, demonstrates that the public
consistently exaggerates levels of immigration, crime, teenage pregnancy and
welfare fraud – precisely the kinds of issues that absorb many tabloid agendas
and provides proof of the misinformation and sensationalism doled out by the
mainstream media. This, surely, is an example of media power at its most
pernicious: dividing communities, looking for scapegoats and mystifying, rather
than illuminating, social relations. In particular, it lends support to the proponents
of a 'control' paradigm of power, like the advocates of the propaganda model
(Herman and Chomsky 1988), for whom the media perform a crucial ideological
role in reproducing the status quo.

However, there is also evidence that audiences are equally prepared to question media content and to adopt frames that run directly counter to those pursued by mainstream media organizations. Perhaps the clearest example of this is the refusal by British audiences to share the initial enthusiasm of the majority of the political and media establishments for the 2003 Iraq War. Researchers found evidence in the UK broadcast news coverage of a 'subtle but clear bias towards those pro-war assumptions' concerning the existence of weapons of mass destruction while, according to Robinson et al. (2010: 104), 'British news coverage of the Iraq invasion conformed to the prediction of the elite-driven model. Press and television news relied heavily on coalition sources and supportive battle coverage prevailed even among newspapers that had opted to oppose the war.' Famously, all but one of the 175 newspapers owned by Rupert Murdoch around the world supported the war (Greenslade 2003).

British public opinion, on the other hand, stubbornly refused to throw itself into the pro-war camp. There was a solid anti-war majority in the build-up to the invasion followed by a short period, when the troops went in to Iraq, where there was a majority in support of the war. The last poll showing a pro-war majority dates from May 2004; from that point on, opposition to the war hardened without interruption. Even with all the supportive and wall-to-wall coverage of troops in combat operations in the middle of 2003, the proportion of the British public backing the war *never* reached above two-thirds of the population (Wells n.d.). Indeed, as I will discuss later, there is evidence to suggest that anti-war public opinion helped to shape at least parts of the media rather than media power being deployed unambiguously on a 'vulnerable' public.

News audiences, in fact, are prepared not just to reject the imperial adventures of their governments but the more day-to-day aspirations of the titles to which they attach themselves. Readers, for example, have regularly refused to toe the editorial line of their own newspapers when it comes to proposals for a new system of independent press regulation following the phone-hacking scandal. Despite vigorous lobbying campaigns by the *Daily Mail* and the *Sun* against the Leveson-compliant Royal Charter, 59 per cent of *Mail* readers and 52 per cent of *Sun* readers nevertheless argue that the titles should accept the new system in contrast to only one-fifth that believes that the titles should be able to establish their own system (YouGov 2013a: 4). Following the creation by leading news publishers (including those of the *Mail* and the *Sun*) of the Independent Press Standards Organisation (IPSO), set up directly to compete with and undermine the Royal Charter system, 54 per cent of *Mail* readers and 40 per cent of *Sun* readers insisted that they wanted their titles to participate in the Royal Charter system and would be 'disappointed' if they did not, with only a tiny proportion of readers arguing that they should do the opposite (YouGov 2013b: 6). This represents a straightforward slap in the face for the editors and publishers who have campaigned tirelessly against the Royal Charter.

One of the key reasons for this divergence between titles and their readers is the growing level of distrust in major social and political institutions and a recognition that ordinary people and media executives do not share the same interests. So, for example, as we saw in Chapter 3, only 21 per cent of the UK population 'trusts' the press as an institution – the second-lowest across the whole of Europe (European Commission 2012: 19) – exactly the same figure as those who trust journalists to 'tell the truth' (Ipsos MORI 2013). This is a pattern we are seeing reproduced internationally where the media's legitimacy increasingly appears to be a minority perspective. The Edelman Trust Barometer which tracks public opinion across twenty-five countries (including the US and China) reports that 46 per cent of the public trusts the media as a whole (Edelman 2012: 7) while Gallup reports that 44 per cent of Americans have either a 'great deal' or a 'fair amount' of trust in media (Mendes 2013). Of course this is somewhat skewed by Republican voters, many of whom continue to insist that the US media is dominated by a 'liberal' cabal, but it is also true that only 37 per cent of 'independents' trust the media (Mendes 2013). In Australia, the figures are even more startling. While 30 per cent of the public has 'total trust' either in the press or in the TV news media (with approximately 20 per cent having 'no trust' at all) (Essential Media Communications 2013a), an astonishing 34 per cent of Australians see the media as 'extremely corrupt', the highest in the poll and substantially higher than the figures for the finance and construction industries (Essential Media Communications 2013b) – an indictment perhaps of the concentrated nature of the Australian news media in which two owners (News Corp and Fairfax) control 86 per cent of sales (Flew 2013).

Of course, as Bourdieu reminds us with his provocative argument that 'public opinion does not exist' (Bourdieu 1972), opinion polls do not reveal the full dynamics of any situation – they provide at best a rather crude snapshot of public sentiment at any one time and are open to manipulation by those who frame the questions. But, there is nothing fictional about the size of anti-war sentiment and nothing invented about the anger expressed in recent years towards unaccountable media moguls and unscrupulous journalists. And if media audiences are willing to be not just active in their media consumption but, at times, downright skeptical of the institutions, individuals and texts associated with the media, then it suggests that media power cannot be as predictable, solid or immoveable as, for example, advocates of the propaganda model and other radical critics argue. We should be careful *not* to exaggerate the significance of audience activity, and Hackett and Carroll are right to caution that audiences 'actively interpret media texts, but not under conditions of their own choosing. Unless we have access to contrary experiences or discursive resources, they tend to work with the raw material provided' (Hackett and Carroll 2006: 30). Nevertheless, particularly in conditions of profound economic and political insecurity, the existence of this kind of 'contradictory consciousness' has major implications for resisting media power as long as we are able to identify the mechanisms through which media control is exerted as well as the circumstances and tensions which allow for a challenge to this process.

Several chapters in this book have illustrated how media power – vested in and circulating through corporate institutions, policy networks, professional routines and technological developments – assists in the reproduction of elite power more generally. This chapter, however, sets out to investigate not the expression and operation of this power so much as the opportunities for resistance to it that are mobilized at specific moments of crisis. The chapter highlights the explicit challenges to established media institutions posed by media reform movements as well as those rare instances where mainstream media outlets express critical views about state and corporate power, notably the anti-war coverage inside the British tabloid newspaper the *Daily Mirror* at the time of the invasion of Iraq in 2003. I counter the arguments that these spaces exist simply as a result of market relations that see a viable audience for this sort of 'radical' content as well as the opposite argument made by proponents of the propaganda model: that 'liberal' critiques of the elite merely constitute an effective means by which a market system is able to legitimate itself as pluralistic and democratic. The chapter seeks instead to argue that the possibilities for critical content and democratic structures exist precisely as a result of the contradictory, not smooth, dynamics of media power that I outlined in general in Chapter 1 and in relation to social media in Chapter 4.

These dynamics are directly related to the structural contradictions of capitalist society: between the social character of production and its private appropriation, between the utility of goods and their exchange value in a market, between the real value of human labour and the mystical properties of the commodities that labour produces, and between the possibilities afforded by technological development and their capacities in a capitalist market. These contradictions are neither external nor accidental to capitalism but part of its DNA. Given the constant interplay between social reproduction and private property that is subjugated not 'to the needs of society at large but to the social conditions that determine the imperatives of competition and the possibilities of realization', Ellen Wood concludes that '[i]t is difficult to think of a system more riddled with contradictions than this' (2002: 286). The media are fully implicated in this environment and suffused by contradictions between, for example, the desire for 'consensus' and the pursuit of difference; between a professional commitment to hold power to account and an institutional entanglement with power; and between the commodification of media audiences and their reluctance passively to accept this process (see Sparks 2006 for a further discussion of the media's contradictions).

For the most part, however, media institutions are intimately connected to networks of prestige and power and their output is, not surprisingly, associated with a hegemonic project that is designed to legitimize elite frames and assumptions. Powerful interests deploy a range of institutions and instruments, the media central among them, to naturalize their views of the world and to inculcate a 'common sense', described by Gramsci as the 'diffuse, unco-ordinated features of a general form of thought common to a particular period and a particular popular environment' (Gramsci 1971: 330n), that restricts the emergence of more radical forms of consciousness. There are, however, two ways – both related to social contradiction – in which this project, at least as it is carried out through the media, may be disrupted.

First, given that these networks are far from harmonious and are riven with sectional interests, the media are able, albeit mostly unwittingly, to articulate elite tensions and to reveal glimpses of the limitations of liberal conceptions of democracy and freedom. As Todd Gitlin puts it (1980: 11):

> The media create and relay images of order. Yet the social reality is enormously complex, fluid and self-contradictory, even in its own terms. In liberal capitalist society, movements embody and exploit the fact that the dominant ideology enfolds contradictory values: liberty versus equality, democracy versus hierarchy, public rights versus property rights, rational claims to truth versus the arrogations and mystifications of power.

One need only think of the main government and industry protagonists for an 'open' internet being involved in extensive systems of surveillance, of the use of the First Amendment by corporations in order to defend their commercial speech rights or of the championing of 'press freedom' by millionaire media moguls in order to ward off more robust forms of press regulation to see how true this is.

Second, the structural contradictions of capitalism give rise to the emergence of uneven forms of consciousness which means that, as we saw with the opinion polls earlier in this chapter, media institutions are *not* viewed as intrinsically credible by audiences and do *not* exert an inexorable power over society – indeed one of the main tasks of media power is precisely to seek this legitimacy and influence. Instead the media are open to challenge, particularly when the frames they propose do not seem to match the experiences or aspirations of their audiences. This is all the more likely at times of social struggle and political instability when existing narratives are under stress and when audiences themselves are actively seeking out new perspectives that better fit with changing circumstances. 'Common sense', never the most stable or homogeneous of phenomenon – which Gramsci, for example, describes as 'fragmentary, incoherent and inconsequential, in conformity with the social and cultural position of the those masses whose philosophy it is' (1971: 419) – is, in these circumstances, particularly vulnerable to more radical expressions of 'good sense' (Ytterstad 2012).

Contradiction, then, does not just refer to the underlying 'chaos' of a complex society or to the multiple, and seemingly irreconcilable, perspectives on power in the contemporary world but to a productive process in which conflicting systemic pressures create the conditions for constant disruption and potential change. Mike Wayne argues that one way of understanding contradiction is as a 'process, social force or agent [that] negates certain aspects of itself and/or wider society in the course of pursuing its own reproduction within that society' (Wayne 2003: 262). This is most obvious in the theory of commodity fetishism in which human subjects, whose labour is central to the production of commodities, become commodities while commodities themselves become subjects (2003: 219). Commodity fetishism both naturalizes market exchange (by making the objects of production seem external and strange to those who produce them while making their interaction in a market seem entirely logical) *and* stores up a reservoir of alienation and unfulfilled expectations that always has the potential to explode. Little wonder that Ellen Wood argues that contradictions give capitalism its 'unprecedented strength and dynamism' at the same time as rendering it vulnerable (2002: 291).

It is these contradictory tendencies at the heart of capitalism and the contradictory forms of consciousness that grip its constituents that provide the context and lay the foundations for the emergence of the spaces and moments in which challenges to media power can be mounted. There is, however, nothing mechanical or predictable about resistance to the dominant media order. Manuel Castells, for example, talks at length about 'counterpower' in the network society which he describes as the 'countervailing processes that resist established domination on behalf of the interests, values and projects that are excluded or under-represented in the programs and composition of the networks' (2009: 47). Counterpower is seen here as effectively the 'flip side' of power, circulating through the same mechanisms and adopting the same logic as its counterpart and linking to it in a mutually reinforcing design. The problem here is that contradiction is not just about reciprocity which, according to John Rees 'can only show mutual interaction not progress' (Rees 1998: 85), but about the specific configurations of material conditions and human agency that give rise to (or suppress) conflict and resistance. 'That is why', according to Rees (1998: 85), 'Marx and Engels say of the contradiction between the proletariat and wealth, "It is not sufficient to declare them two sides of a single whole."'

Castells is rightly absorbed by the possibility of resistance but he talks more about the location and mechanisms of counterpower than how it emerges in concrete circumstances, ignoring Lukes' point that one of the key dimensions of power (as discussed in Chapter 3) is its ability to silence and marginalize challenges to authority. Counterpower, therefore, should be seen as neither instinctual nor inevitable: it cannot be pre-programmed like a digital video recorder. To argue, as Castells does, that both 'official' and resistant forms of power are increasingly networked tells us very little about the sources of power and resistance. There is nothing wrong with stating that '[p]ower rules, counterpowers fight' (2009: 50) but such a conception does little to illuminate the balance of power in capitalist (or indeed networked) societies. Castells is, in this context, far more indebted to Foucault's notion of biopower which insists that '[w]here there is power, there is resistance and yet this resistance is never in a position of exteriority to power' (Foucault 1990: 95), than he is to a materialist understanding of power as subject to the complex interplay of the balance of forces of mutually antagonistic interests.

What we need, therefore, is an approach to media texts and structures that appreciates their interconnections with elite power, as the propaganda model does, but also that recognizes the various contradictions – including the impact of inter-elite tension, the effects of competition and the unevenness of popular consciousness – which undermine their security and efficacy in securing elite reproduction. For this, I turn to Deepa Kumar's 'dominance/resistance model', first outlined in her evaluation of mainstream media coverage of the strike by United Postal Service workers in 1997, which 'allows us to understand both the mechanisms of dominance that justify and reproduce the status-quo, and the mechanisms of resistance that can force through an alternative view' (2008: 56). Adopting what Kumar describes as a 'more dialectical understanding of consent formation' than that offered by the propaganda model (2008: 168) does nothing to underplay the very real and substantial distortion of the communicative environment posed by existing patterns of authority and control but certainly does seek to highlight the potential for challenges to this authority that are facilitated by the very contradictions of media power.

The dominance/resistance model in action: The war in Iraq

On 21 January 2003, the British tabloid newspaper, the *Daily Mirror*, with a readership of over five million people, launched a petition to the then prime minister Tony Blair opposing the proposed invasion of Iraq – a petition that was eventually signed by over 220,000 people. The *Mirror* campaigned tirelessly to rebut the arguments of the British and the US administrations that sought to justify a war in order to neutralize the weapons of mass destruction that were allegedly stockpiled by the Iraqi leader Saddam Hussein. Celebrity gossip and scandal, once the staple of the *Mirror's* news agenda, were kicked off the front page to be replaced by hard-hitting critiques of the pro-war lobby. Memories of front pages dominated by celebrities, the royal family and *Big Brother* goings-on seemed a long way off.

Perhaps the first place to turn to make sense of this unusual news agenda might be *Manufacturing Consent*, the book that first outlined the propaganda model, in which Herman and Chomsky argue that the 'mass media are not a monolith on all issues. Where the powerful are in disagreement, there will be a certain diversity of tactical judgments on how to attain generally shared aims, reflected in media debate' (Herman and Chomsky 1988: xii). Indeed, throughout their writings and that of those who have continued to develop the propaganda model, we find a recognition that, as David Miller puts it, 'It is certainly true that there is some scope for dissent in the mainstream media although this is without doubt limited' (Miller 2004: 95). Herman actually argues that dissent can even go beyond limited, tactical disagreements: '... there are often differences within the elite that open space for some debate and even occasional (but very rare) attacks on the *intent* as well as the tactical means of achieving elite ends' (Herman 2000: 103).

The acknowledgement by the creators of the PM that the mainstream media do sometimes offer up conflicting and oppositional viewpoints offers a pre-emptive strike against those critics who have otherwise described the model as 'perfectly unidimensional' (Hallin 1994: 12) and as proposing an overly instrumental approach that sees media structures as 'solid, permanent and immovable' (Golding and Murdock 2000: 74). Indeed Herman denies that the PM closes off the possibility of oppositional viewpoints or marginalizes the importance of resistance, claiming that it is, instead, 'a model of media *behavior* and *performance*, not of media *effects*' (Herman 2000: 103), that it is about 'how the media work, not how effective they are' (2000: 107). While this may be true – and therefore many of its critics are accusing the model of failing to do something that it never intended to do – it is nevertheless not that easy to insulate the whole question of media performance from that of effectiveness. Indeed, Herman himself immediately follows up his claim about the distinction between 'behavior' and 'effects' with the following assertion:

> The power of the US propaganda system lies in its ability to mobilize an elite consensus, to give the appearance of democratic consent, and to create enough confusion, misunderstanding and apathy in the general population to allow elite programs to go forward. (2000: 103)

The media's performance, in this example, is intimately linked to its ability to generate a compliant citizenry. While resistance may be possible, the PM is predicated on the basis that there is a 'default' position of media consensus, elite power and audience passivity.

My main criticism of the propaganda model is not that it is *unable* to acknowledge the exceptions, gaps and cracks within the corporate media system – as well as the fact that many people over the years have rejected corporate media content and challenged dominant frames. It is rather that, because those activities are not its real focus and its advocates, therefore, rarely provide examples of such exceptions, it finds it difficult to offer a fully worked-out picture of consensus *and* conflict. The real interest of PM supporters lies, understandably enough, in exposing the *lack* of diversity in mainstream media coverage and in laying bare the media's unspoken assumptions about the desirability of market systems and the legitimacy of 'humanitarian intervention'. As Colin Sparks puts it (2007b: 81), 'To the extent that the PM accepts the existence of "tactical" disputes, it is of course prepared to accept some diversity, but it poses uniformity as the normal state of the media.'

I want to do the opposite – to focus on the exceptions, when the 'default' position breaks down, as, for example, with media coverage concerning the Vietnam War and the invasion of Iraq in 2003. My interest in the exceptions is about how meaningful possibilities of transformative action become clearer in moments of crisis than in moments of stability. But what is a 'moment' asks the Hungarian Marxist Georg Lukacs?

> A situation whose duration may be longer or shorter but which is distinguished from the process that leads up to it in that it forces together the essential tendencies of that process, and demands that a *decision* be taken over the *future direction of the process*. That is to say the tendencies reach a sort of zenith, and depending on how the situation concerned is handled, the process takes on a different direction after the 'moment'. (Lukacs 2000: 55)

Because they are about times at which established structures start to wobble, when previously hidden tensions emerge and when new actors are called for, irregular circumstances – like war, scandals and cover-ups – are crucial in alerting us to the possibilities both of new forms of political action and new kinds of media coverage.

Journalistic routines concerning objectivity and balance, so often the professional default mechanism for obstructing more radical views (Cunningham 2003), cannot be fully insulated from such moments. As Todd Gitlin argues (1980: 4), 'The world of news production is not self-enclosed;

for commercial as well as professional reasons, it cannot afford to ignore big ideological change.' So, for example, when there is conflict between elites, when reporters are radicalized by events or when the media are forced to address the problems faced by their audiences, 'the media sometimes present dissenting views' (Kumar 2008: 49). While these are 'criticisms that exist in the margins and are not usually found on page 1' (2008: 50), they nevertheless point to the potential disruption of more consensual news agendas as a result of elite division and wider social conflict.

Justin Schlosberg, in his fascinating examination of the limitations of journalistic contestability (Schlosberg 2013), also looks at those unusual moments when a combination of elite dissent, competitive forces and journalist autonomy allows even mainstream news to challenge official narratives and to ask tough questions of business and government, albeit circumscribed by professional routines and structural constraints. He analyses, for example, television news coverage of the decision by the Serious Fraud Office in 2006 to suspend its investigation into an arms deal between British Aerospace (BAe) and the Saudi government. The BAe scandal was 'exemplary of the cracks in the system that enable radical activists to exploit the mainstream media for resistance effects' (2013: 58) and yet coverage as a whole was marked by its reluctance to investigate broader geopolitical and ethical contexts, not least the merits of selling arms to countries with poor human rights records. He concludes that journalistic contestability is genuine but seriously constrained: the silences and gaps that permeated otherwise critical stories about the corporate sector and government power bear witness to the limitations of pluralist accounts of media power. On the other hand, the scale of critical coverage of corruption and scandal was 'clearly more substantial, prolonged and broader' than is allowed in 'radical functionalist' theories like the propaganda model (2013: 85).

This unsettling of hegemonic agendas and glimpses of more radical content is of course by no means confined to news. Indeed, American-produced entertainment programmes have provided audiences with some of the most hard-hitting critiques of contemporary life in recent years, notably *The Sopranos*, *Mad Men*, *The Wire* and *Breaking Bad*. This is certainly not because drama output is policed more 'liberally' than its news counterpart but simply because niche markets have emerged that can sustain (admittedly very small amounts of) radical output for which there is a clear appetite. This has long been the case in Hollywood in which, even now, a handful of radical voices like Sean Penn, Tim Robbins, Danny Glover and Ed Asner attempt to carve out critical spaces in direct tension with the mass market priorities of the studio system (Dickenson 2006). In the case of *The Wire*, the award-winning drama set in a decaying Baltimore, its creator David Simon acknowledges that he was inspired by Marx's critique of capitalism and that the programme was about 'people who were worth less and who were no longer necessary, as may be 10 or 15 per cent of my country is no longer necessary for the operation of the economy. It was about them trying to solve, for lack of a better term, an existential crisis' (Simon 2013). *Breaking Bad*, the story of a high school chemistry teacher turned illegal drug manufacturer, provides a similarly devastating indictment of capitalism's operating principles, condemning 'the sphere of capital and competitive consumerism, in which business and crime are seen as proximate, intertwined or even synonymous' (Meek 2013).

All of these critically acclaimed series were produced by niche cable channels – HBO made *The Sopranos* and *The Wire* while AMC was responsible for *Breaking Bad* and *Mad Men* – precisely the kind of pay television networks that are symptomatic of the neo-liberal TV markets that I criticized in Chapter 3 for excluding whole sections of the population. Indeed, *Breaking Bad*'s contradictions extend even further. It may equate the 'normal' functioning of capitalism with illegal and destructive market operations but the programme itself was shot in New Mexico, a state that offers substantial tax credits to lucrative productions in order to undercut more expensive locations. *Breaking Bad* does not just represent exploitation and alienation, it actually 'benefits from contexts of racialized low wage labor' (Marez 2013). These programmes have been made not because of an inherent pluralism inside the mainstream media, but because there is currently a business model that rewards critical output at a time when millions of viewers are themselves increasingly aware of capitalism's shortcomings. The degree to which there are non-conformist positions expressed in the media therefore relates to one of the central contradictions of the media industry – the need, in a competitive market, to address (in however a skewed way) the interests of different audiences, even if that means at times generating content that is hostile to the environment in which it is produced.

Notwithstanding these very important programmes, the subject that appears to produce the biggest schisms inside both political and media elites is that of war and its representation in news coverage, particularly when there is a strong anti-war current. For Todd Gitlin, the Vietnam War in the 1960s was a time when, under pressure from both anti-war campaigners and a divided elite, 'journalism itself becomes contested. Opposition groups pressing for social and political change can exploit self-contradictions in hegemonic ideology, including its journalistic codes' (1980: 12), thus accentuating the possibility for further contestation. Gitlin identifies a dominant 'protest paradigm', an approach to reporting on popular mobilizations that follows patterns of deprecation, marginalization, trivialization and polarization (Gitlin 1980: 69). While Gitlin finds evidence of this throughout the coverage of Vietnam, he also shows how this model was unsettled by the struggles that broke out across American society and how audiences reacted very differently to the same images.

The media transmitted images of the turn toward revolutionism as they transmitted images of one of its central rationales: the growing brutality of the police. Together these images helped render the street-fighting style legitimate *within* the movement as they helped render it anathema for the audience *outside*. (1980: 195–196)

The crucial point for Gitlin is that journalists were unable to insulate themselves from this political crisis which was 'not confined to a back-and-forth process between sealed-off elites; the elites experienced political crisis precisely because of the upswelling of opposition – both radical-militant and liberal moderate – throughout the society' (1980: 273). Journalism in this period became a highly unstable source of support for those who wanted most effectively to prosecute the war.

In his analysis of media coverage of the giant demonstrations against British involvement in the Iraq War in 2003, Chris Nineham identifies a 'suspension or breakdown of the protest paradigm in some sections of the media and at least a modification across the board' (2013: 134). Nineham argues that the scale of public opposition to the invasion, together with a resulting outbreak of nerves at the highest levels of the British political establishment, led to unexpectedly sympathetic – or at least serious – coverage of the march on 15 February 2003 that attracted some two million people on to the streets of London. With 37 per cent of stories across the press and the BBC being favourable to the protest (and only 17 per cent unfavourable), Nineham concludes that the march (as well as anti-war public opinion itself) was simply too big to dismiss in the usual terms: 'Not only was it treated in much of the media as a legitimate reaction to important political developments but it was often assumed to have at least the potential to react back on the wider political developments' (2013: 163). In other words, mainstream news outlets took the march seriously because they thought that political elites might take the march seriously.

One newspaper in particular was at the heart of the opposition to the Iraq War, not simply reporting on but mobilizing against the build-up to an invasion. The *Daily Mirror* had actually supported British involvement in the two most recent previous conflicts, the 1991 Gulf War and the 1999 campaign in Kosovo. It did, however, have a long-established anti-war tradition, having opposed both the Suez invasion in 1956 and the Falklands War in 1982. But in opposing the war in Iraq, the traditionally Labour-supporting *Mirror* was confronting the military plans of a *Labour* government for the first time and was in danger of alienating the Labour supporters who formed the core of its readership.

Why would it take such drastic action? The *Mirror's* anti-war stance could be seen as the logical conclusion of a rebranding exercise that had started following the events of 9/11 and the perceived desire among the reading public for a more analytical and serious approach to news in order to understand both the roots and dangers of terrorism. Piers Morgan, the *Mirror's* editor at the time, shifted the paper away from an unremitting emphasis on celebrity scandal and human interest stories towards a focus on international coverage that included a particularly critical stance towards the US and the UK's bombing of Afghanistan in late 2001 and their ever-increasing threats to invade Iraq.

This approach was consolidated with the £19.5 million formal relaunch of the *Mirror* in Spring 2002 when the paper's traditional 'red top' masthead was exchanged for a more sombre black one and when 'heavyweight' journalists like John Pilger (the leading investigative reporter and long-time *Mirror* writer), *Vanity Fair's* Christopher Hitchens and the *Guardian's* Jonathan Freedland were all given regular columns. According to Morgan, the changes were all about the *Mirror* becoming a 'serious paper with serious news, serious sport, serious gossip and serious entertainment' (*Daily Mirror* [*DM*], 16 April 2002). This was an unusual form of 'product differentiation' – a phenomenon more often consisting of 'scoops', competitions and giveaways – but not an entirely unreasonable one, given signs of growing resistance to the Blair government and a fast-growing and very popular anti-war movement that had, up till that moment, little resonance in the mainstream media.

The relaunch and new radical tone was not just in response to a changed political climate but also was a much-needed measure to address the long-term decline in circulation of the *Mirror* and to close the gap with its principal competitor, the *Sun*. In the 1960s, before the *Sun* even existed, the circulation of the *Mirror* exceeded five million; by the mid-1980s and the highpoint of 'Thatcherism', the *Mirror's* circulation was 3.5 million, some 500,000 less than that of the *Sun*; by 1999, the *Mirror* fell into third place behind the *Sun* and the *Daily Mail*; and by 2002, it was hovering just over what was seen as the critical two million mark (Cozens 2003). Indeed, this relaunch was only the latest in a long line of rebranding exercises of the *Mirror*; it had started life in 1903 as a title aimed at women before switching allegiance to Liberal politics and finally settling on a pro-Labour identity. The relaunch of 2001/2002 was, therefore, a business decision supported (at least initially) by its corporate owners at Trinity Mirror.

The *Mirror* followed up its hostility towards the British and American bombing of Afghanistan in 2001 with a series of articles that warned against going to war with Iraq as a distraction from the real fight against international terrorism. The problems involved in challenging George Bush and Tony Blair's war plans soon became clear. The *Mirror* celebrated American Independence Day in 2002 with the headline MOURN ON THE FOURTH OF JULY (*DM*, 4 July 2002) and a two-page article by John Pilger that described the US as 'the world's leading rogue state...out to control the world'. In response, the fund manager of one of Trinity Mirror's large American investors, Tweedy Browne, phoned up the *Mirror's* chief executive to complain about the article – a very clear example of the kind of flak talked about in the propaganda model (Herman and Chomsky 1988: 26). Morgan defended Pilger and emphasized his popularity with *Mirror* readers (if not Americans investors) but the episode showed that an anti-Bush, let alone an anti-imperialist, position would generate real resistance.

Throughout the rest of 2002, the paper developed its argument that an attack on Iraq would be counterproductive and would 'make us less secure, not more' (*DM*, 1 January 2003). Responding to opinion polls showing a lack of popular support for an invasion of Iraq, the *Mirror* attempted to articulate this anti-war sentiment in bold and imaginative ways. On 6 January the paper adapted a cartoon by the US Labour cartoonist Gary Huck that suggested that Bush's motive for attacking Iraq lay with his desire to control oil resources in the region, and ran it on the front page. As preparations for war intensified, the *Mirror* escalated its own anti-war profile by launching its 'No War' petition – that allowed it to feature pictures of celebrities signing the petition every day – and distributing a free 'No War' poster. Morgan records in his diary: 'This is going to be massive, and I see a real opportunity for the *Mirror* to become the anti-Iraq war paper and give a voice to the millions who clearly agree with me' (2005: 374). The first six or so pages of the paper each morning became devoted to the subject of the impending war and how to resist it. Morgan sanctioned further polemical, campaigning and highly controversial front pages, including one featuring Tony Blair with the headline BLOOD ON HIS HANDS (*DM*, 29 January 2003) and lots of red ink on the prime minister's hands.

The *Mirror's* coverage in the early part of 2003 failed to stem the decline in circulation but did, at least, win it critical acclaim and much-needed publicity. David Seymour, the Mirror Group's then political editor and leader writer, recalls that the anti-war position was 'overwhelmingly supported by the readers' and that editorial staff were encouraged by opinion polls showing a significant anti-war constituency in the UK.

> I was at a conference with the political editor of the *Sun* in the run-up to war and he said to me 'how many readers have you lost because of your stance on Iraq?' I said 'why should we lose readers when what we're saying is what the British public is saying?' It was the *Sun* that was flying in the face of British public opinion. (Quoted in Freedman 2003: 100)

This confidence encouraged the *Mirror* to venture into other controversial areas, most notably over the issue of asylum seekers and refugees. On 20 January, the paper ran a full-page feature on 'Why immigration is good for Britain' and followed this up in early March with a three-page special exposing the myths and reality about asylum seekers and pointing out Britain's poor record of accepting refugees despite the contribution they make to the country (*DM*, 3 March 2003). The *Mirror* was, for a time, the model of an accessible, popular, campaigning and challenging daily newspaper.

Furthermore, the *Mirror* did not simply challenge the arguments for going to war but helped to mobilize opposition to the US and the UK governments. It reported on the global anti-war protests in January and firmly identified itself with the national demonstration due to take place in London on 15 February. Two days before, it published a four-page guide to the march that included a map of the route and the contact details of local transport to get to London. The *Mirror* paid for the video screen in Hyde Park at the end of the march and, after meeting with the organizers of the protest (Nineham 2013: 8), printed thousands of 'No War' placards with the paper's logo at the top. The following Monday, the paper featured ten pages on preparations for war as well as a twelve-page commemorative report on the protest march. By the time the war started, the *Mirror* was devoting up to fifteen pages a day in a popular tabloid condemning the arguments of the US and the UK administrations and urging the public to raise its voice against a war.

However, as soon as the war started, the *Mirror* adopted a far more cautious political position. It maintained opposition to the war itself but focused more on celebrating the courage and dedication of British soldiers. As the conflict continued, its coverage and editorial position became less distinctive, reducing its identification with the anti-war movement, curtailing its criticism of Tony Blair and returning gossip and showbiz news to more prominent positions in the paper. On 11 April, it was revealed that the *Mirror's* circulation had dropped below the key psychological barrier of two million copies a day while its main rival, the pro-war *Sun*, had actually added readers during the war (Cozens 2003). The following morning saw the paper's first non-war related front page since the beginning of March and the emergence of a more 'balanced' news agenda juggling celebrity stories, domestic news and the aftermath of the Iraq War.

There are some key lessons about the role of the press to be learned from the *Mirror's* performance during the Iraq War. The first is to repeat once again that at a time of profound social crisis when elites are divided among themselves and the public is willing to challenge and mobilize against these elites, a space can open up in which radical ideas start to circulate. In the context of a mass movement against Tony Blair's attempt to involve Britain in a US-led invasion of Iraq and serious international disagreement about the legitimacy of such military action, the *Mirror* was able to articulate and reinforce the views of this movement and to air opinions that would otherwise have been marginalized in the mainstream media. When the movement was on the up in the months preceding an invasion, the *Mirror* was happy to draw on a wide range of anti-war voices and to organize opposition to an invasion.

It shifted from a newspaper which addressed its readers in fairly passive and restricted terms to one in which readers were conceptualized as active, thoughtful and capable of making an informed contribution to both the paper and the wider world. The significance of a mass-circulation tabloid newspaper, with approximately five million readers, taking on such a perspective should not be underestimated.

However, when 'product differentiation' takes a highly political form that has already antagonized investors, shareholders and government itself, it becomes clear that a newspaper whose ultimate responsibility is to make a profit is not a reliable ally for an anti-war movement and that spaces for radical content are always going to be very fragile in the existing social order. Although the *Mirror* was initially keen to express the overwhelming anti-war sentiment in the UK, when military action started and opinion polls revealed a more ambivalent attitude towards the war among both its own readers and the general public, the *Mirror* was less willing to be identified with what it saw as minority views. Constrained by a 'responsibility' towards the bottom line, the paper was unable to maintain a consistent opposition towards the war and changed its coverage. Such is the logic of the newspaper business. Moments of social crisis can open up spaces for innovative and radical coverage, but they sit uneasily with the ideological commitments of a 'free press' that privilege, above all, profitability and the 'national interest'.

Given this argument, how useful is it to concentrate on how well the *Mirror* performed and not how badly the rest of the British press did in relation to the Iraq War? Perhaps the main reason is to help to refine and expand on political economy approaches, most notably the propaganda model, that explain why mainstream media coverage so often reproduces the agendas and narratives of the most powerful groups in society. But despite Herman and Chomsky's insistence that 'the U.S. media do not function in the manner of the propaganda system of a totalitarian state' (1988: 302), there is a strong sense in the writing of PM advocates that, because of the structural features revealed in the PM, the media – in their everyday behaviour – tend to act as a sealed unit and that departures from the norm are not dynamic and critical moments but serve only to publicize the idea that the bourgeois media are free and diverse and, therefore, to legitimate them as democratic and pluralistic institutions.

Consider, for example, one 'alert' on the Media Lens site (Cook 2008) that initially acknowledges the vital contribution of radical journalists like John Pilger, Seamus Milne, George Monbiot and Robert Fisk, who are virtually unique in stepping outside the boundaries of 'acceptable debate' and challenging mainstream agendas. The article then goes on to warn that their existence at the fringe of the liberal press unwittingly provides the mainstream media with a radical fig leaf.

However grateful we should be to these dissident writers, their relegation to the margins of the commentary pages of Britain's 'leftwing' media serves a useful purpose for corporate interests. It helps define the 'character' of the British media as provocative, pluralistic and free-thinking – when in truth they are anything but. It is a vital component in maintaining the fiction that a professional media is a diverse media. (Cook 2008)

Now there is nothing new, in my opinion, in this rather despairing account of the position of radical ideas within a mainstream environment. It reminds me, in particular, of Herbert Marcuse's concept of 'repressive tolerance' where,

within a repressive society, even progressive movements threaten to turn into their opposite to the degree to which they accept the rules of the game. To take a most controversial case: the exercise of political rights (such as voting, letter-writing to the press, to Senators, etc., protest-demonstrations with a priori renunciation of counterviolence) in a society of total administration serves to strengthen this administration by testifying to the existence of democratic liberties which, in reality, have changed their content and lost their effectiveness. In such a case, freedom (of opinion, of assembly, of speech) becomes an instrument for absolving servitude. (Marcuse 1969: 97)

Certainly, such warnings about the danger of co-option are useful, but they tell us little about how best to maximize the divisions within elites, to mobilize popular forces in favour of social justice, to expose journalists to these divisions and movements, and to create mediated spaces within which new sets of ideas can emerge and circulate to wide numbers of people. The logical consequence of arguing that a system of 'total administration' is able to neutralize and marginalize virtually all forms of political action is to downplay attempts to build mass movements and campaigns in favour of more atomized challenges to political – and, in this case media – power.

At moments where elite disagreements connect with mass opposition, we see the emergence of tensions that are more likely both to generate pressure for change and to offer the possibility for strategic questions about the future direction of society, so often marginalized from mainstream media, to be debated and publicized. 'What is needed', argues Nineham (2013: 187), 'is a theoretical framework that can explain both the norms of media behaviour which tend in general to exclude popular protest and the processes by which suddenly, protest can suddenly move centre stage, reverse the normal circuits of communication and start shaping media output.' An analysis of the media informed by an understanding of contradiction rather than one of 'total administration' allows us not only to press for different kinds of media content but also to imagine new, and more democratic, media structures and institutions.

The politics of media reform

Attempts to democratize actually existing media through initiatives like diversifying media ownership, campaigning for new forms of funding for marginalized content, opposing surveillance, challenging existing copyright regimes, defending net neutrality and pressing for more ethical forms of journalism are central priorities for media reform movements. This kind of campaigning often requires an engagement with official structures – with formal legislative processes, with parliaments and policymakers, with lobbyists and lawyers – in order words, with the very constituents of the system that are responsible for a diminished and degraded media culture. Perhaps not surprisingly then, it is often *not* the preferred route for media activists who are more likely to be engaged in producing alternative content than in lobbying existing institutions to change. For example, Cammaerts et al. in their introduction to *Mediation and Protest Movements* identify four key themes for activists in relation to the media: questions of movement visibility, the nature of symbolic power, the possibilities afforded to protest by networked technologies and the role of audiences and publics (Cammaerts, Mattoni and McCurdy 2013: 10–16). The authors note that capturing the attention of mainstream media is often just as crucial as producing our own images and performing our own communicative practices, but there is scarcely any attention paid to the fact that we might want, or be able, to change the practices and priorities of the media as it currently exists.

This is critical because social movements, whether they like it or not, are forced to relate to mainstream media, either proactively (usually through public relations strategies) or reactively (often in terms of damage limitation). Cammaerts et al. acknowledge this: 'mainstream media representations remain important for movements to gain visibility and publicity because it precisely mediates communication beyond the cosy circle of sympathizers encompassing the like-minded and already converted' (2013: 10). This follows Gitlin's earlier perception that, in a 'floodlit society, it becomes increasingly difficult, perhaps unimaginable, for an opposition movement to define itself and its world view, to build up an infrastructure of self-generated cultural institutions, outside the dominant culture' (Gitlin 1980: 3). While, for the majority of time, this 'dominant culture' is likely either to ignore or to trivialize these movements, even mainstream coverage can have unexpected, and certainly unintended, consequences. Just as the corporate media in the US initially stereotyped the membership and the objectives of the anti-war movement in the 1960s, Gitlin insists that '[p]ublicity helped antiwar feeling become a normal fact of American public life. In the South, television brought startling news of civil rights activity to the cabins of illiterate sharecroppers;

and it brought images of repression ... to the living rooms of Northern liberals, and helped mobilize them into the financial base of the movement' (1980: 243).

In a reflection on the relationship between contemporary activists and the media, Donatella della Porta makes the important point that both media studies and social movement theory tend to 'pay limited and selective attention to democracy, and consider both political institutions and mass media as given structures' (2013: 28). However, she then fails to consider what the consequences of this might be in terms of struggles over the shape of the media in the pursuit of democracy. She insists that we need to get to grips with 'the agency of social movements in the construction of democracy and communications' (2013: 33), but of course this is a very tricky task if, by and large, social movement activists and social movement theory itself have little appetite to attempt to modify the structures and institutions as they are currently organized and instead prefer, almost exclusively, to (re)construct communications from the bottom up.

For many activists, this type of media reform – of trying to democratize the media – is actually seen as potentially counterproductive in that activists are likely either to be incorporated into official channels or to tailor their demands to meet the values and demands of vested interests. Thinking, in particular, of the US media reform group Free Press, Mickey Huff of *Project Censored* warns of the dangers of 'working through the system' and of attempting merely to fix, rather than to replace, a social system that has been found to be demonstrably unfair and unequal (Huff 2011). This lends itself to reformist illusions both that the system can indeed be repaired and that, even if we do fix media institutions, they will ever deliver social justice within the existing frame of capitalism. As Huff argues, we need to 'Be the Media in word and deed...not lobby those in power to reform their own current establishment megaphones for their own power elite agendas, as that will not happen, and indeed, has not, for the most part, in the past' (Huff 2011).

I want to examine these debates – whether we should attempt to 'work through the system' or not – and investigate this particular strand of media reform in relation to another unusual 'moment' in contemporary media and politics: the efforts to produce a more responsible and ethical press in the light of the phone hacking crisis and, in particular, the legacy and the implications of the Leveson Inquiry into press standards and practices.

Few could have predicted that when the *Guardian* first broke the phone hacking story in July 2011, it would have led to such a huge reaction including, as I have already pointed out, the resignation of several senior police officers; the closure of Britain's top-selling title, the *News of the World*; and the year-long public inquiry led by Lord Justice Leveson that saw newspaper editors, media moguls, current and former prime ministers and high-profile victims of press intrusion give evidence before the televised proceedings. Leveson reported in November 2012 and recommended the establishment of a new system of independent press self-regulation, underpinned by a recognition body established in law, together with a low-cost arbitration service and the possibility of third party complaints. After a huge campaign by the press, the government was forced to compromise and instead to work Leveson-like proposals through a mediaeval instrument, a Royal Charter, that was finally agreed in October 2013. This has been studiously ignored by the press, who still maintain that they will refuse to abide by it and have instead set up their own self-regulator, the Independent Press Standards Organisation, in a determined effort to maintain a status quo that is generally agreed to have failed readers (Freedman 2013).

The reaction from many social movement activists, particularly those who are most concerned with the media, was that Leveson was about 'ruling class recuperation' in which one faction of the state sought to discipline and humble the 'unruly elements' of the Murdoch empire (Garland and Harper 2012: 419). A focus on challenging just one element of private power, it was argued, ran the risk of marginalizing the more essential surveillance and consensus-building roles of the state itself. The celebrated investigative journalist John Pilger accused Leveson of being essentially concerned with 'the preservation of the system' and noted that 'Leveson has asked nothing about how the respectable media complemented the Murdoch press in systematically promoting corrupt, mendacious, often violent political power whose crimes make phone-hacking barely a misdemeanour' (Pilger 2012). The monitoring site Media Lens argued that the Leveson Inquiry constituted 'yet another instance of established power investigating itself', while the academic Richard Keeble insisted that the inquiry should be understood as 'spectacular theatre' that provided 'the illusion of moral intent by the state and its propaganda institutions – the leading media corporations – when in reality the system is run on ruthless profit-oriented principles' (quoted in *Morning Star* 2012: 6).

These are all valuable and legitimate criticisms. The emphasis in the Leveson Inquiry on individual 'bad apples' and its reluctance to confront any structural issues meant that, despite overwhelming evidence to the contrary, corrupt organizations, complicit relationships and corrosive institutions were individualized, decontextualized and stripped of their systemic characters in order to pursue politically pragmatic resolutions. Without challenging the underlying conditions that gave rise to phone hacking – a press system wedded either to private profit or public influence – Leveson was, to a certain extent captured by precisely the power relations it sought to investigate and to hold to account (Freedman 2014).

This kind of criticism of Leveson therefore contains a strong element of truth, but there is a major problem: it underplays the central contradiction of the Leveson Inquiry that, while it was intimately related to establishment politics, it simultaneously highlighted the corruption and collusion at the heart of British media and political culture. The radical rejection of Leveson plays down the possibility that the exposure of media power during the course of the Inquiry might help to radicalize victims' groups, other media reform campaigners and indeed ordinary members of the public to ask more fundamental questions about how best to seek not just a more ethical press but a truly accountable media system, not just to introduce new journalistic codes but to press for a completely different form of political culture. The Leveson Inquiry, far from being a precondition for the restoration of credibility in the corporate media, actually intensified the perception that we have a press that is accountable more to its owners than to its readers. It is true that the structuring of the Inquiry fits the propaganda model notion of containing debate within 'acceptable limits', but it also raised fundamental questions about the source and exercise of power in the UK that, if acted upon by activist organizations, could have laid the basis for a more sustained challenge to the power of corporate media. Media reformers, in this context, have a role in amplifying these arguments about the flaws of an entrenched media power as part of a broader argument about the operation of the capitalist hegemony.

That is why I disagree with *Counterpunch*, who, in a recent article, argued that 'the uproar concerning press regulation is in fact much ado about nothing, because the Royal Charter is frankly useless' (Braich 2013). At one level, this is empirically false: anything that makes it easier for innocent victims of press intrusion to seek some redress or that allows third parties to complain on behalf of groups (like refugees or asylum seekers) about racist coverage is not completely 'useless'. Of course it is true that the Royal Charter will do nothing to change the structures underpinning the press, but it is short-sighted not to welcome small reforms that may protect ordinary people. Indeed, it is significant that the loudest voices against the Charter are those of the press barons spuriously claiming that '300 years of press freedom has been abolished' – a claim the press would be far less likely to make if the Charter was completely 'useless'.

But *Counterpunch*'s dismissal of press regulation debates in the UK is important for another reason – that it fails to pose an alternative solution to the 'problem of the media' and therefore fails to provide an outlet for the public's anger at the failures of the corporate media. Media reform efforts in these circumstances need not take the form simply of a polite request to tone down the worst excesses of the tabloid press or parliamentary lobbying to secure minimal changes to press self-regulation. Instead, media reform campaigners need to broaden the debate and to deepen the crisis that has undermined the legitimacy of the press by campaigning for specific remedies to, for example, media concentration, press scapegoating and the decline of local news while recognizing that these failures are indeed systematic and not incidental or peripheral to the core operations of the media. We need, in other words, to bring more radical politics to questions of reform.

This is a debate that applies not simply to media reform but to the politics of reform in general. The term itself has been rather hijacked in recent years where 'reforms' in the areas of health, education and welfare have concerned the further implantation of market values into public services rather than the democratizing of these institutions (Leys 2001). But these are not so much examples of genuine reform, understood as dealing with the root of a social problem, as attempts to concentrate power and wealth in fewer hands. Just because political reform has been rebranded does not mean, however, that we should abandon the struggle for democratic reforms. The whole point of the anti-slavery movement, attempts to organize labour in the nineteenth century, struggles for the vote for women in the early twentieth century and the civil rights movement later on in the twentieth century was that these were reforms that were fought for by different groups of people using hugely varied tactics from the polite and the parliamentary to the far more risky and revolutionary. That is the nature of reform movements: they combine people who are happy to stick to the immediate demands with those who want to go much further; they consist of fragile coalitions between people who think that the system as it exists can deliver reforms that will satisfy enough people and those who think that there are structural inequalities that cannot be ironed out given the priorities of capitalism. In these circumstances, the best tactic for those who want to see radical and durable change is not to withdraw from reform-minded movements, or simply to dismiss them as 'reformist', but to demonstrate that reforms can only be won and protected through systemic critique and radical action such as the boycotts, marches, occupations and direction action that has won the greatest victories in struggles for social justice.

But what is odd is that while millions of citizens are prepared to engage in anti-war, anti-racist, anti-poverty, environmental and disability campaigns to deal with the injustices meted out every day, far fewer are normally prepared to place such demands on the prospects for media change. Activists appear to be simultaneously fascinated and horrified by the mainstream media: we want our actions to be reported and our lives to be represented but we love to complain when this does not happen; we want to produce our own media but have to deal with the fact that millions of people continue to consume mainstream news. Whether we like it or not, television remains by far the most popular source of news, as we saw in the previous chapter, with 78 per cent of the UK public regularly turning to TV news in contrast to less than one-third of the population who use the internet for news (Ofcom 2013: 107). della Porta actually raises this as an issue when she talks about the difficulties for alternative media 'to reach beyond those already sympathetic to the cause' (2013: 29) and the need to engage with the mass media in order to disseminate progressive messages more widely.

Media reform, as with many other campaigns for social reform and justice, is therefore a response to and an expression of 'contradictory consciousness', and it is a way of involving in debates and action those people who have a healthy and often instinctive critique of the status quo but who also maintain some faith in the existing social order. It offers the possibility, for example, for committed activists to work with those who want to see meaningful change but are not yet prepared to junk existing social, political and cultural institutions. Given the resistance of the media establishment to systemic change as well as its frequently low levels of legitimacy, Deepa Kumar is right to suggest that 'reforming the media is both more difficult than liberal media theorists state and less difficult than political economists expect' (Kumar 2008: ix).

Media reform, therefore, has to negotiate this contradictory state of affairs which is why, as Bob Hackett and Bill Carroll argue, democratic media activism needs to be both defensive and pro-active (2006: 13), both reform-oriented in practice but also visionary and radical in spirit. Media reform involves a redefinition of the very idea of democracy to include new rights such as the right to share meaning as well as an increased emphasis on participation and equality through acts of media-making. The objective for media reformers is 'to build coalitions and campaigns to engage with and transform the dominant machinery of representation, in both the media and political fields' (2006: 16). Indeed, it is increasingly difficult to insulate media reform from wider political reform because of the lack of autonomy of the media 'field' from the actions of the state and the market despite the fact that the media still retain the power to affect the behaviour of other social actors.

Robert McChesney echoes this link between media and political reform. He argues that the contemporary US media reform movement was triggered by the anti-globalization struggles that took place from the late 1990s and that demanded communicative, as well as economic, justice in the struggle against neo-liberal policies. Now, he argues, the goal of media reform 'is simply to make media policy a political issue' (McChesney 2008: 57) – in other words, following up della Porta's point made earlier, to challenge the idea that media are 'given structures' and instead to make their shape and orientation a matter of public debate and action. Media reform, in this context, provides another opportunity for individuals and groups to struggle over the character of the society they inhabit and whether commercial or non-commercial, state or citizen, public or private forces should dominate. 'No one thinks any longer that media reform is an issue to solve "after the revolution",' argues McChesney (2008: 59). 'Everyone understands that without media reform, there will be no revolution.'

This means that media reform needs to have a dual orientation. First, it needs to engage with the policy process as it is and not simply as it would like it to be; it needs to use a vision of what the media *might* look like in the future in order to deal with how they are currently constituted. The movement has to use all available channels to spread its messages, including the movement's own networks as well as more formal political channels inside legislative and executive bodies. Activists need to understand, if not actually to speak, the language of their opponents; to grasp the nature of the political cycles and opportunities that exist; to provide 'facts' and data to support the case for reform; and to develop coalitions that are able to bring these issues to multiple constituencies given the links between 'media' and 'democratic' reform.

Yet, media reform also has to be imaginative and radical and not to tailor its demands simply to 'pragmatic' and reasonable ones in order to be taken more seriously by media and policy elites. After all, no meaningful campaign to change the media is likely to be supported by those with vested interests in the existing structures. Of course, there are exceptions such as the recent movement against NSA surveillance where some corporate interests, including social media companies and internet service providers, have an interest in being part of an anti-surveillance coalition, not least in order to win back some credibility. In fact, the primary audience for media reform activists is not politicians, and certainly not the media themselves, but publics – ordinary citizens whose communicative needs are not being met and, therefore, whose ability to act as informed and engaged citizens is being undermined. The immediate objective is to generate a shift in the public's attitude to questions of, for example, privacy or concentration in order most effectively to apply pressure on the politicians and regulators who have the formal power to act. Media reform, like other areas of social reform, has to be fought at multiple levels, both in the context of those on the left who believe that the media are 'incorrigbly unreformable' (Hackett and Carroll 2006: 17) but, of course, *mainly* against those who have a material stake in its current composition and therefore have no desire to see any changes to the terms and values on which the system is organized.

What this means is that those people who want to see a fundamental democratization of media power need to engage in media reform but not from a reformist perspective. The German revolutionary Rosa Luxemburg, in her short polemic on 'reform or revolution' (Luxemburg 1989 [1899]), distinguished between what she describes as 'revisionist' strategies for reform, which attempt to administer palliative care to the capitalist system, and more radical strategies that seek to win reforms as a fundamental part of a revolutionary strategy to transform the status quo. While the former wants 'to lessen, to attenuate, the capitalist contradictions' (1989: 51) in order to stabilize society and produce consensus, the latter seeks to struggle for reforms as part of a more widespread challenge to capitalist hegemony. The crucial point for Luxemburg however was that movements for reforms were central to a more profound social struggle: 'Between social reforms and revolution there exists for the revolutionary an indissoluble tie. The struggle for reforms is its means; the social revolution, its aim' (1989: 21).

Media reform, like all other forms of social reform, is a contradictory and uneven process that involves a range of groups, strategies and interests. There is a world of difference between a reform campaign which calls on a handful of the 'great and the good' to plead its case and one which seeks to mobilize greater numbers of people using a range of parliamentary and extra-parliamentary tactics – a difference perhaps between 'reform from above' and 'reform from below'. Media reform should not be reduced exclusively to parliamentary campaigns although it would be equally short-sighted to refuse to engage with parliamentary processes as part of a reform campaign. There is, after all, little point in aiming only at the band-aid if you want to cure the ailment just as there is little point in refusing at least to treat the wound. Media reform, by delegitimizing and posing alternatives to the power structures that are responsible for the problems, can help to intensify the contradictions of media in a capitalist society and is, as such, a central feature of resistance to media power.

Conclusion

This chapter has focused on the possibility of resistance to media power that emanates both from the structural contradictions generated by intra-capitalist competition and elite dissensus and in response to opposition movements for whom the 'usual' explanations are found wanting and where there is thus a perceived need for more critical and unorthodox media. That is why moments of crisis, like the British government's decision to go to war in Iraq in 2003 or the period following the uncovering in 2011 of phone hacking at the *News of the World*, are so important. They are likely to involve not simply a public scepticism towards mainstream agendas and established structures but a willingness on the part of large numbers of people to consider alternatives to the status quo and to participate in movements that expose them to new ideas. According to the broadcaster John Pilger (quoted in Media Lens 2009):

My experience in popular journalism, in the press and on television, is that when people are engaged on issues that touch their lives and move them, and help them make sense of the world, they respond in remarkable ways and never cynically ... When the *Daily Mirror* devoted almost an entire issue to stricken Cambodia, it not only sold out completely, it raised millions of pounds, unsolicited, mostly from readers who could ill afford to help a faraway people. When my film on East Timor, *Death of a Nation*, was broadcast late at night on ITV, it was followed by 4,000 phone calls every minute into the early hours – a storm of public interest and concern. That's the 'hidden public' that's so often well ahead of journalists who dismiss or patronise its power.

When this public emerges from its hiding places, as it did so notably and powerfully with the two-million strong march in London in February 2003 against the invasion of Iraq, this creates unparalleled opportunities not just for alternative and grass roots media outlets but also for activists trying to exploit mainstream media's *contradictory* desire to maintain 'normal' conditions of service at the same time as wanting to relate to a shift in popular consciousness. This is precisely what the *Daily Mirror* did in the conditions of anti-war radicalization and its own declining circulation. This single (and rather exceptional) example illustrates the argument that the media – and those that work within it – are far from a homogeneous and static bloc but a series of groups and institutions that, while overwhelmingly tied to powerful interests, are not immune from the movements and social forces who wish to challenge these interests.

We need an approach to the media that focuses on its internal contradictions – tensions that are most clearly expressed in moments of crisis – that not only explains the failures of mainstream media in representing 'ordinary' lives and holding power to account but also encourages us to mobilize with others in seeking to open up critical spaces, to press for more accountability and to inspire a democratic and genuinely diverse media. This requires a set of ideas that emphasizes both structure *and* agency, contradiction *and* action, consensus *and* conflict, and that rejects the identification of the media with pluralist accounts of a robust and competitive media as well as with more critical perspectives of the media as an instrument of 'total administration'. As Justin Schlosberg argues (2013: 247), 'The paradox of hegemonic power is that ideology is likely to be most effective when it is *not* total, absolute or consistent. It likely to depend on the very demonstrations of antagonism that give rise to pluralist notions of contest' and which remain at the heart of the struggle over media power.

6

Conclusions – Media Power Paradigms Revisited

Contradiction is active opposition, driving towards resolution.

MARX (1976A: 293)

In January 2014, millions of UK viewers were both gripped and outraged by a new documentary series that sought to highlight the lives of a working-class community on one street in Birmingham blighted by poverty and unemployment. *Benefits Street* focused attention on a handful of individuals allegedly involved in irresponsible parenting, drug-taking, cheating the welfare system and generally 'scrounging' off the public purse. Watched by a huge audience of over seven million, the programme – depending on your perspective – either confirmed popular prejudices about a 'feckless' urban poor or provided a sensationalist and heavily skewed account of the lives of vulnerable people. It was, as the *Guardian* put it, a 'lightning rod for attitudes towards state welfare' where 'the first programme polarised opinion between critics who said it demonised the poor and unemployed, and those who said it highlighted a social security system in need of reform' (Plunkett 2014). Such was the furore generated by the programme that death threats were issued to local residents, and children living on the street were bullied at school. While debate raged on- and offline, a petition condemning the programme gathered more than 50,000 signatures and a protest outside the office of the programme's producers generated yet more column inches and digital buzz. In terms of a single programme's ability to shape popular discussion of a key public issue from Parliament (the prime minister admitted to having watched it) to the pub and, further, to cement the media's authority to represent and capture the lives of ordinary people, this was a clear example of the complexities of media power.

Let us examine the programme with reference to the paradigms of power developed throughout this book. A pluralist account would draw attention to the public purposes of the programme: its ability to reflect divergent views on the subject of welfare in order to foster public debate, social action and political consensus. The programme was, after all, commissioned by Channel 4, a state-owned public service broadcaster with a remit to make controversial and challenging programmes. This was also the line adopted, not surprisingly, by the production team who claimed that their main objective was to stimulate a discussion about poverty in austerity-ridden Britain. According to the head of documentaries at Channel 4, 'I don't think there is a more important job for programme makers than to record what life is like on the receiving end of the latest tranche of benefit cuts. In fact, it's not just important, it's essential' (Mirsky 2014).

Proponents of the chaos paradigm might doubt the good intentions of the producers but would nevertheless argue that the programme has to be understood in the context of a more fluid communications environment in which the blogging and tweeting that accompanies any popular programme modifies its reception and allows for multiple points of engagement. As long as the programme was trending, the ambitions of the producers were likely to be countered by the vast amount of response and counter-response that dilutes the power of the initial source. Instead of a single programme setting an 'agenda', we have the prospect of different perspectives contributing to a far more frenzied interaction in which people are equally free to propose a 'Parasite Street' (composed of corporate tax-dodgers and bonus-stuffed bankers) as they are to reproduce the official government agenda on the need to cut welfare benefits for the poorest.

Neither of these approaches, it seems to me, do justice to the operation of media power in these particular circumstances. The debate, such as it exists, is firmly framed by assumptions that the unemployed consists exclusively of those who will do anything to avoid work and to 'game' a system that rewards them handsomely should they succeed; it accepts the starting point that unemployment is a problem less for the individuals concerned than for a society that can allegedly no longer afford the benefits to be handed out. This assumption is not borne out by an examination of the welfare budget which shows that unemployment is responsible for only a tiny proportion of the welfare bill, some 2.6 per cent in contrast to the 42.3 per cent paid out in pensions, the 20.8 per cent used to support those on low incomes or the 18.4 per cent paid to families (Coote and Lyall 2013: 4). The terms of debate, in other words, are firmly those of the government and selected tabloids with an insatiable appetite for stories about 'scroungers' and 'skivers' and no end of social media chat can compensate for the agenda-setting power of the producers. The frame, furthermore, is hardly one originated or structured by the participants themselves, despite the claim by its producers that the 'series gives a voice to the disenfranchised' (Mirsley 2014), not least because of criticisms by participants that the programme makers misrepresented the series to them as one about community spirit and *not* about benefits (Plunkett 2014).

The programme has, however, been a huge success both for its producers and for Channel 4, which is eager for public-oriented yet sensationalist output to grab attention and maintain ratings in a highly volatile environment. In this atmosphere, controversy can be highly lucrative, whatever the ethical or political consequences of the act. According to Richard McKerrow, creative director of the programme's producers: 'I don't want to say I am actively looking to be controversial because I'm not but I slightly think if you are not doing something that gets attention, then why do it?' (quoted in Plunkett 2014). When asked on BBC Radio whether he was 'proud' of the programme despite all the controversy it had attracted, another of the production company's creative directors responded positively and referred immediately to the millions of people who are watching the series as evidence of its success (Radio 4, *Today*, 16 January 2014). The programme's political economy – its mining of dominant tropes about unemployment and an 'underclass' in order to produce substantial revenue for its producers – positions it, therefore, less as meaningful dialogue than as a form of prime-time propaganda designed (perhaps) to get people talking but certainly to make sure they are watching. This interplay between political contexts and economic considerations in the service of hegemonic power arrangements is at the heart of the control paradigm.

In its capacity to engage both media audiences and opinion formers in a (unbalanced) discussion about social priorities and to inscribe itself as a vehicle for social reproduction, *Benefits Street* is an everyday story of media power. But, as well as polluting the environment it has also destabilized it. When the writer Owen Jones argued in his *Independent* column that a 'healthy media would stand up to the powerful and wealthy. Ours targets the poor and voiceless' (Jones 2014), he also captured the potential contradiction: 'Columns like this one could be passed off by disingenuous TV executives as a sign of the "debate" that their trash has helped to provoke. But the only debate to be opened is why we let our media get away with it' (Jones 2014). A significant section of the public response to the programme started to shift from blaming 'skivers' to condemning the media for stereotyped representations of the poor and a lack of emphasis in the media on corporate, as opposed to unemployed, 'scroungers', for example in relation to bankers' bonuses and tax evasion by some of the largest companies in the country. Media power, in this context, while overwhelmingly tied to established agendas concerning welfare and class, can be unsettled when the media's representations, *as well as their own legitimating authority*, is questioned and confronted. The media are, of course, comfortable with making the news but are far more nervous when, challenged by social movements, their own status becomes the news, as happened with *Benefits Street*. The contradiction paradigm seeks both to illuminate the processes through which elite interests are realized through the media and to highlight the tensions that may well emerge inside any hegemonic project.

The paradigms I have provided in this book are, I hope, useful and coherent frameworks for assessing the relationships mobilized through media power between producers and audiences in specific economic, political, regulatory and cultural contexts. They reflect, of course, the existence of very different ideological perspectives. The consensus approach continues to provide policymakers and industry voices in particular with a 'common sense' narrative about the balance between state and market in contemporary communications systems. Media power is seen here as a benign form of consensus-building: of giving voice to a range of groups and to a variety of 'problems' in pursuit of common solutions and shared spaces. The media provide us as citizens and consumers with opportunities for creation and reception; diversion and information; and monitoring and entertaining in order that conflicts may be resolved and differences redeemed. Power, from this perspective, refers to the ability to transform mediated situations in the interests of the continuing stability of the existing system.

The chaos paradigm allows us better to theorize the non-linearity and multidimensional nature of power flows in a digital and dispersed communications environment in which centralized coordinating structures and authoritative gatekeepers have been eclipsed by fluid structures and disintermediating agents. The very notion of media power here is virtually redundant as established 'sources' and 'centres' of power are undermined by a far more complex and vigorous collision of actors in the online world. No one is able to determine the future or fully to control the present; media moguls are replaced by 'innovators' whose own shelf-life is limited and therefore need constant reinvention. Traditional sources of authority – whether they be daily newspapers, network news organizations, Hollywood studios or major record labels – are all vulnerable as power shifts from the centre to the edge; from hierarchies to networks; from the 'mass' to the 'niche'. This may be experienced by all concerned as highly unsettling and unpredictable but is seen as potentially more democratic in the sense that media power is less a force to be imposed on unwilling audiences than a capacity to be struggled over (and ideally to be shared) by decentred publics. This is precisely the conception at the heart of what have been described as 'Twitter revolutions' and digital uprisings.

Both of these paradigms marginalize what I consider to be a central dimension of the dynamics of media power: the fact that, despite 'pluralistic' political arrangements and the potential disruption to media moguls posed by digital technologies, access to media power is highly unequally distributed and remains out of reach for most people. The material resources needed to amplify one's voice in an increasingly noisy communications environment do not come cheap and are shaped at present by a neo-liberal consensus that ordinarily rewards profitability and facilitates state control at the expense of more collective and not-for-profit uses. This is precisely what advocates of a control paradigm have long argued: that power has to be understood in relation to its material configuration in specific political and economic contexts. In a capitalist society, the media are answerable to the fundamental requirements of capital accumulation and commodity production and function as vital ideological sources of reinforcement for the current economic order. This approach provides critics of a market system with a vocabulary with which to highlight the democratic deficit caused by private ownership and unaccountable state coordination of the media and to identify the institutional, organizational and textual means through which social control is reproduced.

Proponents of the contradiction school endorse this critique and echo the structural entanglements of media power with a ruling elite. At a time when both commodity production *and* state power are increasingly wrapped up with processes of mediation, the media are indeed vital sources of legitimacy and authority. But, while sympathetic to these critical political economy critiques, I argue that it is essential, at the same time, to focus on the uneven consciousness – and therefore the limits on the media's authority – that is associated with the systemic contradictions of capitalism, for example between 'use' and 'exchange' value and between the socialized nature of production and its individualized appropriation. These tensions give capitalism both its remarkable dynamism as well as its underlying volatility. This is the result of its inability to meet the needs of its constituents and instead its tendency to deliver poverty alongside wealth and huge inequality alongside its claims to deliver justice for all. As Mike Wayne argues (2003: 264), capitalism's cracks are exposed especially 'where liberalism runs up against the realities of widening social inequalities'. These contradictions, in other words, simultaneously galvanize the productivity of the system *and* create the conditions in which the system may be challenged.

The crucial point is that the media are not immune from these tensions and, while intimately connected to established patterns of privilege, they are far from able fully to exorcize the contradictions of the society to which they are tied. As Todd Gitlin concluded in his assessment of the impact of news coverage of the anti-war movements in the 1960s, the media

> produce self-contradictory artifacts, balancing here, absorbing there, framing and excluding and disparaging, working in complicated ways to manage and contain cultural resistance, to turn it to use as a commodity

and to take and isolate intractable movements and ideas. In the process, they may actually magnify and hasten manageable forms of political change.

(Gitlin 1980: 292)

This is clearly not the everyday impression we get of the mainstream media but in moments when social tensions are at their most exaggerated – notably in wars, recessions and class conflict – it is vital to reveal and act on the instability and contingency of existing forms of media control. Perhaps no single model can do justice to the heterogeneity of media flows and the complexity of media power, but the contradiction paradigm, with its emphasis on both the constitution of and the cracks in media power, provides by far the most persuasive account of how best to challenge the traditions, institutions and practices that underpin it.

I have argued throughout this book that media power is irreducible to any single place or person or text and that it is instead organized more like a force field – the meeting point of institutions and individuals in defined contexts struggling to dominate creative and symbolic production. There is nothing inevitable or predetermined about its effectiveness or legitimacy as a source of information, identity, inspiration or, indeed, ideological control. Nick Couldry is, therefore, absolutely right to argue that media power needs to be regularly reproduced in order to naturalize its authority so as to make its news credible and its fictions relevant, and he is completely justified in focusing on the 'universe of beliefs, myths, and practices that allows a highly unequal media system to seem legitimate' (Couldry 2003a: 41).

But media power refers, quite crucially, to more than the cultural processes by which established patterns of media power come to be accepted. It is also about the material relations that underlie this inequality and which then structure the complex operations of media as power holders in their own right. Just as we need to take seriously the more 'intimate' parts of media power – the circulation of meaning, the production of texts and the characteristics of media forms – we need to highlight and evaluate those dimensions and practices which are crucial in shaping the composition, role and impact of media in public life more generally: questions of ownership and control, policymaking and regulation, technological development and, crucially, the contradictory consciousness of the audiences on which the media depend. In order to challenge what Couldry himself describes as the fundamental inequality of media power concerning 'who can effectively speak, and be listened to' (2000: 192), we need to focus on those situations where power is most overwhelmingly concentrated: in the operations of the state, the belly of the market and the transactions that take place in elite networks – which brings us back to Raisa the horse and the 'problem' of media power.

References

Aaron, C. (2013), 'Spin the Revolving Door: Tribune Hires FCC Chairman's Right-Hand Man', *Huffington Post*, 30 January. http://www.huffingtonpost.com/craig-aaron/spin-the-revolving-door-t_b_2584529.html?view=print&comm_ref=false [14 August 2013].

ACLU vs Reno (1996), 11 June, 96–963. http://www.pas.rochester.edu/~mbanks/CDA/decision/dalzell.html [14 January 2014].

Adorno, T. (2001), *The Culture Industry: Selected Essays on Mass Culture*, London: Roultledge.

Ahmed, A. and Olander, S. (2012), *Velocity: Seven New Laws for a World Gone Digital*, London: Vermilion.

Akers, S. (2012), Evidence to Leveson Inquiry, 27 February. http://www.levesoninquiry.org.uk/wp-content/uploads/2012/02/lev270212am.pdf [14 January 2014].

Alcatel-Lucent. (2009), *Targeted Investment in Broadband Infrastructure*. http://www3.alcatel-lucent.com/economicrecovery/targ_invest_bb_swp.pdf [6 September 2013].

Alford, M. (2009), 'A Propaganda Model for Hollywood', *Westminster Papers in Culture and Communication*, 6 (2): 144–156.

Alloway, T. and Massoudi, A. (2012), 'Morgan Stanley Fined Over Facebook IPO', *Financial Times*, 17 December. http://www.ft.com/cms/s/0/4bd127b2-4891-11e2-a6b3-00144feab49a.html?siteedition=uk [5 September 2013].

Anderson, C. (2009 [2006]), *The Longer Long Tail: How Endless Choice Is Creating Unlimited Demand*, London: Random House Business Books.

Associated Press (2006), 'FCC Chair Orders Probe into Why Media Ownership Studies Were Destroyed', *Fox News.com,* 19 September. http://www.foxnews.com/printer_friendly_story/0,3566,214392,00.html [14 August 2013].

——— (2012), 'Facebook Stock Down for 3rd Consecutive Day', 5 June. http://bigstory.ap.org/article/facebook-stock-down-3rd-consecutive-day [5 September 2013].

Bachrach, P. and Baratz, M. (1970), *Power and Poverty: Theory and Practice*, New York: Oxford University Press.

Bagdikian, B. (2000 [1983]), *The Media Monopoly*, sixth edition, Boston: Beacon Press.

Balbus, I. (1971), 'Ruling-Class Elite Theory vs Marxian Class Analysis', *Monthly Review*, 23 (1): 36–46.

Ball, J., Harding, L. and Garside, J. (2013), 'BT and Vodafone among Telecoms Companies Passing Details to GCHQ', *Guardian*, 2 August. http://www.theguardian.com/business/2013/aug/02/telecoms-bt-vodafone-cables-gchq/print [14 January 2014].

Band, J. and Gerafi, J. (2013), 'CEO Compensation in Copyright Industries', *policybandwidth*, August. http://infojustice.org/wp-content/uploads/2013/08/band-gerafi082013.pdf [14 January 2014].

Barach, P. and Baratz, M. (1962), 'Two Faces of Power', *American Political Science Review*, 56 (4): 947–952.

Bard, A. and Soderqvist, J. (2002), *Netocracy: The New Power Elite and Life After Capitalism*, London: Reuters.

Barwise, P. (2009), 'New Forms of Funding for PSB', Speech to Federation of Entertainment Unions, 22 June. http://writersguild.blogspot.co.uk/2009/06/why-levies-make-sense-ii.html [16 December 2013].

Baudrillard, J. (1994), *Simulacra and Simulation*, Ann Arbor: University of Michigan Press.

BBC. (2011), 'George Osborne Met News Corporations Executives 16 Times', *BBC News*, 26 July. http://www.bbc.co.uk/news/uk-politics-14290322 [14 January 2014].

Beck, U. (1992), *Risk Society: Towards a New Modernity*, London: Sage.

Beckett, C. (2008), *Supermedia: Saving Journalism So It Can Save the World*, Malden: Wiley.

———. (2012), *WikiLeaks: News in the Networked Era*, Cambridge: Polity.

Beevolve. (2012), 'An Exhaustive Study of Twitter Users Across the World', 10 October. http://www.beevolve.com/twitter-statistics/ [6 January 2014].

Bell, D. (1958), 'The Power Elite – Reconsidered', *American Journal of Sociology*, 64 (3): 238–250.

Benkler, Y. (2006), *The Wealth of Networks: How Social Production Transforms Markets and Freedom*, New Haven: Yale University Press.

Bennett, W. L. (2003), 'New Media Power: The Internet and Global Activism', in N. Couldry and J. Curran (eds), *Contesting Media Power: Alternative Media in a Networked World*, Lanham: Rowman & Littlefield, 17–37.

Berger, G. and Masala, Z. (2012), *Mapping Digital Media: South Africa*, London: Open Society Media Program.

Bezos, J. (2012), 'The Power of Invention', Form 8-K, 13 April. http://www.sec.gov/Archives/edgar/data/1018724/000119312512161812/d329990dex991.htm [4 September 2013].

Bilderberg. (2013), 'Media Lobby'. http://bilderberg2013.co.uk/media-lobby/ [14 August 2013].

BIS/DCMS (Department for Business, Innovation and Skills/Department for Culture, Media and Sport). (2009), *Digital Britain*, London: The Stationery Office.

Blair, T. (2007), 'Speech on Public Life', London, 12 June. http://image.guardian.co.uk/sys-files/Politics/documents/2007/06/12/BlairReustersSpeech.pdf [14 January 2014].

———. (2012), 'Oral Evidence to the Leveson Inquiry', 28 May. http://www.levesoninquiry.org.uk/wp-content/uploads/2012/05/Transcript-of-Morning-Hearing-28-May-2012.pdf [14 January 2014].

Bordo, S. (2003[1993]), *Inbearable Weight: Feminism, Western Culture, and the Body*, tenth anniversary edition, Berkeley: University of California Press.

Boston Consulting. (2013), *The Internet Economy in the G-20: The $4.2 Trillion Growth Opportunity*, Boston: BCG.

———. (2013), *Global Wealth 2013: Maintaining Momentum in a Complex World*, Boston: BCG.

Bourdieu, P. (1972), 'Public Opinion Does Not Exist', in A. Mattelart and S. Siegelaub (eds), *Communication and Class Struggle*, Vol 1, New York: International, 121–130.

———. (1991), *Language and Symbolic Power*, Cambridge: Polity.

Bradshaw, T. and Dembosky, A. (2012), 'Social Media Adverts Turf War Heats Up', *Financial Times*, 14 October. http://www.ft.com/cms/s/0/6968092c-14d8 -11e2-aa93-00144feabdc0.html?siteedition=uk#axzz2qQCAY39n [14 January 2014].

Braich, S. (2013), 'Media Bias in Britain', *counterpunch*, 8–10 November. http://www.counterpunch.org/2013/11/08/media-bias-in-britain/ [6 January 2014].

Braman, S. (2004), 'Where Has Media Policy Gone? Defining the Field in the Twenty-First Century', *Communication Law and Policy*, 9 (2): 153–182.

brandongaille.com. (2013), http://brandongaille.com/twitter-user-audience -demographics-and-statistics/ [18 December 2013].

Bureau of Labor Statistics. (2012), 'Consumer Expenditure 2011', *News Release*, 25 September. http://www.bls.gov/news.release/cesan.nr0.htm [10 August 2013].

Burston, J., Dyer-Witherford, N. and Hearn, A. (2010), 'Digital Labour: Workers, Authors, Citizens', *Ephemera*, 10 (3/4), 214–221.

Burton-Jones, A. (1999), *Knowledge Capitalism: Business, Work and Learning in the New Economy*, Oxford: Oxford University Press.

Cairncross, F. (1997), *The Death of Distance: How the Communications Revolution Will Change Our Lives*, London: Orion.

Calabrese, A. and Mihal, C. (2011), 'Liberal Fictions: The Public-Private Dichotomy in Media Policy', in J. Wasko, G. Murdock and H. Sousa (eds), *The Handbook of Political Economy of Communications*, Chichester: Wiley-Blackwell, 226–263.

Cameron, D. (2011), 'Speech on Phone Hacking', *guardian.co.uk*, 8 July. http:// www.guardian.co.uk/politics/2011/jul/08/david-cameron-speech-phone-hacking [14 January 2014].

Cammaerts, B., Mattoni, A. and McCurdy, P. (2013), 'Introduction', in B. Cammaerts, A. Mattoni and P. McCurdy (eds), *Mediation and Protest Movements*, Bristol: Intellect, 3–19.

Campbell, T. (2001), 'Internet Trolls', 13 July. http://curezone.org/forums/troll.asp [14 January 2014].

Caraway, B. (2011), 'Audience Labor in the New Media Environment: A Marxian Revisiting', *Media, Culture & Society*, 33 (5): 693–708.

Carey, J. (1992), *Communication as Culture: Essays on Media and Society*, London: Routledge.

Carr, D. (2012), 'Newspaper as Business Pulpit', *New York Times*, 10 June. http:// www.nytimes.com/2012/06/11/business/media/san-diego-union-tribune-open -about-its-pro-business-motives.html?_r=0 [14 August 2013].

———. (2013), 'For Media Moguls, Paydays That Stand Out', *New York Times*, 5 May. http://www.nytimes.com/2013/05/06/business/media/for-media-moguls -paydays-that-outstrip-other-fields.html [13 August 2013].

Carroll, W. (2010), *The Making of a Transnationalist Capitalist Class: Corporate Power in the 21st Century*, London: Zed.

Carswell, D. (2012), *The End of Politics and the Birth of Democracy*, London: Biteback.

Castells, M. (2000), *The Rise of the Network Society: The Information Age: Economy, Society and Culture*, Oxford: Wiley.

———. (2007), 'Communication, Power and Counter-power in the Network Society', *International Journal of Communication* 1, 238–266.

———. (2009), *Communication Power*, Oxford: Oxford University Press.

———. (2011), 'A Network Theory of Power', *International Journal of Communication*, 5, 773–787.

———. (2012), *Networks of Outrage and Hope*, Cambridge: Polity.

Cater, D. (1965), *Power in Washington: A Critical Look at Today's Struggle to Govern in the U.S.A*, London: Collins.

Chakravartty, P. and Schiller, D. (2010), 'Global Financial Crisis: Neoliberal Newspeak and Digital Capitalism in Crisis', *International Journal of Communication*, 4: 670–692.

Chon, G., Strasburg, J. and Das, A. (2012), 'Some Big Firms Got Facebook Warning', *Wall Street Journal*, 24 May. http://online.wsj.com/article/SB1000142 405270230470760457742269091718950 0.html [5 September 2013].

Clegg, N. (2012), 'Witness Statement to Leveson Inquiry', 13 June. http://www .levesoninquiry.org.uk/wp-content/uploads/2012/06/Witness-Statement-of -Nick-Clegg-MP2.pdf [30 November 2013].

Clinton, H. (2010), 'Remarks on Internet Freedom', speech, Washington, DC, 21 January. http://www.state.gov/secretary/rm/2010/01/135519.htm [16 December 2013].

Cockburn, C. and Loach, L. (1986), 'In Whose Image?', in J. Curran, J. Ecclestone, G. Oakley and A. Richardson (eds), *Bending Reality: The State of the Media*, London: Pluto, 15–26.

Compaine, B. (2001), 'The Myths of Encroaching Global Media Ownership', *OpenDemocracy*, 8 November. http://www.opendemocracy.net/media -globalmediaownership/article_87.jsp [14 January 2014].

——— and Gomery, D. (2000[1979]), *Who Owns the Media? Competition and Concentration in the Mass Media Industry*, third edition, Mahwah, NJ: Lawrence Erlbaum.

Competition Commission. (2012), *Movies on Pay TV Market Investigation*, London: Competition Commission. http://www.competition-commission.org .uk/our-work/directory-of-all-inquiries/movies-on-pay-tv-market-investigation [15 January 2014].

comScore. (2013), 'comScore Releases "2013 UK Digital Future in Focus" report', 14 February. comScore_Releases_2013_UK_Digital_Future_in_Focus_Report [6 January 2014].

Cook, J. (2008), 'Intellectual Cleansing: Part Two', *Media Lens*, 7 October. http:// www.medialens.org/alerts/08/081007_intellectual_cleansing_part2.php [6 January 2014].

Cookson, R. (2012), 'Publishers' Talk to Unlock Ebook Market', *Financial Times*, 12 November. http://www.ft.com/cms/s/0/a8f285ee-2370-11e2-bb86 -00144feabdc0.html#axzz2qQCAY39n [6 January 2014].

Coote, A. and Lyall, S. (2013), *Strivers v. Skivers: The Workless Are Worthless*, London: New Economics Foundation. http://dnwssx4l7gl7s.cloudfront.net/ nefoundation/default/page/-/images/publications/Strivers%20vs.%20skivers _final.pdf [16 January 2014].

Corner, J. (2011), *Theorising Media: Power, Form and Subjectivity*, Manchester: Manchester University Press.

Couldry, N. (2000), *The Place of Media Power: Pilgrims and Witnesses of the Media Age*, London: Routledge.

———. (2003a), 'Beyond the Hall of Mirrors? Some Theoretical Reflections on the Global Contestation of Media Power', in N. Couldry and J. Curran (eds), *Contesting Media Power: Alternative Media in a Networked World*, Lanham: Rowman & Littlefield, 39–54.

———. (2003b), *Media Rituals: A Critical Approach*, London: Routledge.

———. (2009), 'Teaching Us to Fake It: The Ritualized Norms of Television's "Reality" Games', in S. Murray and L. Ouellette (eds), *Reality TV: Remaking Television Culture*, New York: New York University Press, 82–99.

———. (2010), *Why Voice Matters: Culture and Politics after Neoliberalism*, London: Sage.

———, and Curran, J. (2003), 'The Paradox of Media Power', in N. Couldry and J. Curran (eds), *Contesting Media Power: Alternative Media in a Networked World*, Lanham: Rowman & Littlefield, 3–15.

Cozens, C. (2003), 'Daily Mirror Sales Fall below 2m', *Guardian*, 11 April. http://www.guardian.co.uk/media/2003/apr/11/pressandpublishing.mirror [6 January 2014].

Craufurd Smith, R. and Tambini, D. (2012), 'Measuring Media Plurality in the United Kingdom: Policy Choices and Regulatory Challenges', *Journal of Media Law*, 4 (1): 35–63.

Crenson, M. (1971), *The Un-Politics of Air Pollution: A Study of Non-Decisionmaking in the Cities*, Baltimore: Johns Hopkins Press.

Cunningham, B. (2003), 'Re-thinking Objectivity', *Columbia Journalism Review*, 11 July. http://www.cjr.org/feature/rethinking_objectivity.php?page=all [16 January 2014].

Curran, J. (2002), *Media and Power*, London: Routledge.

———. (2012a), 'Witness Statement to the Leveson Inquiry', May. http://www.mediareform.org.uk/wordpress/wp-content/uploads/2013/04/Curran-statement-to-Leveson-Inquiry.pdf [14 August 2013].

———. (2012b), 'Rethinking Internet History', in J. Curran, N. Fenton and D. Freedman (eds), *Misunderstanding the Internet*, London: Routledge, 34–65.

———, Coen, S., Aalberg, T., Hayashi, K., Jones, P., Splendore, S., Papathanassopoulos, S., Rowe, D. and Tiffen, R. (2013), 'Internet Revolution Revisited: A Comparative Study of Online News', *Media, Culture and Society*, 35 (7): 880–897.

———, Fenton, N. and Freedman, D. (2012), *Misunderstanding the Internet*, London: Routledge.

Dahl, R. (1958), 'A Critique of the Ruling Elite Model', *American Political Science Review*, 52 (2): 463–469.

———. (2005[1961]), *Who Governs?: Democracy and Power in an American City*, second edition, New Haven: Yale University Press.

Davidoff, S. (2011), 'Gro17uponomics and Zyngametrics, but Few Sound Numbers', 12 October. http://query.nytimes.com/gst/fullpage.html?res=9C0DE2DD1638F931A25753C1A9679D8B63 [15 January 2014].

Davies, N. (2012), 'The Moment a Cynical Press Was Stopped in Its Tracks', *Guardian*, 28 February.

Davies, W. (2013), 'Neoliberalism and the Revenge of the "Social"', *openDemocracy*, 16 July. http://www.opendemocracy.net/william-davies/neoliberalism-and-revenge-of-"social" [14 January 2014].

Davis, A. (2007), *The Mediation of Power*, London: Routledge.

———. (2012), 'The Shifting Contours of Elite Power', *New Left Project*, 4 December. http://www.newleftproject.org/index.php/site/article_comments/the_shifting_contours_of_elite_power [14 January 2014].

Dayan, D. and Katz, E. (1992), *Media Events: The Live Broadcasting of History*, Cambridge: Harvard University Press.

DCMS (Department for Media, Culture and Sport). (2003), *Privacy and Media Intrusion. Cm 5985*, Norwich: The Stationery Office.

———. (2012), 'Competition in Content Markets', *Communications Review Seminar Series*. http://dcmscommsreview.readandcomment.com/wp-content/uploads/2012/06/seminar2_competition_paper_alt.pdf [16 December 2013].

———. (2013a), *Connectivity, Content and Consumers: Britain's Digital Platform for Growth*, July, London: DCMS.

———. (2013b), *Media Ownership and Plurality*, July, London: DCMS.

DeCarlo, S. (2013), 'The World's Biggest Companies', *Forbes*, 17 April. http://www.forbes.com/sites/scottdecarlo/2013/04/17/the-worlds-biggest-companies-2/ [13 August 2013].

della Porta, D. (2013), 'Bridging Research on Democracy, Social Movements and Communication', in B. Cammaerts, A. Mattoni and P. McCurdy (eds), *Mediation and Protest Movements*, Bristol: Intellect, 23–37.

Der Derian, J. (2009), *Virtuous War: Mapping the Military-Media-Industrial-Entertainment Network*, New York: Routledge.

De Tocqueville, A. (2003[1838]), *Democracy in America*, Clark, NJ: Lawbook Exchange.

Diakopoulos, N. (2012), 'Understanding Bias in Computational News Media', Nieman Journalism Lab, 10 December. http://www.niemanlab.org/2012/12/nick-diakopoulos-understanding-bias-in-computational-news-media/ [4 September 2013].

Diamandis, P. and Kotler, S. (2012), *Abundance: The Future Is Better than You Think*, New York: Free Press.

Dickenson, B. (2006), *Hollywood's New Radicalism: War, Globalisation and the Movies from Reagan to George W. Bush*, London: I.B. Tauris.

Dimaggio, A. (2008), *Mass Media, Mass Propaganda: Examining American News in the 'War on Terror'*, Lanham, MD: Lexington.

Ding, J. and Koh, L. (2013), *Mapping Digital Media: Malaysia*, London: Open Society Media Program.

Domhoff, W. (1967), *Who Rules America?*, Englewood Cliff, NJ: Prentice-Hall.

———. (2013), 'Wealth, Income and Power', *Who Rules America?* http://whorulesamerica.net/power/wealth.html [12 August 2013].

Downes, L. (2009), *The Laws of Disruption: Harnessing the New Forces That Govern Life and Business in the Digital Age*, New York: Basic Books.

Downie, Jr., L. and Schudson, M. (2009), 'The Reconstruction of American Journalism', *Columbia Journalism Review*, 19 October. http://www.cjr.org/reconstruction/the_reconstruction_of_american.php?page=all [13 August 2013].

Downing, J. (2001), *Radical Media: Rebellious Communication and Social Movements*, London: Sage.

Dullforce, A. (2013), 'FT 500 2013', *ft.com*, 22 July. http://www.ft.com/cms/s/0/16f6d1bc-f2c4-11e2-a203-00144feabdc0.html#axzz2bwL8nTIN [13 August].

Dye, T. (1976), *Who's Running America?*, Englewood Cliff, NJ: Prentice-Hall.

Economist. (2012), 'Another Game of Thrones', 1 December 2012. http://www
.economist.com/news/21567361-google-apple-facebook-and-amazon-are-each
-others-throats-all-sorts-ways-another-game [14 January 2014].

Edelman. (2012), *Edelman Trust Barometer: Global Results*. http://www
.slideshare.net/EdelmanInsights/2012-edelman-trust-barometer-global-deck [6
January 2014].

Edmonds, R. (2013), 'New Research Finds 92 Per cent of Time Spent on News
Consumption Is Still on Legacy Platforms', *Poynter*, 13 May. http://www
.poynter.org/latest-news/business-news/the-biz-blog/212550/new-research
-finds-92-percent-of-news-consumption-is-still-on-legacy-platforms/ [6 January
2014].

Edwards, D. and Cromwell, D. (2006), *Guardians of Power: The Myth of the
Liberal Media*, London: Pluto.

Eggerton, J. (2013), 'Cross-Ownership Study: Impact on Minority/Female
Ownership "Probably Negligible"', *Broadcasting & Cable*, 30 May. http://www
.broadcastingcable.com/article/493763-Cross_Ownership_Study_Impact_on
_Minority_Female_Ownership_Probably_Negligible_.php [14 August 2013].

Elberse, A. (2008), 'Should You Invest in the Long Tail?', *Harvard Business
Review*, July–August, 1–11.

Essential Media Communications. (2013a), *Essential Report: Trust in Institutions*,
18 March. http://essentialvision.com.au/trust-in-institutions-3 [6 January 2014].

———. (2013b), *Essential Report: Corruption – in Industries*, 15 October. http://
essentialvision.com.au/corruption—in-industries [6 January 2014].

European Commission. (2012), *Standard Eurobarometer 78: Media Use in the
European Union*. Brussels: EC. http://ec.europa.eu/public_opinion/archives/eb/
eb78/eb78_media_en.pdf [6 January 2014].

———. (2013), *Preparing for a Fully Converged Audiovisual World: Growth,
Creation and Values*, green paper. COM(2013) 231 final, 24 April. Brussels: EC.
http://eur-lex.europa.eu/LexUriServ/LexUriServ.do?uri=COM:2013:0231:FIN:E
N:PDF [14 January 2014].

FCC (Federal Communications Commission). (2005), *Internet Policy Statement*,
FCC 05–151, 5 August. http://hraunfoss.fcc.gov/edocs_public/attachmatch/
FCC-05-151A1.pdf [16 December 2013].

———. (2011), *Quadrennial Regulatory Review of Broadcast Ownership
Rules*, FCC 11–186, 22 December. http://hraunfoss.fcc.gov/edocs_public/
attachmatch/FCC-11-186A1.pdf [16 December 2013].

Facebook. (2014),'Facebook Principles'. https://www.facebook.com/principles.php
[15 January 2014].

Fenton, N. (2012), 'The Internet and Radical Politics', in J. Curran, N. Fenton and
D. Freedman (eds), *Misunderstanding the Internet*, London: Routledge, 149–176.

Financial Times. (2013), 'FT 500', n.d. http://www.ft.com/indepth/ft500 [13 August
2013].

Fischer, F. (2003), *Reframing Public Policy*, Oxford: Oxford University Press.

Fisher, M. (2013), 'How to Kill a Zombie: Strategizing the End of Neoliberalism',
openDemocracy, 18 July. http://www.opendemocracy.net/mark-fisher/how-to
-kill-zombie-strategizing-end-of-neoliberalism [14 January 2014].

Fiske, J. (1989), *Television Culture*, London: Routledge.

Fitzgerald, S. (2012), *Corporations and Cultural Industries*, Lanham: Lexington Books.

Fleming, P. (2013), 'Common as Silence', *Ephemera*, 13 (3): 627–640.

Flew, T. (2008), 'A Game of Two Halves', *Australian Journalism Review*, 30 (2): 127–129.

———. (2013), 'Factcheck: Does Murdoch Own 70% of Newspapers in Australia?', *The Conversation*, 7 August, http://theconversation.com/factcheck -does-murdoch-own-70-of-newspapers-in-australia-16812 [6 January 2014].

Forbes. (2013a), 'The World's Biggest Public Companies', n.d. http://www.forbes .com/global2000/list/ [13 August 2013].

———. (2013b), 'The Richest People on the Planet 2013', *Forbes*, 25 March. http://www.forbes.com/sites/luisakroll/2013/03/04/inside-the-2013-billionaires -list-facts-and-figures/ [14 August 2013].

Foucault, M. (1977), *Discipline and Punish: The Birth of the Prison*, London: Allen Lane.

———. (1979), *The History of Sexuality, Vol 1*, London: Allen Lane.

———. (1980), *Power/Knowledge: Selected Interviews and Other Writings 1972–1977*, Brighton: Harvester.

———. (1990), *The History of Sexuality: An Introduction*, New York: Vintage.

Freedman, D. (2003), 'The Daily Mirror and the War on Iraq', *Mediactive*, issue 3, London: Barefoot, 95–108.

———. (2008), *The Politics of Media Policy*, Cambridge: Polity.

———. (2012a), 'Measuring Media Plurality Isn't Enough', LSE Media Policy Project, 25 June. http://blogs.lse.ac.uk/mediapolicyproject/2012/06/25/ measuring-media-plurality-isnt-enough/ [14 January 2014].

———. (2012b), 'Web 2.0 and the Death of the Blockbuster Economy', in J. Curran, N. Fenton and D. Freedman (eds), *Misunderstanding the Internet*, London: Routledge, 69–94.

———. (2013), 'Year After Leveson: Has British Press Cleaned Up Its Act?', *CNN Online*, 29 November. http://edition.cnn.com/2013/11/29/opinion/uk-leveson -press-opinion/index.html?iref=allsearch [30 November 2013].

———. (forthcoming 2014), 'Truth Over Justice: The Leveson Inquiry and the Implications for Democracy', in C. Greenfield and P. Dearman (eds), *How We Are Governed*, Cambridge: Cambridge Scholars.

Freeman, J. L. (1965), *The Political Process: Executive Bureau-Legislative Committee Relations*, New York: Random House.

Friedman, W. (2012), 'TV News Shows Spike in Viewers, Ratings', *mediapost. com*, 19 March. http://www.mediapost.com/publications/article/170550/tv -news-shows-spike-in-viewers-ratings.html [14 January 2014].

Fuchs, C. (2009), 'Information and Communication Technologies and Society: A Contribution to the Critique of the Political Economy of the Internet', *European Journal of Communication*, 24 (1): 69–87.

———. (2013), *Digital Labour and Karl Marx*, London: Routledge.

Fund, J. (2010), 'The Net Neutrality Coup', *Wall Street Journal*, 21 December. http://online.wsj.com/news/articles/SB10001424052748703886904576031512 110086694 [16 December 2013].

Galloway, A. (2004), *Protocol: How Control Exists after Decentralization*, Boston: MIT Press.

Galperin, H. (2004), *New Television, Old Politics: The Transition to Digital TV in the United States and Britain*, Cambridge: Cambridge University Press.

Garfield, B. (2009), *The Chaos Scenario*, Nashville: Stielstra Publishing.

Garland, C. and Harper, S. (2012), 'Did Somebody Say Neoliberalism?: On the Uses and Limitations of a Critical Concept in Media and Communications', *tripleC*, 10 (2): 413–424.

Garnham, N. (1990), *Capitalism and Communication*, London: Sage.

Gauntlett, D. (2011), *Making Is Connecting: The Social Meaning of Creativity from DIY and Knitting to YouTube and Web 2.0*, Cambridge: Polity.

Genachowski, J. (2009), 'The Open Internet: Preserving the Freedom to Innovate', *Huffington Post*, 21 September. http://www.huffingtonpost.com/ julius-genachowski/the-open-internet-preserv_b_293147.html [16 December 2013].

———. (2010), 'Remarks on Preserving Internet Freedom and Openness', Washington, DC, 1 December. http://www.fcc.gov/document/federal -communications-commission-chairman-julius-genachowski-remarks -preserving-internet-f [16 December 2013].

Giddens, A. (1979), *Central Problems in Social Theory: Action, Structure and Contradiction in Social Analysis*, London: Macmillan.

Gillmor, D. (2011), '2012 Will Be the Year of the Content-controller Oligopoly', *Nieman Journalism Lab*, 20 December. http://www.niemanlab.org/2011/12/ dan-gillmor-2012-will-be-the-year-of-the-content-controller-oligopoly/ [4 September 2013].

Gilroy, A. (2013), 'Access to Broadband Networks: The Net Neutrality Debate', 14 February, Washington, DC: Congressional Research Service.

Ginsborg, P. (2005), *Silvio Berlusconi: Television, Power and Patrimony*, London: Verso.

Gitlin, T. (1980), *The Whole World Is Watching: Mass Media in the Making & Unmaking of the New Left*, Berkeley: University of California Press.

———. (2013), 'The Washington Post Doesn't Need a New-Media Mogul – It Needs an Old-Fashioned One', *New Republic*, 13 August. http://www .newrepublic.com/article/114286/jeff-bezos-washington-post-needs-old -fashioned-mogul [14 January 2014].

Golding, P. and Murdock, G. (2000), 'Culture, Communications and Political Economy', in J. Curran and M. Gurevitch (eds), *Mass Media and Society*, third edition, London: Arnold, 70–92.

Gomez, R. and Sosa-Plata, G. (2011), *Mapping Digital Media: Mexico*, London: Open Society Media Program. http://www.opensocietyfoundations.org/sites/ default/files/mapping-digital-media-mexico-20130605_0.pdf [14 August 2013].

Google. (n.d.), 'Ten Things That We Know to Be True', Google. http://www.google .co.uk/about/company/philosophy/ [14 January 2014].

Gorman, S. and Valentino-Devries, J. (2013), 'New Details Show Broader NSA Suerveillance Reach', *Wall Street Journal*, 20 August. http://online.wsj .com/news/articles/SB1000142412788732410820457902287409173247 0?mg=reno64-wsj&url=http%3A%2F%2Fonline.wsj.com%2Farticle%2 FSB10001424127887324108204579022874091732470.html [14 January 2014].

Gramsci, A. (1971), *Selections from the Prison Notebooks*, London: Lawrence & Wishart.

———. (1985), *Selections from Cultural Writings*, London: Lawrence & Wishart.

Grayson, D. and Freedman, D. (2013), 'Leveson and the Prospects for Media Reform', *Soundings*, 53 Spring, 69–81.

Greenslade, R. (2003), 'Their Master's Voice', *The Guardian*, 17 February. http://www.theguardian.com/media/2003/feb/17/mondaymediasection.iraq [6 January 2014].

Groksop, V. (2010), 'David Yelland: Rupert Murdoch Is a Closet Liberal', *Evening Standard*, 29 March. http://www.standard.co.uk/lifestyle/david-yelland-rupert-murdoch-is-a-closet-liberal-6732847.html [14 August 2013].

Grossman, L. (2006), 'You – Yes, You – Are TIME's Person of the Year', *Time*, 25 December. http://content.time.com/time/printout/0,8816,1570810,00.html [3 September 2013].

Groupon. (n.d.), Mission Statement. http://www.techvibes.com/company-directory/groupon [15 January 2014].

Guardian. (2013a), 'The NSA Files', *Guardian*, n.d. http://www.theguardian.com/world/the-nsa-files [14 August 2013].

———. (2013b), 'MediaGuardian 100', *Guardian*, 2 September.

Gye, H. and Boyle, L. (2012), 'The Blunder that Cost Google $24 BILLION in EIGHT minutes', *Mail Online*, 18 October. http://www.dailymail.co.uk/news/article-2219751/Google-shares-suspended-20-drop-profits-accidentally-revealed-early.html [5 September 2013].

Hackett, R. and Carroll, W. (2006), *Remaking Media: The Struggle to Democratize Public Communication*, London: Routledge.

Hall, S. (1986), 'Media Power and Class Power', in J. Curran, J. Ecclestone, G. Oakley and A. Richardson (eds), *Bending Reality: The State of the Media*, London: Pluto, 5–14.

Hallin, D. (1986), *The Uncensored War*, Oxford: Oxford University Press.

———. (1994), *We Keep America on Top of the World: Television Journalism and the Public Sphere*, London: Routledge.

Harris, J. (2011), 'How the Phone-hacking Scandal Unmasked the British Power Elite', *Guardian*, 18 July. http://www.theguardian.com/media/2011/jul/18/phone-hacking-british-power-elite [14 January 2014].

Harvey, D. (2005), *A Brief History of Neoliberalism*, Oxford: Oxford University Press.

———. (2014), *Seventeen Contradictions and the End of Capitalism*, London: Profile.

Havens, T., Lotz, A. and Tinic, S. (2009), 'Critical Media Industry Studies: A Research Approach', *Communication, Culture & Critique*, 2: 234–253.

Helm, T., Doward, J. and Boffey, D. (2011), 'Rupert Murdoch's Empire must be Dismantled – Ed Miliband', *Guardian*, 16 July. http://www.guardian.co.uk/politics/2011/jul/16/rupert-murdoch-ed-miliband-phone-hacking [14 January 2014].

Herman, E. (2000), 'The Propaganda Model: A Retrospective', *Journalism Studies*, 1 (1): 101–112.

———. and Chomsky, N. (1988), *Manufacturing Consent: The Political Economy of the Mass Media*, New York: Pantheon.

Hermida, A. (2010), 'From TV to Twitter: How Ambient News Became Ambient Journalism', *M/C Journal*, 13 (2). http://www.journal.media-culture.org.au/index.php/mcjournal/article/viewArticle/220 [14 January 2014].

Hesmondhalgh, D. (2001), 'Ownership Is Only Part of the Picture', *openDemocracy*, 28 November. http://www.opendemocracy.net/media-globalmediaownership/article_46.jsp [14 August 2013].

———. (2013), *The Cultural Industries*, third edition, London: Sage.

Hickman, M. (2012), 'Rupert Murdoch Did Try to Dictate Government Policy on EU, Says Sir John Major', *Independent*, 13 June. http://www.independent.co.uk/news/uk/politics/rupert-murdoch-did-try-to-dictate-government-policy-on-eu-says-sir-john-major-7845036.html [14 August 2013].

Hiltzik, M. and Eller, C. (1995), 'Chemistry Made Talks Quick, Quiet', *Los Angeles Times*, 1 August. http://articles.latimes.com/1995-08-01/news/mn-30183_1_walt-disney [14 August 2013].

Hood, S. (1980), *On Television*, London: Pluto.

Hopewell, L. (2013), 'Turnbull: Our Broadband Plan Could Cost Same as NBN, but with a Catch', *Gizmodo*, 16 April. http://www.gizmodo.com.au/2013/04/turnbull-our-broadband-plan-could-cost-the-same-as-the-nbn-but-with-a-catch/ [15 September 2013].

Horwitz, R. (1989), *The Irony of Regulatory Reform: The Deregulation of American Telecommunications*, Oxford: Oxford University Press.

Hounshell, B. (2011), 'The Revolution Will Be Tweeted', *Foreign Policy*, 20 June. http://www.foreignpolicy.com/articles/2011/06/20/the_revolution_will_be_tweeted [14 January 2014].

Huff, M. (2011), 'Project "Censored 2012": Moving Beyond Media Reform. *truthout.org*, 7 September. http://www.truth-out.org/opinion/item/3160:project-censored-2012-moving-beyond-media-reform [6 January 2014].

Hunt, J. (2011), 'A Communications Review for the Digital Age', *open letter*, 16 May. https://www.gov.uk/government/uploads/system/uploads/attachment_data/file/72929/commsreview-open-letter_160511.pdf [16 December 2013].

Institute for Public Policy Research (2009), *Mind the Funding Gap: The Potential of Industry Levies for Continued Funding of Public Service Broadcasting*, London: IPPR.

Interactive Advertising Bureau. (2013), *IAB Internet Advertising Revenue Report: 2012 Full Year Results*. http://www.iab.net/media/file/IAB_Webinar_PWC_Presentation_FY2012_April_16_2013.pdf [3 September 2013].

International Telecommunication Union. (2012), *The State of Broadband 2012: Achieving Digital Inclusion for All. A Report by the Broadband Commission*, Geneva: ITU.

Ipsos, MORI. (2013), 'Trust in Professions', 3 December. http://www.ipsos-mori.com/researchpublications/researcharchive/15/Trust-in-Professions.aspx?view=wide [6 January 2014].

Jakubowski, F. (1976), *Ideology and Superstructure in Historical Materialism*, London: Allison & Busby.

Janeway, W. (2012), *Doing Capitalism in the Innovation Economy*, Cambridge: Cambridge University Press.

Jansen, S. (1991), *Censorship: The Knot That Binds Power and Knowledge*, Oxford: Oxford University Press.

Jarvis, J. (2009), *What Would Google Do?*, New York: Harper Collins.

——. (2011), *Public Parts: How Sharing in the Digital Age Improves the Way We Work and Live*, New York: Simon & Schuster.

Jenkins, H. (2006), *Convergence Culture*, New York: New York University Press.

Jenkins, S. (2011), 'This Is Not a Berlin Wall Moment – Just Daft Hysteria', *Guardian*, 20 July.

——. (2013), 'Is Glenn Greenwald's Journalism Now Viewed as a "terrorist" Occupation?', *Guardian*, 19 August. http://www.theguardian.com/

commentisfree/2013/aug/19/glenn-greenwald-journalism-david-miranda
-detention [19 August 2013].

Jones, O. (2014), 'Benefits Street', *Independent*, 8 January. http://www
.independent.co.uk/voices/comment/benefits-street-a-healthy-media
-would-stand-up-to-the-powerful-and-wealthy-ours-targets-the-poor-and
-voiceless-9046773.html [16 January 2014].

Kampfner, J. (2011), 'The Phone Hacking Inquiry Must Shackle Corporate
Power, not Journalists', *Guardian*, 9 November. http://www.guardian.co.uk/
commentisfree/2011/nov/09/leveson-james-murdoch-phone-hacking [6 January
2014].

Kerr, D. (2013), 'App Market Soars with 13.4 Billion Downloads in Q1 2013', *CNET*,
8 April. http://news.cnet.com/8301-1035_3-57578563-94/app-market-soars
-with-13.4-billion-downloads-in-q1-2013/ [14 January 2014].

Kirkpatrick, B. (2013), 'Vernacular Policymaking and the Cultural Turn in Media
Policy Studies', *Communication, Culture and Critique*, 6: 634–647.

Kroes, N. (2010), 'Net neutrality in Europe', speech to ARCEP Conference, Paris,
13 April. http://europa.eu/rapid/press-release_SPEECH-10-153_en.htm [16
December 2013].

Kroll, L. (2013), 'Mapping the Wealth of the World's Billionaires', *Forbes.com*, 9
March. http://www.forbes.com/sites/luisakroll/2013/03/09/mapping-the-wealth
-of-the-worlds-billionaires/ [13 August 2013].

Kumar, D. (2008), *Outside the Box: Corporate Media, Globalization, and the UPS
Strike*, Chicago: University of Illinois Press.

Kunzler, M. (2012), '"It's the Idea, Stupid!" How Ideas Challenge Broadcasting
Liberalization', in N. Just and M. Puppis (eds), *Trends in Communication Policy
Research*, Bristol: Intellect, 55–74.

Lanier, J. (2013), 'Fixing the Digital Economy', *New York Times*, 8 June. http://
www.nytimes.com/2013/06/09/opinion/sunday/fixing-the-digital-economy
.html?pagewanted=all&_r=0 [5 September 2013].

Lazarsfeld, P. and Merton, R. (2004 [1948]), 'Mass Communication, Popular Taste
and Organized Social Action', in J. D. Peters and P. Simonson (eds), *Mass
Communication and American Social Thought: Key Texts, 1919–1968*, Lanham,
MD: Rowman & Littlefield, 230–242.

Leadbeater, C. (2008), *We-Think*, London: Profile.

Lebedev, E. (2012), 'Written Submission to the Leveson Inquiry', 18 July. http://
www.levesoninquiry.org.uk/wp-content/uploads/2012/10/Further-Witness
-Statement-from-Evgeny-Lebedev.pdf [14 January 2014].

Lee, D. (2013), 'App Stores "full of zombies" Claim on Apple Anniversary', *BBC
News*, 10 July. http://www.bbc.co.uk/news/technology-23240971 [14 January
2014].

Leigh, D. (2012), 'David Cameron Admits to Private Dinners for Tory Donors',
Guardian, 27 March.

Lens, Media. (2009), 'Putting Out the People's Eyes', *Media Lens Alert*, 17
February. http://www.medialens.org/index.php/alerts/alert-archive/2009/560
-putting-out-the-peoples-eyes.html [8 January 2014].

Lentz, B. (2013), 'Excavating Historicity in the U.S. Network Neutrality Debate:
An Interpretive Perspective on Policy Change', *Communication, Culture &
Critique*, 6, December, 568–597.

Leonard, T. (1986), *The Power of the Press: The Birth of American Political Reporting*, New York: Oxford University Press.

Lessig, L. (2006), *Code*, New York: Basic Books.

———. (2008), *Remix: Making Art and Commerce Thrive in the Hybrid Economy*, London: Bloomsbury.

———. and McChesney, R. (2006), 'No Tolls on the Internet', *Washington Post*, 8 June. http://www.washingtonpost.com/wp-dyn/content/article/2006/06/07/AR2006060702108.html [16 December 2013].

Lessin, J. and Ante, S. (2013), 'Apps Rocket Toward $25 Billion in Sales', *Wall Street Journal*, 4 March. http://online.wsj.com/news/articles/SB10001424127887323293704578334401534217878 [14 January 2014].

Leveson, Lord Justice. (2012), *An Inquiry into the Culture, Practices and Ethics of the Press*, Executive Summary, November, London: The Stationery Office.

Lewis, G. (2007), *Virtual Thailand: The Media and Cultural Politics in Thailand, Malaysia and Singapore*, New York: Routledge.

Leys, C. (2001), *Market-driven Politics: Neoliberal Democracy and the Public Interest*, London: Verso.

Lichter, S. R., Rothman, S. and Lichter, L. (1986), *The Media Elite*, Chevy Chase, MD: Adler & Adler.

Lieberman, D. (2013), 'Comcast and Carmike Steal the Show in an Unusually Good Year for Media Stocks', *Deadline Hollywood*, 1 January. http://www.deadline.com/2013/01/media-stocks-performance-2012/#more-394050 [14 August 2013].

Lindblom, C. (1977), *Politics and Markets: The World's Political and Economic Systems*, New York: Basic Books.

Lloyd, J. (2004), *What the Media Are Doing to Our Politics*, London: Constable.

Lukacs, G. (2000 [1925/1926]), *A Defence of History and Class Consciousness: Tailism and the Dialectic*, London: Verso.

Lukes, S. (2005 [1974]), *Power: A Radical View*, second edition, Basingstoke: Palgrave.

———. (2012), 'Dimensions of Elite Power', *New Left Project*, 7 December. http://www.newleftproject.org/index.php/site/article_comments/dimensions_of_elite_power [14 January 2014].

Luxemburg, R. (1989 [1899]), *Reform or Revolution*, London: Bookmarks.

MacAskill, E. (2013), 'NSA Paid Millions to Cover Prism Compliance Costs for Tech Companies', *Guardian*, 23 August. http://www.theguardian.com/world/2013/aug/23/nsa-prism-costs-tech-companies-paid/print [14 January 2014].

Mair, J. and Keeble, R. (2012), *The Phone Hacking Scandal: Journalism on Trial*, Bury St Edmunds: Abramis.

Management Today. (2013), 'Hollywood's Dwindling Share of Global Box Office Revenue', 26 April. http://www.managementtoday.co.uk/features/1178997/hollywoods-dwindling-share-global-box-office-revenue/ [14 August 2013].

Mandelson, P. (2009), 'Mandelson Warns against "Clumsy" Web Regulation', *Financial Times*, 18 May. http://www.ft.com/cms/s/0/cc77881a-43f0-11de-a9be-00144feabdc0.html?siteedition=uk#axzz2njaYr0Ex [15 December 2013].

Mansell, R. (2004), 'Political Economy, Power and New Media', *New Media and Society*, 6 (1): 96–105.

Marcuse, H. (1969 [1965]), 'Repressive tolerance', in R. Wolff, B. Moore and H. Marcuse (eds), *A Critique of Pure Tolerance*, London: Cape, 95–137.

Marez, C. (2013), 'From Mr Chips to Scarface, or Racial Capitalism in Breaking Bad', *Critical Inquiry*, 25 September. http://critinq.wordpress.com/2013/09/25/breaking-bad/ [6 January 2014].

Margolis, M. (1998), 'In the Company of Giants', in N. Woodhull and R. Snyder (eds), *Media Mergers*, New Brunswick: Transaction Publishers, 143–151.

Martin, R. (2002), *Financialization of Daily Life*, Philadelphia: Temple University Press.

Marx, K. (1909), *Capital: A Critique of Political Economy*, Vol 3, Chicago: Charles A. Kerr.

———. (1963), *Selected Writings in Sociology and Social Philosophy*, Harmondsworth: Penguin.

———. (1969 [1865]), *Value, Price and Profit*, New York: International Publishers.

———. (1973 [1858]), *Grundrisse: Foundations of the Critique of Political Economy*, London: Allen Lane.

———. (1976a), *Marx and Engels Collected Works*, Vol 3, New York: International Publishers.

———. (1976b), *Marx and Engels Collected Works*, Vol 32, New York: International Publishers.

———. and Engels, F. (1975 [1848]), *Manifesto of the Communist Party*, Peking: Foreign Languages Press.

Mason, P. (2012), *Why It's Kicking Off Everywhere: The New Global Revolutions*, London: Verso.

———. (2013), 'Which Should I Leave First, Twitter or Facebook?' *Guardian*, 19 August. http://www.theguardian.com/commentisfree/2013/aug/19/leave-twitter-facebook-paul-mason [6 April 2014].

Mastrini, G. and Becerra, M. (2011), 'Media Ownership, Oligarchies, and Globalization: Media Concentration in South America', in D. Winseck and D. Jin (eds), *The Political Economies of Media: The Transformation of the Global Media Industries*, London: Bloomsbury, 66–83.

Mayer-Schonberger, V. (2009), *Delete: The Virtue of Forgetting in the Digital Age*, Princeton: Princeton University Press.

McChesney, R. (2000), *Rich Media, Poor Democracy*, New York: New Press.

———. (2004), *The Problem of the Media*, New York: Monthly Review Press.

———. (2008), 'The U.S. Reform Movement: Going Forward', *Monthly Review*, 60 (4): 51–59.

———. (2013), *Digital Disconnect: How Capitalism Is Turning the Internet against Democracy*, New York: The New Press.

———. and Nichols, J. (2010), *The Death and Life of American Journalism*, New York: Basic Books.

McCullagh, C. (2002), *Media Power: A Sociological Introduction*, Basingstoke: Palgrave.

McKnight, D. (2013), *Murdoch's Politics; How One Man's Thirst for Wealth and Power Shapes Our World*, London: Pluto.

McLuhan, M. (1964), *Understanding Media: The Extensions of Man*, London: Routledge & Kegan Paul.

McNair, B. (2006), *Cultural Chaos*, New York: Routledge.

Media Reform Coalition. (2012), *Time for Media Reform: Proposals for a Free and Accountable Media*, London: Media Reform Coalition. http://www.mediareform.org.uk/wp-content/uploads/2012/09/time-for-media-reform.pdf [14 January 2014].

Meek, J. (2013), 'It's the Moral Thing to Do', *London Review of Books*, 3 January. http://www.lrb.co.uk/v35/n01/james-meek/its-the-moral-thing-to-do [6 January 2014].

Mele, N. (2013), *The End of Big: How the Internet Makes David the New Goliath*, New York: St Martins Press.

Mendes, E. (2013), 'In U.S., Trust in Media Recovers Slightly from All-Time Low', gallup.com, 19 September. http://www.gallup.com/poll/164459/trust-media-recovers-slightly-time-low.aspx. [6 January 2014].

Meyer, D. (2013), 'Microsoft down to fifth place in comScore's global search stats, thanks to Yandex', GigaOM, 6 February. http://gigaom.com/2013/02/06/microsoft-down-to-fifth-place-in-comscores-global-search-stats-thanks-to-yandex/ [2 September 2013].

Miliband, R. (1962), 'Tribute to C. Wright Mills', originally published in *New Left Review* 15, 1962. http://www.newleftproject.org/index.php/site/article _comments/tribute_to_c_wright_mills [14 January 2014].

———. (1969), *The State in Capitalist Society*, London: Camelot Press.

Miller, D. (2002), 'Media Power and Class Power: Overplaying Ideology', in L. Panitch and C. Leys (eds), *Socialist Register*, Woodbridge: Merlin Press, 245–264.

———. (2004), 'The Propaganda Machine', in D. Miller (ed.), *Tell me Lies: Propaganda and Media Distortion in the Attack on Iraq*, London: Pluto, 80–99.

———. (2011), *Tales from Facebook*, Cambridge: Polity.

———. and Dinan, W. (2008), *A Century of Spin*, London: Pluto.

Miller, P. and Rose, N. (1997), 'Mobilising the Consumer: Assembling the Subject of Consumption', *Theory, Culture and Society*, 14 (1): 1–36.

Mills, C. Wright, (1959), *The Power Elite*, New York: Oxford University Press.

Mirowski, P. (2013), *Never Let a Serious Crisis Go to Waste: How Neoliberalism Survived the Financial Meltdown*, London: Verso.

Mirsky, N. (2014), 'Benefits Street Struck a Nerve – Exposing How Vital a Documentary It Is', *Guardian*, 10 January. http://www.theguardian.com/commentisfree/2014/jan/10/benefits-street-documentary-reality [16 January 2014].

Moore, A. (2011), *No Straight Lines: Making Sense of our Non-linear World*, Cambridge: Bloodstone Books.

Moore, C. (2011), 'I'm Starting to Think That the Left Might Actually be Right', *Telegraph*, 22 July. http://www.telegraph.co.uk/news/politics/8655106/Im-starting-to-think-that-the-Left-might-actually-be-right.html [14 August 2013].

Morgan, P. (2005), *The Insider*, London: Ebury Press.

Morning Star. (2012), 'Leveson: A Tiger with No Teeth?', 9 July.

Morozov, E. (2011), *The Net Delusion: How Not to Liberate the World*, London: Allen Lane.

———. (2012), 'Muzzled by the Bots', *Slate*, 26 October. http://www.newrepublic.com/article/113045/free-speech-internet-silicon-valley-making-rules [4 September 2013].

———. (2013), *To Save Everything, Click Here: Technology, Solutionism, and the Urge to Fix Problems That Don't Exist*, London: Allen Lane.

Mosco, V. (2009), *The Political Economy of Communication*, second edition, London: Sage.

Murdoch, R. (2009), 'The Future of Journalism Is More Promising than Ever', *Speech to the Federal Trade Commission*, 3 December. http://www.pressgazette.co.uk/story.asp?sectioncode=6&storycode=44737&c=1 [14 January 2014].

———. (2012), 'Oral Evidence to the Leveson Inquiry', 25 April. http://www.levesoninquiry.org.uk/wp-content/uploads/2012/04/Transcript-of-Morning-Hearing-25-April-2012.pdf [14 January 2014].

Murdock, G. and Golding, P. (1977), 'Capitalism, Communication and Class Relations', in J. Curran, M. Gurevitch and J. Woollacott (eds), *Mass Communication and Society*, London: Arnold, 12–43.

———. (2005), 'Culture, Communications and Political Economy', in J. Curran and M. Gurevitch (eds), *Mass Media and Society*, fourth edition, New York: Hodder Arnold, 60–83.

Murthy, D. (2013), *Twitter: Social Communication in the Twitter Age*, Cambridge: Polity.

Naim, M. (2013), *The End of Power: From Boardrooms to Battlefields and Churches to States, Why Being in Charge Isn't What It Used to Be*, New York: Basic Books.

Naughton, J. (2012), *From Gutenberg to Zuckerberg: What You Really Need to Know About the Internet*, London: Quercus.

Neate, R. (2012), 'Facebook Paid £2.9m Tax on £840m Profits Made Outside US, Figures Show', *Guardian*, 23 December. http://www.theguardian.com/technology/2012/dec/23/facebook-tax-profits-outside-us [5 September 2013].

Negroponte, N. (1996), *Being Digital*, London: Coronet.

netmarketshare. (2013), *Market Share Reports*, December. https://www.netmarketshare.com [14 January 2014].

Nichols, J. (2010), 'In a Year of Deep Disappointments, The Deepest: Obama Pledged to Protect Internet Freedom, But His FCC Put It at Risk', *The Nation*, 31 December.

———. and McChesney, R. (2013), *Dollarocracy: How the Money and Media Complex Is Destroying America*, New York: Nation Books.

Nineham, C. (2013), *Making the News: The Media and the Movement against the Iraq War*, unpublished PhD dissertation, University of Westminster.

Nunberg, G. (2009), *The Years of Talking Dangerously*, New York: Public Affairs.

Nye, J. (2011), *The Future of Power*, New York: Public Affairs.

OECD. (2013), *OECD Communications Outlook 2013*, Paris: OECD Publishing.

Ofcom. (2012), *Measuring Media Plurality*, June, London: Ofcom.

———. (2013), *Communication Market Review 2013*, London: Ofcom.

Ohmae, K. (1996), *The End of the Nation State: The Rise of Regional Economies*, New York: Free Press.

O'Neill, O. (2004), *Rethinking Freedom of the Press*, Dublin: Royal Irish Academy.

Paige, J. (2013), 'British Public Wrong about Nearly Everything, Survey Shows', *The Independent*, 9 July. http://www.independent.co.uk/news/uk/home-news/british-public-wrong-about-nearly-everything-survey-shows-8697821.html [6 January 2014].

Parenti, M. (1993), *Inventing Reality: The Politics of News Media*, New York: St Martins Press.

Parsons, T. (1963), 'On the Concept of Political Power', *Proceedings of the American Philosophical Society*, 107 (3): 232–262.

———. (1967), *Sociological Theory and Modern Society*, New York: Free Press.

Peck, J. (2008), *The Age of Oprah: Cultural Icon for the Neoliberal Age*, Boulder: Paradigm.

———. and Brenner, N. (2009), 'Postneoliberalism and Its Malcontents', *Antipode*, 41 (6): 1236–1258.

Pew (2012a), *In Changing News Landscape, Even Television Is Vulnerable*, Washington, DC: Pew Research Centre for the People & The Press. http://www.people-press.org/files/legacy-pdf/2012%20News%20Consumption%20Report.pdf [4 September 2013].

———. (2012b), 'Trend Data (Teens)', Pew Internet & American Life Project. http://www.pewinternet.org/Static-Pages/Trend-Data-(Teens)/Online-Activites-Total.aspx [4 September 2013].

———. (2013), 'Trend Data (Adults)', Pew Internet & American Life Project. http://www.pewinternet.org/Static-Pages/Trend-Data-(Adults)/Online-Activites-Total.aspx [4 September 2013].

Pham, A. (2013), 'iTunes Market Share Still Dominant after a Decade, Study Says', *Hollywood Reporter*, 17 April. http://www.hollywoodreporter.com/news/itunes-market-share-still-dominant-441063 [6 January 2014].

Philip, P. and Karaganis, J. (2007), 'Toward a Federal Data Agenda for Communications Policymaking', *CommLaw Conspectus*, 16: 53–96.

Philo, G., Briant, E. and Donald, P. (2013), *Bad News for Refugees*, London: Pluto.

Pickard, V. (2014), *Media, Democracy and Market Failure: The Postwar Triumph of Corporate Libertarianism in America*, Cambridge: Cambridge University Press.

Pilger, J. (1999), *Hidden Agendas*, London: Vintage.

———. (2012), 'The Leveson Inquiry into the British Press – Oh, What a Lovely Game', *johnpilger.com*, 31 May. http://johnpilger.com/articles/the-leveson-inquiry-into-the-british-press-oh-what-a-lovely-game [6 January 2014].

Plunkett, J. (2005), 'Murdoch Calls for "Bonfire" of Media Regulations', *Guardian*, 22 September. http://www.theguardian.com/media/2005/sep/22/broadcasting.bskyb2 [15 December 2013].

———. (2014), 'Benefits Street Boss: "There isn't Enough Aftercare for People Who've Been on TV"', *Guardian*, 12 January. http://www.theguardian.com/media/2014/jan/12/benefits-street-richard-mckerrow-channel-4 [16 January 2014].

Qualman, E. (2009), *Socialnomics: How Social Media Transforms the Way We Live and Do Business*, Hoboken, NJ: Wiley.

Quiggin, J. (2010), *Zombie Economics: How Dead Ideas Still Walk among Us*, Princeton: Princeton University Press.

Ray, T. (2013), 'Google Off 5%: Q2 Misses as "Cost-Per-Click" Falls 6%', *Tech Trader Daily*, 18 July. http://blogs.barrons.com/techtraderdaily/2013/07/18/google-off-5-q2-misses-as-cost-per-click-falls-6/ [15 January 2014].

Rees, J. (1998), *The Algebra of Revolution: The Dialectic and the Classical Marxist Tradition*, London: Routledge.

Richards, E. (2010), 'Speech on Net Neutrality', *Cable Congress*, 3 March. http://media.ofcom.org.uk/2010/03/03/cable-congress-2010-speech-on-net-neutrality-3-march-2010/ [16 December 2013].

Rifkin, J. (2000), *The End of Work: The Decline of the Global Labour Force and the Dawn of the Post-Market Era*, London: Penguin.

Robinson, J. (2010), 'BSkyB buys Complete HBO TV Catalogue', *Guardian*, 29 July. http://www.theguardian.com/media/2010/jul/29/bskyb-buys-hbo-tv-catalogue [14 January 2014].

———. (2011), 'David Cameron, Ed Miliband and Co Flock to Pay Home at Rupert Murdoch's Summer Party', *Guardian*, 20 June. http://www.theguardian.com/media/2011/jun/20/david-cameron-rupert-murdoch-party?guni=Article:in%20body%20link [14 August 2013].

Robinson, M. (2012), 'The Wealth Gap – Inequality in Numbers', *BBC News Online*, 17 January. http://www.bbc.co.uk/news/business-16545898 [12 August 2013].

Robinson, P., Goddard, P., Parry, K., Murray, C. and Taylor, P. M. (2010), *Pockets of Resistance: British News Media, War and Theory in the 2003 Invasion of Iraq*, Manchester: Manchester University Press.

Rogers, S. and Burn-Murdoch, J. (2012), 'Murdoch Meetings: The List of Meets with Prime Ministers and Leaders of the Opposition', *Guardian*, 27 April. http://www.theguardian.com/media/datablog/2012/apr/27/murdoch-meetings-list [14 January 2014].

Rosen, J. (2008), 'Google's Gatekeepers', *New York Times*, 28 November. http://www.nytimes.com/2008/11/30/magazine/30google-t.html?pagewanted=all&_r=0 [4 September 2013].

———. (2013), 'The Delete Squad', *New Republic*, 29 April. http://www.newrepublic.com/article/113045/free-speech-internet-silicon-valley-making-rules [4 September 2013].

Rothkopf, D. (2009), *Superclass: How the Rich Ruined Our World*, London: Abacus.

Rowe, A. and Malhotra, S. (2013) 'Still the Silence: Feminist Reflections at the Edges of Sound', in S. Malhotra and A. Rowe (eds), *Silence, Feminism, Power: Reflections at the Edge of Sound*, Houndmills, Basingstoke: Palgrave Macmillan, 1–24.

Sabbagh, D. (2011), 'How Proprietors are Taking over the Biggest Media Companies in the UK', *Guardian*, 20 June. http://www.theguardian.com/media/2011/jun/20/media-ownership-proprietors-families [14 August 2013].

Scannell, P. (1989), 'Public Service Broadcasting and Modern Public Life', *Media Culture and Society*, 11 (2): 135–166.

Schattschneider, E. (1960), *The Semi-Sovereign People: A Realists' View of Democracy in America*, New York: Holt, Rhinehart & Winston.

Schiller, H. (1969), *Mass Communications and American Empire*, Boston: Beacon Press.

———. (1989), *Culture, Inc.: The Corporate Takeover of Public Expression*, New York: Oxford University Press.

Schiller, D. (2000), *Digital Capitalism: Networking the Global Market System*, Boston: MIT Press.

———. (2007), *How to Think About Information*, Urbana: University of Illinois Press.

———. (2011), 'Power Under Press: Digital Capitalism in Crisis', *International Journal of Communication*, 5: 924–941.

Schlosberg, J. (2013), *Power Beyond Scrutiny: Media, Justice and Accountability*, London: Pluto.

Schmidt, E. and Cohen, J. (2013), *The New Digital Age*, London: John Murray.

Schudson, M. (1982), *The Power of News*, Cambridge, MA: Harvard University Press.

Schumpeter, J. (1994), *Capitalism, Socialism & Democracy*, London: Routledge.

Schuster, T. (2006), *The Markets and the Media: Business News and Stock Market Movements*, Lanham: Lexington.

Scott, J. (2001), *Power*, Cambridge: Polity.

Seymour-Ure, C. (1991), *The British Press and Broadcasting since 1045*, Oxford: Blackwell.

Siebert, F., Peterson, T. and Schramm, W. (1963 [1956]), *Four Theories of the Press*, Chicago: University of Illinois Press.

Simon, D. (2013), 'There Are Now Two Americas. My Country Is a Horror Show', *Observer*, 8 December. http://www.theguardian.com/world/2013/dec/08/david-simon-capitalism-marx-two-americas-wire [6 January 2014].

Sklair, L. (2001), *The Transnational Capitalist Class*, Oxford: Blackwell.

Sky. (2013), 'Amazon Paid £2.4m Tax on £4.2bn Sales in 2012', *Sky News*, 15 May. http://news.sky.com/story/1091370/amazon-paid-2-4m-tax-on-4-2bn-sales-in-2012 [5 September 2013].

Smythe, D. (1981), *Dependency Road: Communications, Capitalism, Consciousness, and Canada*, Norwood: Ablex.

Spar, D. (2001), *Ruling the Waves: Cycles of Discovery, Chaos and Wealth from the Compass to the Internet*, New York: Harcourt.

Sparks, C. (1986), 'The Media and the State', in J. Curran, J. Ecclestone, G. Oakley and A. Richardson (eds), *Bending Reality: The State of the Media*, London: Pluto, 76–86.

———. (2006), 'Contradictions in Capitalist Media Practices', in L. Artz, S. Macek and D. Cloud (eds), *Marxism and Communication Studies: The Point Is to Change It*, New York: Peter Lang, 111–132.

———. (2007a), *Globalization, Development and the Mass Media*, London: Sage.

———. (2007b), 'Extending and Refining the Propaganda Model', *Westminster Papers in Communication and Culture*, 4 (2): 68–84.

Sreberny, A. and Khiabany, G. (2010), *Blogistan: The Internet and Politics in Iran*, London: I. B. Tauris.

Stadd, A. (2013), '50 Twitter Fun Facts', 11 January. http://www.mediabistro.com/alltwitter/50-twitter-fun-facts_b33589 [6 January 2014].

Starr, P. (2004), *The Creation of the Media: Political Origins of Modern Communications*, New York: Basic Books.

Starr, C. (2009), '70 Year Old Man Shoots TV Over Digital Transition Frustration', *Yahoo! Voices*, 22 February. http://voices.yahoo.com/70-year-old-man-shoots-tv-over-digital-transition-2710336.html [6 April 2014].

Stephens, P. (2011), 'Nemesis Chases Murdoch's Hubris', *Financial Times*, 8 July.

Stiglitz, J. (2008), 'The End of Neo-liberalism?', *Project Syndicate*, 7 July. http://www.project-syndicate.org/commentary/the-end-of-neo-liberalism- [13 August 2013].

Streeter, T. (1996), *Selling the Air: A Critique of the Policy of Commercial Broadcasting in the United States*, Chicago: University of Chicago Press.

———. (2013), 'Policy, Politics, and Discourse', *Communication, Culture and Critique*, 6: 488–501.

Streitfeld, D. (2013), 'E-Book Ruling Gives Amazon an Advantage', *New York Times*, 10 July. http://www.nytimes.com/2013/07/11/business/e-book-ruling-gives-amazon-an-advantage.html [4 September 2013].

Strupp, J. (2012), 'The Fall of the San Diego Union-Tribune', *Media Matters for America*, 6 December. http://mediamatters.org/blog/2012/12/06/the-fall-of-the-san-diego-union-tribune/191710 [18 August 2013].

Sunday Times. (2012), 'Rich List 2012', *Sunday Times*, 29 April.

Tambini, D. and Craufurd-Smith, R. (2012), 'Measuring Media Plurality in the United Kingdom: Policy Choices and Regulatory Challenges', *Journal of Media Law*, 4 (1): 35–63.

Tan, T. and Netessine, S. (2009), Is Tom Cruise Threatened? Using Netflix Prize Data to Examine the Long Tail of Electronic Commerce', http://knowledge.wharton.upenn.edu/papers/1361.pdf [3 September 2013].

Tapscott, D. and Williams, D. (2008), *Wikinomics: How Mass Collaboration Changes Everything*, London: Atlantic.

Tarde, G. (2010), *On Communication and Social Influence: Selected Papers*, Chicago: University of Chicago Press.

Telegraph. (2012), 'Google's Tax Avoidance Is Called "Capitalism"', *Daily Telegraph*, 12 December. http://www.telegraph.co.uk/technology/google/9739039/Googles-tax-avoidance-is-called-capitalism-says-chairman-Eric-Schmidt.html [5 September 2013]. Says chairman Eric Schmidt.

Thierer, A. and Eskelsen, G. (2008), *Media Metrics: The True State of the Modern Media Marketplace*, Social Science Research Network. http://ssrn.com/abstract=1161312 [14 August 2013].

Thompson, J. (1995), *The Media and Modernity: A Social Theory of the Media*, Stanford: Stanford University Press.

Toffler, A. (1990), *Power Shift: Knowledge, Wealth. And Violence at the Edge of the 21st Century*, London: Bantam.

Tunstall, J and Palmer, J. (1991), *Media Moguls*, London: Routledge.

Turkle, S. (2011), *Alone Together: Why We Expect More from Technology and Less from Each Other*, New York: Basic Books.

Turner, S. D. (2007), *Off the Dial: Female and Minority Radio Station Ownership in the United States*, Florence, MA: Free Press. http://www.freepress.net/sites/default/files/resources/off_the_dial.pdf [14 August 2013].

Turow, J. (1992), *Media Systems in Society: Understanding Industries, Strategies, and Power*, New York: Longman.

Van Natta, D. (2011), 'Stain from Tabloids Rubs Off on a Cozy Scotland Yard', *New York Times*, 16 July. http://www.nytimes.com/2011/07/17/world/europe/17police.html?_r=4& [14 January 2014].

Verizon. (2012), 'Verizon v. Federal Communications Commission', No. 11–1355, 2 July. http://hraunfoss.fcc.gov/edocs_public/attachmatch/DOC-317120A1.pdf [16 December 2013].

Warner, J. (2009), 'Digital Britain Is Already a Success: Why Interfere?', *Independent*, 17 June.

Wasko, J., Murdock, G. and Sousa, H. (eds). (2011), *The Handbook of Political Economy of Communications*, Oxford: Blackwell.

Watt, N. (2012), 'The Campbell Diaries: Bush Left in No Doubt over Blair's Support for Iraq War', *Guardian*, 15 June. http://www.theguardian.com/politics/2012/jun/15/campbell-blair-bush-iraq-war [17 August 2013].

Wayne, M. (2003), *Marxism and Media Studies: Key Concepts and Contemporary Trends*, London: Pluto.

Webb, S. (2012), 'Microsoft Avoids Paying £159MILLION Corporation Tax EVERY YEAR Using Luxembuourg Tax Loophole', *Mail Online*, 9 December. http://www.dailymail.co.uk/news/article-2245412/Microsoft-avoids-paying -159MILLION-corporation-tax-EVERY-YEAR-using-Luxembourg-tax-loophole .html [5 September 2013].

Weinberger, D. (2011), *Too Big to Know*, New York: Basic Books.

Wells, A. (n.d.), 'UK Polling Report'. http://ukpollingreport.co.uk/iraq [6 January 2014].

Williams, R. (1968 [1962]), *Communications*, Harmondsworth: Penguin.

———. (2005 [1980]), *Culture and Materialism: Selected Essays*, London: Verso.

Williams, H. (2006), *Britain's Power Elites: The Rebirth of a Ruling Class*, London: Constable.

Winter, J. (2007), *Lies the Media Tell Us*, Montreal: Black Rose Books.

Wolff, M. (2008), *The Man Who Owns the News: Inside the Secret World of Rupert Murdoch*, London: Bodley Head.

———. (2012), 'The Facebook Fallacy', *MIT Technology Review*, 22 May. http:// www.technologyreview.com/news/427972/the-facebook-fallacy/ [5 September 2013].

Wood, E. M. (2002), 'Contradictions: Only in Capitalism?', in L. Panitch and C. Leys (eds), *Socialist Register*, Woodbridge: Merlin Press, 275–293.

Wright, Mills, C. (1959 [1956]), *The Power Elite*, New York: Galaxy.

Wu, T. (2010), *The Master Switch: The Rise and Fall of Information Empires*, London: Atlantic.

———. (2013), 'The Right to Evade Regulation: How Corporations Hijacked the First Amendment', 3 June. http://www.newrepublic.com/article/113294/how -corporations-hijacked-first-amendment-evade-regulation# [15 December 2013].

Wu, S., Mason, W., Hofman, J. and Watts, D. (2011), 'Who Says What to Whom on Twitter', 20th Annual World Wide Web Conference, Hyderabad. http://labs .yahoo.com/publication/who-says-what-to-whom-on-twitter/ [14 January 2014].

Wyatt, E. (2014), 'Court Rejects Equal Access Rules for Internet Providers', *New York Times*, 14 January. http://www.nytimes.com/2014/01/15/ technology/appeals-court-rejects-fcc-rules-on-internet-service-providers .html?ref=netneutrality&_r=0 [14 January 2014].

YouGov. (2013a), 'YouGov/Media Standards Trust Survey Results', 17–18 July. http://d25d2506sfb94s.cloudfront.net/cumulus_uploads/document/41whd9glei/ YG-Archive-Media-Standards-Trust-results-180713-press-regulation.pdf [6 January 2014].

———. (2013b), 'YouGov/Media Standards Trust Survey Results', 9–10 October. http://d25d2506sfb94s.cloudfront.net/cumulus_uploads/ document/5je3dagqcz/YouGov-survey-Media-Standards-Trust-press -regulation-131010.pdf [6 January 2014].

Ytterstad, A. (2012), *Norwegian Climate Change Policy in the Media: Between Hegemony and Good Sense*, unpublished PhD dissertation, University of Oslo.

———. and Eide, E. (2011), 'The Tainted Hero: Frames of Domestication in Norwegian Press Representation of the Bali Climate Summit', *International Journal of Press/Politics*, 16 (1): 50–74.

Zittrain, J. (2008), *The Future of the Internet*, London: Penguin.

Index